Literature and Justice in
Mid-Twentieth-Century Britain

OXFORD MID-CENTURY STUDIES

The **Oxford Mid-Century Studies** series publishes monographs in several disciplinary and creative areas in order to create a thick description of culture in the thirty-year period around the Second World War. With a focus on the 1930s through the 1960s, the series concentrates on fiction, poetry, film, photography, theatre, as well as art, architecture, design, and other media. The mid-century is an age of shifting groups and movements, from existentialism through abstract expressionism to confessional, serial, electronic, and pop art styles. The series charts such intellectual movements, even as it aids and abets the very best scholarly thinking about the power of art in a world under new techno-political compulsions, whether nuclear-apocalyptic, Cold War-propagandized, transnational, neo-imperial, super-powered, or postcolonial.

Series Editors
Allan Hepburn, McGill University
Adam Piette, University of Sheffield
Lyndsey Stonebridge, University of East Anglia

Literature and Justice in Mid-Twentieth-Century Britain

Crimes and War Crimes

VICTORIA STEWART

OXFORD
UNIVERSITY PRESS

OXFORD
UNIVERSITY PRESS

Great Clarendon Street, Oxford, OX2 6DP,
United Kingdom

Oxford University Press is a department of the University of Oxford.
It furthers the University's objective of excellence in research, scholarship,
and education by publishing worldwide. Oxford is a registered trade mark of
Oxford University Press in the UK and in certain other countries

Impression: 1

Published in the United States of America by Oxford University Press
198 Madison Avenue, New York, NY 10016, United States of America

British Library Cataloguing in Publication Data
Data available

Library of Congress Control Number: 2022945199

ISBN 978-0-19-285823-8
DOI: 10.1093/oso/9780192858238.001.0001

Printed and bound by
CPI Group (UK) Ltd, Croydon, CR0 4YY

Acknowledgements

Many thanks to Professor Allan Hepburn, Professor Adam Piette, and Professor Lyndsey Stonebridge for their support and careful feedback during the development and writing of this book. Thanks to Jacqueline Norton and Jo Spillane at Oxford University Press, and Priyan Gopathy at Integra for their help and patience.

Thanks to Professor Dan Stone for inviting me to contribute to a 2019 Special Issue of *Patterns of Prejudice* which was dedicated to the memory of Professor David Cesarani. Chapter 4 of this book develops some of the ideas I first explored in that article. Dan Stone also organized the Royal Holloway, University of London Holocaust Research Institute memorial event for Professor Cesarani, held at Senate House, in April 2017, and I was extremely grateful for the chance to discuss there some of the material that features in Chapters 2 and 3, and which in a different form was the basis for an article that appeared in the journal *Law and Literature* in 2019. I spoke again on this material at the British Association for Holocaust Studies conference, held at the University of Leeds in July 2018, and input from other attendees was important in developing my thinking. Thanks to them, and to Dr Dominic Williams who hosted this event. Thanks to Beatriz Lopez for inviting me to speak about detective fiction and the Holocaust at the READ Seminar, University of Durham in February 2020, and to all those who attended and offered thoughts and suggestions, especially Kate Jackson. Professor Alaric Searle of the University of Salford took the trouble to provide me with a copy of his 1998 article on Basil Liddell Hart and I'm very grateful for this kind gesture. Thanks to Professor David Hendy for his advice relating to the BBC Written Archives. I'm extremely grateful to Charlotte Hollister for answering my inquiries about her father Derrick Sington.

Thanks to the staff who helped me to access material at the BBC Written Archives, Caversham, the Gerald Duckworth & Co Archives, Senate House, University of London, the Churchill Archives Centre, Churchill College, University of Cambridge, the Imperial War Museum Archives, the National Archives, and the Penguin Books Archive, University of Bristol.

This book was completed during study leave granted by the College of Social Sciences, Arts and Humanities, University Leicester. Thanks to Professor Richard Thomas and Professor Martin Halliwell for assisting me in securing this leave.

Contents

Introduction
Understanding War Crimes Trials in Postwar Britain

This book considers how ideas about crime, criminality, and judicial procedure that had developed in a domestic setting influenced the representation and understanding of war crimes trials, victims of war crimes, and war criminals in 1940s and 1950s Britain. Taking account of these ideas helps to explain why the fate of the Jews and other victims of the Nazis was sometimes brought starkly into focus and sometimes marginalized in public discourse at this period. What remain are glimpses of the events now called the Holocaust, but glimpses that can be as powerful and as meaningful as more direct or explicit representations.

Writing in 2010, David Cesarani argues for a modification of the prevailing view that the Holocaust was largely absent from British culture in the period between the Allied trials of major war criminals at the end of the Second World War and the 1961–1962 trial of Adolf Eichmann in Jerusalem. He points out that 'we should not expect to find a fully formed historical narrative of "the Holocaust"' in the immediate post-war period, and reminds us that, for commentators in 1945–1946:

> [a]t such close proximity to the undiscriminating horrors of the war [...] it was not self-evident that the Jews had been differentiated from all other victims. Patchiness or 'marginalisation' may have seemed to contemporaries like the proper perspective.[1]

While the Eichmann trial was undoubtedly an important moment in establishing the Holocaust as what Shoshana Felman calls a 'semantically authoritative story', this occurred in the light of earlier engagements with the

[1] David Cesarani, 'How Post-War Britain Reflected on the Nazi Persecution and Mass Murder of Europe's Jews: A Reassessment of Early Responses', *Jewish Culture and History* 12.1–2 (2010): pp. 95–130 (p. 99, p. 98).

Literature and Justice in Mid-Twentieth-Century Britain. Victoria Stewart, Oxford University Press.

persecution of the Jews and others which, in the British context, were often entangled with broader questions about the reshaping of Europe in the wake of the war.[2]

Cesarani's own research into what he characterizes as the 'simultaneous presence/absence' of the Holocaust in British culture in the 1940s and 1950s takes him to medical journals, sociological works, and autobiographies spanning a range of wartime experiences, and he mentions the 'traditional discourse of legal studies and law reports', though he situates this as principally a 'source for historical research'.[3] In fact, as I will show, the legal and judicial aspects of war crimes were discussed not only in law reports and academic articles but in a range of other genres aimed at nonspecialist readers, including journalistic accounts of trials, life-writing, and the novel, which authors adapted to accommodate what was widely felt to be unprecedented subject matter. As Dan Stone has noted, at this period, 'Holocaust memory in Britain was not absent, but nor was it ubiquitous and well informed. It was subject to distortions and awkward silences.'[4] These distortions were not necessarily deliberate or intended to mislead, and silences or absences could themselves be telling.

War crimes are a specific type of crime, but the manner in which war crimes trials and those accused of war crimes were depicted in press reports and other texts often drew on dominant pre-existing cultural understandings of criminality. Equally, understandings of domestic criminality, and in particular, debates about the abolition of the death penalty, were affected by decisions that had been made about the treatment of war criminals. Comparing one criminal to another may seem to help in grasping the types of aberrant behaviour that are under scrutiny, but it can downplay the specificity of individuals' actions. The law acts as a means of restoring order, but both judicial procedure, and understandings of 'order', are culturally constructed, and debates about these issues were also part of the attempt to establish what might constitute the shared values of post-war Europe.

---

[2] Shoshana Felman, 'Theaters of Justice: Arendt in Jerusalem, the Eichmann Trial, and the Redefinition of Legal Meaning in the Wake of the Holocaust', *Critical Inquiry* 27.2 (2001): pp. 201–38 (p. 233).

[3] Cesarani, 'How Post-War Britain', p. 122; p. 105. Cesarani states that 'Sir David Maxwell Fyfe edited the *War Crimes Trials* series' which ran 'to nearly 20 volumes' (p. 105). As I will explain in Chapter 1, Maxwell Fyfe was a consultant rather than an active editor on this series, which was published by William Hodge & Co and ran to nine volumes, with another six announced but never actually appearing.

[4] Dan Stone, '"The Greatest Detective Story in History": The BBC, the International Tracing Service, and the Memory of Nazi Crimes in Early Postwar Britain', *History & Memory* 29.2 (2017): pp. 63–89 (p. 67).

Defining and Prosecuting War Crimes

Holding war crimes trials is a way of marking certain types of behaviour as beyond the pale even by the standards of an activity—war—which endorses actions that would not be acceptable in civilian life. This reinforces the idea that, as Marco Duranti suggests, in the 1940s war crimes trials were conceived as having not only 'a punitive function [but] a pedagogical one as well'; it was believed that they could assist in re-educating Germany about western democratic values.[5] 'Re-education' was itself a far from unproblematic aim, not least because, as Nicholas Pronay has argued, an understanding of education as being able to mould character 'which the British approach implied' could from another perspective be seen as 'indoctrination'.[6] In relation to war crimes, raising the issue of where the boundary of 'acceptable' and 'unacceptable' lies in wartime opens up the question of how those who have been involved on active service in the war on either side might be reincorporated into civilian life. Positioning oneself on the side of 'right' and justice can result in feelings of guilt and shame for not having done more to prevent the crimes under investigation.

Dealing with war criminals was identified as a war aim in a joint statement made by United States President Franklin D. Roosevelt and British Prime Minister Winston Churchill on 25 October 1941. The language used by implication set these crimes apart from 'civilised' standards of behaviour: 'The atrocities committed in Poland, Yugoslavia, Norway, Holland, Belgium, and particularly behind the German front in Russia, exceed anything that has been known since the darkest and most bestial ages of humanity. The punishment of these crimes should now be counted among the major goals of the war.'[7] The Einsatzgruppen ('Special Squads') had been established in March 1941, and the first news of mass killings of Jews in Poland reached the British government in mid-October, so could possibly be alluded to here.[8] The form any punishment might take was not specified at this point.

---

[5] Marco Duranti, *The Conservative Human Rights Revolution: European Identity, Transnational Politics, and the Origins of the European Convention* (Oxford: Oxford University Press, 2017), p. 140.

[6] Nicholas Pronay, 'Introduction: To Stamp out the Whole Tradition', in *The Political Re-Education of Germany and Her Allies after World War II*, edited by Nicholas Pronay and Keith Wilson (London: Croom Helm, 1985), pp. 1–36 (p. 9).

[7] Qtd in Ann Tusa and John Tusa, *The Nuremberg Trial* (London: Macmillan, 1983), p. 21.

[8] Dariusz Stola, 'Early News of the Holocaust from Poland', *Holocaust and Genocide Studies* 11.1 (1997): pp. 1–27 (p. 4).

In November 1943, Roosevelt, Churchill, and the Soviet leader Stalin issued the Moscow Declaration, which distinguished 'major' war criminals, broadly speaking, the Nazi hierarchy, whose crimes had no specific geographical location and who would be dealt with jointly by the Allies, from 'minor' war criminals, who could be connected to specific incidents or series of events and would be 'returned to the scene of the crime to stand trial'.[9] In spring 1944, both Churchill and the British Lord Chancellor Sir John Simon were among those who argued that summary execution without trial of 'a dozen or so leading members of the Nazi apparatus [...] would be a tangible punishment of a state's most visible functionaries'.[10] This course of action, which was also supported by the Soviets, was seen as a political solution which would avoid the difficulties of attempting to mount a trial that, as Judith Shklar puts it, 'was not part of a legal system'.[11] In addition, the Nazi leadership would be denied the opportunity to mount a public defence of their actions. Ultimately, the United States' view that a trial could provide a 'valuable opportunity to apply, extend, and enforce principles of international law' was the one that prevailed.[12]

Meanwhile, where 'minor' war criminals were concerned, the Soviets had begun a programme of trials in mid-1943. The other Allied nations were opposed to this course of action, partly, as Bradley Smith notes, because of the fear of 'enemy reprisals against Allied prisoners of war', but also because of 'a degree of skepticism regarding war crimes reports, the legacy of the exaggerated tales of German atrocities in Belgium which the Anglo-Americans themselves had circulated during World War I'.[13] Wariness about potential propaganda was supplemented by more basic kinds of prejudice.

---

[9] Devin O. Pendas, 'Retroactive Law and Proactive Justice: Debating Crimes against Humanity in Germany, 1945–1950', *Central European History* 43 (2010): pp. 428–63 (p. 428).

[10] Lawrence Douglas, *The Memory of Judgment: Making Law and History in the Trials of the Holocaust* (New Haven: Yale University Press, 2001), p. 38. See also Bradley F. Smith, *Reaching Judgment at Nuremberg* (London: Andre Deutsch, 1977), pp. 29–33.

[11] Judith N. Shklar, *Legalism: Law, Morals, and Political Trials* (Cambridge, MA: Harvard University Press, 1986 [1964]), p. 159.

[12] Douglas, *The Memory of Judgment*, p. 41.

[13] Alexander Victor Prusin, '"Fascist Criminals to the Gallows!": The Holocaust and Soviet War Crimes Trials, December 1945–February 1946', *Holocaust and Genocide Studies* 17.1 (2003): pp. 1–30 (p. 5); Smith, *Reaching Judgment*, p. 21. Prusin notes that an extension of martial law after the German invasion of the USSR, which enabled these trials, was at least partly aimed at discouraging collaboration, and many defendants in these early trials were Soviet citizens. The British resisted the Soviets' suggestion that Rudolf Hess should be put on trial after he came into British custody in November 1942. See Ariel J. Kochavi, *Prelude to Nuremberg: Allied War Crimes Policy and the Question of Punishment* (Chapel Hill: University of North Carolina Press, 1998), p. 44.

Dariusz Stola quotes comments made by Victor Cavendish-Bentinck of the Joint Intelligence Committee, in 1943: 'It is incorrect to describe Polish information regarding German atrocities as trustworthy. The Poles, and to a far greater extent the Jews, tend to exaggerate German atrocities in order to stoke us up.'[14] As I will show, the belief that victims were given to exaggeration persisted even after the end of the war.

By the autumn of 1944, in the knowledge that nationality was not a primary factor in the targeting of Jews by the Nazis, Jewish groups and European governments in exile in London were pressuring the British and the Americans to agree to 'punish crimes by Germans against Germans or other Axis nationals', a course of action that would not be usual under existing war crimes legislation. The response to this pressure led to 'a dual strategy: military courts and special courts with jurisdiction for more than war crimes alone', and this meant that British courts in occupied Germany eventually dealt with some cases that did not involve any British victims or witnesses.[15] This allowed for a demonstration of the principles of 'British justice' that both filled the vacuum left by the collapse of the Nazi regime and, in theory, contributed to denazification and re-education efforts. As Mary Fulbrook notes, however, where the formalized process of denazification was concerned, people 'generally saw the procedures as a hurdle to be jumped rather than an occasion for serious confrontation with the past'.[16]

As my discussion of the Belsen Trial, held at Lüneberg in the autumn of 1945, will show, even though these British-run prosecutions were military tribunals rather than trials, the procedure followed would have been broadly

---

[14] Stola, 'Early News', p. 2. The British government received information about the treatment of the Jews from the Polish underground, as well as other sources, including decrypted Enigma intercepts. See Robert J. Hanyok, *Eavesdropping on Hell: Historical Guide to Western Communications Intelligence and the Holocaust* (2005; New York: Dover, 2012) especially pp. 147–51, and Michael Smith, 'Bletchley Park and the Holocaust', in *Understanding Intelligence in the Twenty-First Century: Journeys in Shadows*, edited by Peter Jackson and L. V. Scott (London: Routledge, 2004), pp. 111–21.

[15] Michael Bryant and Wolfgang Form, 'Victim Nationality in US and British Military Trials: Hadamar, Dachau, Belsen', in *Justice, Politics and Memory in Europe after the Second World War: Landscapes after Battle Volume 2*, edited by Suzanne Bardgett, David Cesarani, Jessica Reinisch, and Johannes-Dieter Steinert (London: Vallentine Mitchell, 2011), pp. 19–42 (pp. 28–29). These included the 'Velpke Baby Home Case' which centred on the mistreatment of the children of Polish forced labourers in Germany, and which was one of the cases included in Hodge & Co's *War Crimes Trials* series. I discuss this further in Chapter 1.

[16] Mary Fulbrook *Reckonings: Legacies of Nazi Persecution and the Quest for Justice* (Oxford: Oxford University Press, 2018), p. 211.

recognizable to the British public from its use in civilian courts at home.[17] The same can be said of the Nuremberg International Military Tribunal (IMT), which began sitting in late 1945, shortly after the conclusion of the Belsen Trial. The charges laid at the Belsen Trial were of war crimes, specifically the mistreatment of named Allied nationals who were prisoners of war at either Belsen or Auschwitz. As Caroline Sharples notes, in both the naming of individuals in the indictment and in the use of existing international law, the Belsen Trial 'differed sharply' from the IMT.[18] The drawing up of the Rules of Procedure for the IMT necessitated 'reaching compromises between four national systems of conducting a trial'.[19] These compromises were by no means incidental, given the fundamental differences between the inquisitorial approach adopted in trials on the continent and the Anglo-American adversarial system, and there was considerable debate about the charges to be laid. As Lawrence Douglas notes, the charges of conspiracy to wage aggressive war and of crimes against humanity, the result of 'legal haggling', laid the IMT open to accusations of creating law after the event.[20] Aside from these judicial challenges, the IMT's focus on 'major' war criminals, figureheads representing different aspects of the Nazi infrastructure, meant that there was a certain amount of horse trading between the Allies in relation to the identification of defendants.[21]

Over the course of the Allies' involvement in the war crimes trials, particular concerns were raised about the appropriateness of putting members of the military on trial. Sharples notes that some members of the British public interviewed by the social survey organization Mass-Observation 'appeared very reluctant to countenance the involvement of the [German] Armed Forces in the perpetration of Nazi atrocities',[22] reflecting not just a view

---

[17] Although the proceedings at Lüneberg were a military tribunal and scrutinized actions that had been taken at Auschwitz, as well as at Belsen, for ease of reference, I will adopt the common usage 'Belsen Trial' here.

[18] Caroline Sharples, '"Where, Exactly, Is Auschwitz?" British Confrontation with the Holocaust through the Medium of the "Belsen" Trial', in *The Palgrave Handbook of Britain and the Holocaust*, edited by Tom Lawson and Andy Pearce (Basingstoke: Palgrave, 2021), pp. 181–200 (p. 191).

[19] Tusa and Tusa, *The Nuremberg Trial*, p. 116.

[20] Douglas, *The Memory of Judgment*, p. 43. David Margolies, a member of the American legal team, recalled that the conspiracy charge, 'a favourite American legal device for dealing with organized crime', was unfamiliar to both the British and to the defendants. Qtd in Hilary Gaskin, *Eyewitnesses at Nuremberg* (London: Arms and Armour, 1990), p. 55.

[21] Accommodating the Soviets presented its own challenges. See Francine Hirsch, *Soviet Judgment at Nuremberg* (New York: Oxford University Press, 2020).

[22] Caroline Sharples, 'Holocaust on Trial: Mass Observation and British Media Responses to the Nuremberg Tribunal', in *Britain and the Holocaust: Remembering and Representing War*

that soldiers of whatever nationality should not be treated like common criminals, but an implicit fear that the actions of Allied soldiers could in turn come under scrutiny. This opinion was shared, as Donald Bloxham points out, by some of those responsible for overseeing the trials, who saw them as a potentially dangerous precedent: 'Soldiers, after all, were meant to carry out unpleasant tasks under orders.'[23]

Bloxham discusses the trial of Erich von Manstein, which took place in the summer of 1949, and saw the former Field-Marshal being defended by British Labour MP and barrister Reginald Paget. In his book on the case, Paget expressed the view that the trial was a 'political as opposed to a judicial process' and critiqued the basis under which the British had established courts in Germany as 'an exercise of the power of the victor over the vanquished.'[24] As Bloxham shows, by the time of Manstein's trial, the British were in any case keen to bring their involvement in war crimes trials to an end. The Soviets had wanted to try Manstein themselves, but the British refused to allow his extradition, believing that he would not receive a fair trial.[25] This illustrates how the context of the nascent Cold War exerted an influence on the Allied trials.

Attitudes to the German military, and especially to career soldiers like Manstein, were one site for the emergence in some quarters of a desire to separate Nazis from 'Good Germans'. The suggestion that all Germans had inherent Nazi tendencies underpinned the shrill rhetoric of Lord Vansittart's *Black Record* (1941), which positioned Nazism as the inevitable culmination of historic German militarism. But countering this type of prejudice could bring its own problems, especially when it involved an appeal to other kinds of stereotype, albeit of an ostensibly more positive kind.[26] Petra Rau has argued that the 'Good German is largely a product of the 1950s', and cites, for instance, the popularity of Desmond Young's 1950 English-language

---

and Genocide, edited by Caroline Sharples and Olaf Jensen (Basingstoke: Palgrave, 2013), pp. 31–50 (p. 44).

[23] Donald Bloxham, 'Punishing German Soldiers during the Cold War: The Case of Erich von Manstein', *Patterns of Prejudice* 33.4 (1999): pp. 25–45 (p. 32).

[24] R. T. Paget, *Manstein: His Campaigns and His Trial* (London: William Collins, 1951), p. 1, p. 68.

[25] Bloxham, 'Punishing German Soldiers', p. 31.

[26] One common counter to the image of the militaristic German is the sensitive music lover; these stereotypes persist in film and novels. See Richard Falcon, 'Images of Germany and the Germans in British Film and Television Fictions: A Brief Chronological Overview', in *Anglo-German Attitudes*, edited by Cedric Cullingford and Harald Husemann (Aldershot: Avebury, 1995), pp. 67–89, and Victoria Stewart *The Second World War in Contemporary British Fiction: Secret Histories* (Edinburgh: Edinburgh University Press, 2010).

biography of Erwin Rommel and subsequent film representations of the Field Marshall's life and career (he died by suicide in the wake of the 1944 July Plot).[27] But a desire to separate specific individuals from the taint of Nazism, which, as Patrick Major notes, took on a particular inflection in the 1950s, when the war was seen via the 'prism' of the Cold War, certainly has its roots in the late 1940s.[28]

Alaric Searle highlights the significance of the work of military historian Basil Liddell Hart. *The Other Side of the Hill* (1948), based on the Liddell Hart's interviews with German Generals who were being held at a prisoner of war camp near his home in the Lake District, focuses on military strategy rather than ideological considerations. Searle notes that Liddell Hart was not unaware that he might be manipulated by the Generals for their own ends, but was in any case keen to offer them support in negotiating their way through any judicial proceedings that they might eventually face.[29] Searle argues that as well as refurbishing Liddell Hart's own profile in both Britain and Germany, *The Other Side of the Hill* led to him participating in debates about German rearmament in both the British and German press. This extended, controversially, to him deploring the demoralizing effects on ordinary German soldiers of seeing Generals put on trial. While, as Searle notes, the Generals may have been 'cynical' in exploiting 'Liddell Hart's name in the selling of their version of the history of the war', this was evidently a version that could find an audience in both Germany and Britain.[30]

These various tactics for classifying and discriminating between individuals and groups, together with the separation of the Holocaust from other aspects of the war, had their advantages because they helped to defuse anxieties that might be circulating in Britain about British soldiers' actions or the British conduct of the war. From a political perspective, they additionally assisted in the goal of establishing good relations with the Federal Republic

---

[27] Petra Rau, *Our Nazis: Representations of Nazism in Contemporary Literature and Film* (Edinburgh: Edinburgh University Press, 2013), p. 128. Rau cites comments by Labour MP and former psychological warfare officer Richard Crossman, who identifies the roots of this way of thinking in wartime, and especially in attitudes towards Rommel: 'During the war we adopted Rommel [...] and made him an honorary Englishman by picturing him as the one German who played war according to the rules of cricket.' Crossman, writing in 1950, qtd in Rau, *Our Nazis*, p. 130.

[28] Patrick Major, '"Our Friend Rommel": The *Wehrmacht* as "Worthy Enemy" in Postwar British Popular Culture', *German History* 26.4 (2008): pp. 520–35 (p. 520).

[29] Alaric Searle, 'A Very Special Relationship: Basil Liddell Hart, Wehrmacht Generals and the Debate on West German Rearmament, 1945–1953', *War in History* 5.3 (1998): pp. 327–57 (p. 333).

[30] Searle, 'A Very Special Relationship', p. 356.

of Germany. But as I will show, this separation was rarely an absolute one, and writers employed a range of tactics for incorporating aspects of the Holocaust, and questions of guilt and responsibility, into war narratives while not necessarily engaging with these issues directly.

Representing the Camps in Britain

The handing over of Belsen to the British on 15 April 1945, like the subsequent trial of its personnel, received extensive press coverage in Britain, and as Tony Kushner notes, 'from 1945 onwards [Belsen] had a particular resonance and centrality in the British imagination. It took many years before Auschwitz would become a metonym either for the crimes of the Nazi regime or more generally as [sic] a symbol of mankind's capacity to commit evil deeds.'[31] The place that 'Auschwitz' now has as an emblem in Anglo-American memorial culture, with, for example, Holocaust Memorial Day being marked on 27 January, the date of American troops' arrival at the camp in 1945, was thus, for a time at least, occupied by 'Belsen' in British culture.

But despite the importance of the Belsen Trial, which will be a key focal point for this book, one of the problems with how the camps were represented in the press at the end of the war was that different types of camp were not always properly distinguished from each other.[32] In Mark Rawlinson's view, this is not simply a case of a lack of distinction between concentration camps and death camps, an issue to which I will return. Another type of camp, the prisoner of war camp, loomed much larger in British culture: 'There is no room for what Holocaust survivor David Rousset dubbed "*l'univers concentrationnaire*" in the war represented by reimagined POW camps, corners of foreign fields that remain defiantly English.'[33] This observation about the competing narratives that formed the British memory of

---

[31] Tony Kushner, 'From 'This Belsen Business" to "Shoah Business": History, Memory and Heritage, 1945–2005', in *Belsen 1945: New Historical Perspectives*, edited by David Cesarani and Suzanne Bodgett (London: Vallentine Mitchell, 2006), pp. 189–216 (p. 196). See also, Kushner, 'The Memory of Belsen', in *Belsen in History and Memory*, edited by David Cesarani, Tony Kushner and Jo Reilly (Florence: Routledge, 2013), pp. 181–205.

[32] See Dan Stone, *Concentration Camps: A Short History* (Oxford: Oxford University Press, 2017), especially Chapter 3, 'The Third Reich's World of Camps', pp. 34–56, for an explanation of how this confusion came about. Caroline Sharples notes that matters were further complicated in the case of Belsen by shifts in how the camp was used over the course of the 1930s and 1940s. 'Where, Exactly, Is Auschwitz?', p. 182.

[33] Mark Rawlinson, 'This Other War: British Culture and the Holocaust', *Cambridge Quarterly* 25.1 (1996): pp. 1–25 (p. 11).

the war is further complicated, as Rawlinson acknowledges, and as I will show in Chapter 3, by the fact that some British prisoners were in fact kept in concentration camps, though their conditions were often very different from those of the other inmates.

Rawlinson's argument is supported by the observations of Ken Worpole, who in 1983 surveyed what he believed to have been the 'most widely read books in Britain' in the 1950s, a selection of predominantly non-fiction paperbacks, nearly all of which 'dealt with the experiences of male combatants in the Second World War'.[34] Worpole notes: 'Women's experiences [...] were largely ignored, except for the translation of a small number of accounts by women of involvement in European resistance movements or as survivors of the Nazi concentration camps.'[35] Somewhat misleadingly, the examples he gives of female-authored texts include Anne Frank's *The Diary of a Young Girl* (1952), which fits neither of these categories, and Anne-Marie Walters's *Moondrop to Gascony* (1947), an account of experiences in the Special Operations Executive's French section by a British agent (and therefore not a translation). But Worpole's list is striking because it encompasses texts such as Ka-Tzetnik's *House of Dolls* (1953, as *Beit habubot*; English translation 1955) and Micheline Maurel's memoir *Ravensbrück* (1957, as *Un camp très ordinaire*; English translation 1958), alongside Paul Brickhill's *The Great Escape* (1950) and Eric Williams's *The Wooden Horse* (1950). Worpole suggests that these represent 'four distinct genres' of popular representations of war: 'escape stories, heroism in war, stories of resistance, and testimonies of German and Japanese war crimes.'[36] Worpole does not allow for types of writing that either embrace one or more of these genres or, in the case of Anne Frank's diary or Ka-Tzetnik's fictionalized memoir, cannot easily fit into any of them.[37] There is little space in Worpole's typology for the resistance memoir that, for example, includes a description of concentration camp experience. But Worpole, like Rawlinson, nevertheless reminds us that war crimes, the treatment of the Jews and others, and the manner in which these were depicted need to be situated within a network of representations of British war experience, one which views the camps from a British perspective.

[34] Ken Worpole, *Dockers and Detectives* (London: Verso, 1983), p. 50.
[35] Worpole, *Dockers*, p. 50
[36] Worpole, *Dockers*, p. 52.
[37] For debates about Ka-Tzetnik's work and its reception, see Annette F. Timm, ed., *Holocaust History and the Readings of Ka-Tzetnik* (London: Bloomsbury, 2018).

Aside from depictions in various kinds of war narrative, some of which I will examine in later chapters, there are other more indirect ways that the concentration camps were referenced in post–war British discourse. Illustrating the prominence of Belsen in British culture, Kushner identifies allusions to the camp in a range of contexts in the late 1940s, with its name rapidly becoming a shorthand way of describing 'anything in an abused state'.[38] Kushner characterizes figurative language as distancing the reader from the object of the comparison and eroding its particularity. To borrow one of his examples, describing the interwar treatment of Britain's architectural heritage as 'Belsen-like' diminishes Belsen, reducing it to one 'horror' with which another can easily be compared.[39] Elsewhere, Kushner cites examples of exposure to images of Belsen prompting either empathy or its 'reverse', noting a tendency towards a focus 'on the motives of the perpetrators rather than the impact on the victims'.[40] Like the other uses of 'Belsen' he identifies, this results in an erosion of the specificity of what happened at the camp.

Another way of considering apparently insensitive or reductive comparisons is to see them as a means of attempting to control or encompass within discourse events that initially appear uncontrollable and highly dissonant. Writing in May 1945, soon after a visit to Belsen, journalist Patrick Gordon Walker reflected: 'When I was in Belsen camp the only parallel that came to my mind were the holds of the slave ships.' Developing this analogy, he noted what he felt should be a key distinction for his readers: 'The slaves are now among your fellow citizens. The slave ships, driven from the Atlantic, have anchored at Dachau, Belsen and Buchenwald—in the midst of Europe.'[41] This comparison was echoed by, for instance, Ashley Price, in a review of a book about the Atlantic slave trade that appeared in the Times Literary Supplement in 1949: 'The twentieth century was well under way before

---

[38] Tony Kushner, 'From "This Belsen Business"' to "Shoah Business": History, Memory and Heritage, 1945–2005', in Belsen 1945: New Historical Perspectives, edited by Susan Bardgett and David Cesarani (London: Vallentine Mitchell 2006), pp. 189–216 (p. 196). Annette F. Timm, ed., Holocaust History and the Readings of Ka-Tzetnik (London: Bloomsbury, 2018).

[39] Kushner, 'From "This Belsen Business"', p. 196.

[40] Tony Kushner, 'The Holocaust in the British Imagination: The Official Mind and Beyond, 1945 to the Present', Holocaust Studies 23.3 (2017): pp. 364–84 (pp. 367–68). As an example of empathy, Kushner cites the novelist Alan Sillitoe's memory of looking at newspaper photographs of the camp, as well as Sillitoe's acknowledgement that he only understood later that the majority of victims were Jewish. Meanwhile, author Frederic Raphael believed his public school nickname, 'Belsen', was a reference to him being thin rather than to his Jewishness (p. 367).

[41] Patrick Gordon Walker, The Lid Lifts (London: Victor Gollancz, 1945), pp. 64–65.

it was realised that slavery had been scratched and not killed. The same miasmic stenches were to greet the liberators of Belsen as had nauseated the crews of British frigates boarding slave ships in the Bight of Benin.'[42] Each of these examples works in both directions. An attempt is made to bring a remote historical event closer to the reader by drawing a parallel with a more temporally proximate event, and Belsen is situated and contextualized within an historical lineage of inhumanity.[43] This is not to suggest that such a comparison is unproblematic, not least because of the implication that for such things to happen in Europe and to Europeans makes them worse, but, certainly in Walker's case, it is not a comparison that is made casually or unthinkingly, as Kushner suggests his examples often seem to be.[44] As Michael Rothberg has argued, some form of comparison is implied even when uniqueness is being asserted, and expressions of relational, or

---

[42] Anon [Ashley Price], 'Benevolent Crochet' [rev of Christopher Lloyd, *The British Navy and the Slave Trade*] *Times Literary Supplement*, 7 October 1949, p. 650. Later, Derrick Sington, one of the 'liberators of Belsen' mentioned here, argued for involvement in the slave trade as a precedent for the '[s]ystematic, large-scale brutalisation' brought about by Nazism, suggesting that descriptions of 'the "selection" of negroes for shipment' are 'curiously like accounts of selection parades for the gas chambers', and that 'long treks of captives out of the African jungle, with many dropping by the wayside under the lash, clearly resembled the "death marches" from Sachsenhausen'. Giles Playfair and Derrick Sington, *The Offenders: Society and the Atrocious Crime* (London: Secker & Warburg, 1957), pp. 153–54, n. 2.

[43] As Michael Rothberg points out, a visit that the African American scholar W. E. B. Du Bois made to the remains of the Warsaw Ghetto in 1949 led Du Bois to 'rethink his understanding of the African American past and present' bringing 'black and Jewish histories into relation without erasing their differences or fetishizing their uniqueness'. *The Implicated Subject: Beyond Victims and Perpetrators* (Stanford: Stanford University Press, 2019), pp. 126–27. See also W. E. B. Du Bois, 'The Negro and the Warsaw Ghetto', *Jewish Life* (May 1952): pp. 14–15.

[44] This question about the appropriateness of using the Nazi camps as a point of comparison for other historical situations came to the fore in the Anglo-American context in June 2019, when I was first drafting this chapter. After Congresswoman Alexandria Ocasio-Cortez used the term 'concentration camps' to describe refugee detention camps on the southern border of the United States, the United States Holocaust Memorial Museum issued a statement asserting that it 'unequivocally rejects efforts to create analogies between the Holocaust and other events, whether historical or contemporary'. 'Statement Regarding the Museum's Position on Holocaust Analogies', 24 June 2019. https://www.ushmm.org/information/press/press-releases/statement-regarding-the-museums-position-on-holocaust-analogies. Accessed 1 October 2019. This statement prompted an open letter condemning the museum's position, signed by over 550 academics engaged in work on the Holocaust from around the world, and stating that the ban on drawing analogies 'makes learning from the past almost impossible'. Omer Bartov et al., 'An Open Letter to the Director of the US Holocaust Memorial Museum', *New York Review of Books*, 1 July 2019, https://www.nybooks.com/daily/2019/07/01/an-open-letter-to-the-director-of-the-holocaust-memorial-museum/?fbclid=IwAR1AoKWPKzbxZfxd8ia48BuBjDfbyerfRizy7SZziGGWqnCShfUQ8LFZjyY. Accessed 1 October 2019.

what he terms *multidirectional*, memory do not necessarily mean that the historical specificity of events is being denied.[45]

It is also relevant for my discussion that the use of 'Belsen' as a metonymy for Nazi crimes in general is echoed in discourse about domestic murder cases, where the name of either the perpetrator, the place where the crime was committed, or the manner of the crime, is often used as shorthand for both the events themselves and their eventual judicial outcome. I will return later to George Smith, hanged in 1915 after committing a series of killings that are often known as the 'Brides in the Bath' murders. Kushner's examples may seem reductive to us now, but to authors or readers of the time, reduction may have been precisely the point. It signals an attempt, however clumsy, to bring into focus images and descriptions that were unprecedented in their horror. Like the nicknames given to murderers, this use of language is a way of simultaneously acknowledging and keeping at bay or controlling the events to which reference is being made. Minor characters in fiction and 'passing' references in all types of writing can also have a metonymic function, acting as a means of alluding to, without fully exploring or explaining, aspects of historical context; in Chapter 4, I will show how this affects the treatment of refugee characters, especially Jews who had fled mainland Europe, in 1940s and 1950s crime fiction. The question that remains difficult to answer, but which I will begin to explore here, is how a contemporary reader might have decoded such references.

An issue that will re-emerge in relation to representation in both literary and legal senses is who has the right to speak, who can speak on behalf of others, and what cultural work their testimonies are made to do. An acknowledgement of the difficulties of representing the Holocaust, especially the unprecedented horror of what was lived through and seen at the camps, is certainly not a recent development. Where the question of whose voices get to be heard is concerned, it is notable that a number of authors of autobiographical texts to be considered here incorporate first person testimony by survivors into what are principally accounts of how the camps seemed to those who arrived at them as members of the Allied

---

[45] See Michael Rothberg, *Multidirectional Memory: Remembering the Holocaust in the Age of Decolonization* (Stanford: Stanford University Press, 2009). The publication of the German translation of *Multidirectional Memory* in early 2021 saw Rothberg facing accusations of relativism—the opposite of his actual position—partly because the book was drawn into ongoing debates in the German press about Holocaust memory and the legacy of colonialism. For an overview, see Daniel Little, 'The Holocaust "Comparability" Debate', Understanding Society blog, 29 June 2021, https://understandingsociety.blogspot.com/2021/06/the-holocaust-comparability-debate.html. Accessed 1 November 2021.

armed forces. While this technique acknowledges that voices other than those of the primary author are important and indicates a recognition of the need to allow survivors themselves to speak about what they have experienced, rather than speaking on their behalf, it implies selection on the part of the author, and the criteria informing that selection are not always transparent.

This approach is employed by Patrick Gordon Walker in his short article 'What I Saw at Belsen', published in *The Listener* in May 1945. Walker's position as an eyewitness is foregrounded in the title of the article, but about a quarter of its single page consists of direct quotation from a survivor of Belsen. Walker makes his encounter with Czech prisoner Gitta Cartagena, whose words he quotes, seem purely accidental, commenting: 'I talked to a Czech girl as we stood among the corpses and the filth', but the recording of the broadcast on which the article is based reveals that the choice of interviewee must have been at least partly influenced by her ability to speak fluent English.[46] Her words are her own, but they serve, within the context of the report, to evoke the experiences of many other former prisoners, and her individuality is therefore both acknowledged and undercut.

Walker's response to Belsen incorporates two sentiments that arise in many other representations of the camps from 1945–1946 and which persist in later Holocaust writing. He remarks that the British soldiers he spoke to were concerned about whether 'the people at home [would] believe these things'. To illustrate this, in the broadcast Driver Mechanic Payne of the Oxfordshire Yeomanry gives an account in his own words of what he saw, and he ends with the assertion: 'I'm a British soldier and it's not propaganda, it's the truth.'[47] This statement precedes Cartagena's testimony, framing and guaranteeing it. As Joanne Reilly notes, 'attention was given' to 'authenticating' broadcast and newspaper accounts, often, as in Walker's case, through an element of self-referentiality, in an effort to ensure that reports were

[46] Patrick Gordon Walker, 'What I Saw at Belsen', *The Listener*, 31 May 1945, p. 599, and Patrick Gordon Walker, 'Belsen Facts and Thoughts', broadcast 27 May 1945. https://www.bbc.co.uk/archive/patrick-gordon-walker—belsen-facts-and-thoughts/zdsvxyc. Accessed 3 July 2019. A transcript of the broadcast, including descriptions of the musical inserts, in included in Suzanne Bardgett, 'What Wireless Listeners Learned: Some Lesser-Known BBC Broadcasts about Belsen', in *Belsen 1945: New Historical Perspectives*, edited by Suzanne Bardgett and David Cesarani (London and Portland: Vallentine Mitchell, 2006), pp. 123–52 (pp. 137–41).

[47] Walker, 'Belsen Facts and Thoughts'.

believed by the public who heard or saw them.[48] Walker asserts that 'most people' in Britain do believe, but that this is not enough:

> It seems to me that whoever of us has ever shut his ears to these things, or flinched from whatever effort was necessary to put an end to them, now carries part of the responsibility for these things. The world can and must, in a tremendous act of justice, stamp out this horror.[49]

Believing what happened and accepting some share in the responsibility for seeing justice done are in this analysis inseparable from each other, though the violent idiom 'stamp out' sits uneasily next to the more measured phrase 'act of justice'. Walker also moves from 'whoever of us', that is, the individual, to 'the world', blurring the sense of what an individual's 'responsibility' might actually entail.

Rothberg notes that in her response to the Eichmann trial, Hannah Arendt preferred to use the term *responsibility* rather than *guilt* when the individual in question does not have direct involvement in the actions under scrutiny. Rothberg observes that *guilt* has both emotional and legal connotations. This seems to be implied in comments made by Stephen Spender in his account of visiting Germany in the immediate aftermath of the war: 'Everyone is to some extent guilty for the crimes of everyone else', and the Allies have no 'automatic moral ascendency' in the face of German guilt.[50] These remarks illustrate Lyndsey Stonebridge's suggestion that the 'strangely proliferating culpability' in British writing of the post-war period could indicate that 'the acknowledgement of some of kind of guilt [...] at least provided some kind of affective relationship to immediate history'.[51]

Rothberg argues that Arendt's wish to separate guilt from responsibility is 'wrong from a psychological perspective', but he adds that for Arendt, '[u]nlike guilt, which [...] is strictly individual, responsibility does not derive primarily from personal characteristics, but rather from our nature as social

---

[48] Joanne Reilly, *Belsen: The Liberation of a Concentration Camp* (London: Routledge, 1998), p. 57. To give another example, Henry Standish's report from the camp, published in the *News Chronicle* on 21 April 1945, two days after the paper's initial account of Belsen, stated in its third sentence: 'Everything that everybody has written about [Belsen], or has said on the radio, is true.' Henry Standish, 'The Living Dead of Belsen: Allied Rescue Services are Inadequate', p. 1.

[49] Walker, 'What I Saw at Belsen', p. 5

[50] Stephen Spender, *European Witness* (London: Hamish Hamilton, 1946), p. 165.

[51] Lyndsey Stonebridge, *The Writing of Anxiety: Imagining Wartime in Mid-Century British Culture* (Basingstoke: Palgrave, 2006), p. 99.

beings'.[52] This certainly chimes in with how Walker uses the word, as well as with the comments made by *Daily Express* correspondent Alan Moorehead after he visited Belsen in April 1945: 'This touches me and I am responsible. Why has it happened? How did we let it happen?'[53] This type of response, and indeed the work done by individuals such as Walker and Moorehead to inform the general public about the camps and enable even a small number of survivors to talk about what they had seen and experienced, was important. But foregrounding the legal purpose of testimony as Walker does can lead to testimony becoming instrumental, a means to an end, rather than having any other value. The doing of justice may be constructed as an indisputable good, a way of beginning to address the question: How did we let this happen? Yet however well-meant the intentions, this can lead to a focus on the perpetrators rather than the victims.

Questions of competing narratives, not just in relation to what is said by defendants and witnesses in the courtroom but in terms of what stake individuals like Driver Mechanic Payne might have had in the development of a wider understanding of these events, will also be a point at issue here. Considering how the Holocaust has been incorporated into British accounts of the Second World War since the 1990s, Aimee Bunting and Tony Kushner support Rawlinson's contention that the concentration camps were initially overshadowed by other types of camp, noting that the experiences of the British servicemen who were imprisoned at E715, a subcamp of Stalag VIII B that was situated within the Auschwitz complex, were marginalized. In recent years, Kushner observes: 'The increasing awareness of the horrors of the Holocaust creates a narrative challenge for more traditional British readings of the conflict.'[54] As I have argued elsewhere, late twentieth and early twenty-first century fictional accounts of the Second World War evidence a desire to incorporate references to aspects of the war that until recently were not prominent in British culture, including the Holocaust.[55] Cesarani's work shows that the Allies' arrival at Belsen was a key point at which British servicemen, and, via accounts such as Walker's, the British public, were confronted with what had been happening to Europe's Jews

[52] Rothberg, *Implicated Subjects*, pp. 46–47.

[53] Alan Moorehead, 'Glimpses of Germany II - Belsen', *Horizon* 12.67 (July 1945): pp. 26–35 (p. 31).

[54] Aimee Bunting and Tony Kushner, 'Co-Presents to the Holocaust: The British in Auschwitz and Belsen', David Cesarani Memorial Lecture 2018, 30 January 2018. Podcast, backdoorbroadcasting.net. Accessed 12 June 2018.

[55] See Victoria Stewart, *The Second World War in Contemporary British Fiction: Secret Histories* (Edinburgh: Edinburgh University Press, 2011).

and other minorities, even if this awareness appears to have rapidly been displaced by a sense of having seen and heard enough.

In Chapter 2, I will consider an account of the British arrival at Belsen that was produced soon after the event by Derrick Sington who, as Captain in command of No. 14 Amplifying Unit, went into the camp to announce to the inmates that the Allies were now in charge, and who remained to assist with the relief effort for much of the spring and summer of 1945. Sington is an important figure for this study not only because his book *Belsen Uncovered* (1946) is the earliest full-length British-authored account of the camp,[56] but because, both in that book and in his later work, he shows a keen interest in how criminals, including though not exclusively war criminals, might best be dealt with. Sington was far from the only soldier to write an account of what conditions were like at Belsen during the spring and summer of 1945.[57] As Mark Celinscak argues, Belsen became the focus for what might now be termed *dark tourism* for Allied soldiers stationed in surrounding areas, and many were prompted to write about what they saw there. Celinscak explains that 'Thousands of British and Canadian soldiers, airmen, medics, and the like were working and fighting in and around the Lüneburg Heath', and, once news about the camp spread, 'scores of individuals and small groups made their way to the site. Some came to bear witness to a significant crime in history, while others appeared out of a basic human curiosity.'[58] It is not quite accurate to describe the many Allied soldiers who passed through during the spring and summer of 1945, whether on official duties or simply out of an urge to see the 'hell-camp' for themselves, as witnesses or even bystanders. Bunting and Kushner have used the term *co-presents* to describe the situation of those who had 'more agency' than bystanders, as well as in many cases an ongoing affective involvement, even investment, in what they saw at the camp after the collapse of the Nazi regime.[59] The concept of co-presence acknowledges that 'having been at Belsen' could be an important

---

[56] I will discuss in Chapter 2 the significance of the fact that although *Belsen Uncovered* has 1946 as its year of publication on its copyright page, it did not actually appear until March 1947.

[57] My focus is on published accounts; for a consideration of a range of accounts by soldiers, including some that remain unpublished, see Mark Celinscak, *Distance from the Belsen Heap: Allied Forces and the Liberation of a Nazi Concentration Camp* (Toronto: University of Toronto Press, 2015); Ben Flanagan and Donald Bloxham eds., *Remembering Belsen: Eyewitnesses Record the Liberation* (London: Vallentine Mitchell, 2005); and Reilly, *Belsen*. Walker's *The Lid Lifts*, published in 1945, is a much shorter text than Sington's and, as I will show in Chapter 2, it incorporates an account of conditions at the camp immediately after the Allies arrival there that was given to Walker by Sington himself.

[58] Celinscak, *Distance from the Belsen Heap*, p. 79.

[59] Bunting and Kushner, 'Co-Presents to the Holocaust'.

part of the war experience and later life story even of those who were not officially stationed there. This also seems an apt way of describing Sington's engagement with his Belsen experience.

Celinscak notes that at Belsen and indeed other camps, 'Britons and Canadians alike were able to find a reason or confirmation as to why the war needed to be undertaken, and, for the Allies, had to be won.'[60] This sentiment echoes Moorehead's comments following his own visit to Belsen, when he recognizes that seeing the camps might have provided Allied soldiers with a form of belated rationale for the war. He explains the 'shudder of horror' that met the news of the camps by commenting: '[I]t is perhaps not too subtle to say that since Germany was manifestly beaten, people wanted to have a justification for their fight, a proof that they were engaged against evil.'[61] Moorehead's observations underline that any such justification was very much after the fact.

Kushner and Bunting consider the case of Captain Derek van den Bogaerde, later well-known as an actor under his stage name Dirk Bogarde, whose claim to have visited Belsen when he was a reconnaissance officer attached to the Royal Canadian Air Force was for a time doubted by some commentators, and seen as an appropriation on his part of experiences undergone by others.[62] Kushner and Bunting argue that the initial rejection of Bogarde's account indicated 'the unwillingness to imagine the horror of the Holocaust and connect it to those who are also part or were also part of a traditional British war effort'.[63] In other examples discussed by Bunting and Kushner, the opposite tendency prevails. The still-disputed account of prisoner of war Charles Coward's infiltration into Auschwitz is notable in this context.[64] In Coward's case, 'the desire to believe that all

---

[60] Celinscak, *Distance from the Belsen Heap*, p. 102.

[61] Moorehead, 'Glimpses of Germany', p. 35. As is indicated in a note on its first page, this essay is extracted from Moorehead's book *Eclipse* (1945), which describes his travels through Italy, France, and Germany in the final months of the war. The quoted comments are the same in each version. In 'Glimpses of Germany', Moorehead goes on to observe: 'From the German point of view, Belsen was perfectly mistimed. Worse camps like Ausschwitz [sic] existed in Poland and we took no notice' (p. 35). This reference to Auschwitz is not included in *Eclipse*, which reads instead: 'Worse camps existed in Poland and we took no notice.' Moorehead, *Eclipse* (London: Granta, 2000 [1945]), p. 259.

[62] Celinscak notes that Bogarde's biographer initially doubted his claim, but later came to believe that it was true. Celinscak, *Distance from the Belsen Heap*, p. 225, n.113.

[63] Bunting and Kushner, 'Co-Presents to the Holocaust'.

[64] Bogarde starred in the 1962 film adaptation of John Castle's biography of Coward, *The Password Is Courage* (1954), but the film as circulated omits the parts of the narrative relating to Auschwitz. See Malcolm Stollery, '"The Hideous Difficulty of Recreating Nazism at War": Escaping from Europe in *The Wooden Horse* (1950) and the British Prisoner of War Film', *Historical Journal of Film, Radio, and Television* 37.3 (2017): pp. 539–88 (pp. 553–54).

[the] testimony was true highlights not only the ignorance about Holocaust history but also the desperate attempt to connect the British war effort to the saving of the Jews'.[65] Bogarde arrived at Belsen too late to take action and could only observe the aftermath; Coward's story is more comforting, by this analysis, because it offers the hope that Britain—or, at least, some individual Britons—did attempt to take action to prevent the horrors that were unfolding.[66]

Criminals and War Criminals

One of the charges laid at Nuremberg was that Nazi Germany had waged 'aggressive war', an indictment that rests on a distinction between justifiable and unjustifiable uses of force. Writing in 1949, Hartley Shawcross commented:

> At Nuremberg the Defendants, the leaders of Nazi Germany, were charged not only as common murderers, as they all were, but also with the international crime of aggressive war. It is the crime of war which is at once the object and the parent of the other crimes: the crimes against humanity, the war crimes, the common murders. These things occur when men embark on total war as an instrument of policy for national ends.[67]

Quite aside from how different national legal systems might define the apparently straight-forward category of 'common murder', with variations arising from, for instance, whether there is a focus on the intention of the defendant, this comparison illustrates how an appeal to what might ordinarily be seen as constituting criminal behaviour could both help and hinder the understanding of war crimes.

Ten years earlier, in his Penguin Special, *Why Britain is at War* (1939), an account that, even more squarely than Shawcross's short preface, was aimed at a general readership, Harold Nicolson drew a parallel between Hitler and

---

[65] Bunting and Kushner, 'Co-Presents to the Holocaust'.

[66] For an analysis that attempts to establish what Coward may actually have done during his time at Auschwitz, see Joseph Robert White, '"Even in Auschwitz ... Humanity Could Prevail": British POWs and Jewish Concentration-Camp Inmates at IG Auschwitz, 1943–1945', *Holocaust and Genocide Studies* 15.2 (2001): pp. 266–95.

[67] Hartley Shawcross, 'Foreword', in *Trial of Wolfgang Zuess and Others (The Natzweiler Trial)*, edited by Anthony M. Webb (London: William Hodge, 1949), pp. 13–15 (p. 13). Shawcross was a Labour MP, served as Attorney General from 1945–1951 and was Chief Prosecutor for the British at the Nuremberg Trials.

George Smith, the serial bigamist and so-called Brides in the Bath murderer, who was hanged in 1915 having married and then murdered three women in the preceding two years. Interestingly, however, Nicolson's comparison is based not on Hitler and Smith having committed the same type of crime but on them having committed different crimes in a similar way:

> Even as George Smith might have got away with the murder of Margaret Lofty had not his two previous brides [Alice Burnham and Beatrice Munday] been done to death in an identical manner, so also might Adolf Hitler have got away with the seizure of Danzig and the Corridor, had he not already applied the same technique to the destruction of Austria and Czechoslovakia.[68]

Smith's crimes appear to have had a financial motivation, and this sense that a serious crime has been committed for a base reason is part of what underpins Nicolson's comparison. Nicolson goes on to describe Hitler as having committed 'robbery with violence against Austria, Czechoslovakia and Poland'.[69] As Patrick Hamilton reminds us in his novel *Hangover Square* (1941), when a character with fascist sympathies reflects that she 'did not really think that Mussolini looked like a funny burglar', the Italian fascist leader's colonial ambitions led to him being compared to a house-breaker in satirical representations, and Hitler was sometimes depicted in a similar fashion.[70] The point of comparison here lies in the bypassing of diplomatic channels, with the invasion of the home standing for the violation of the homeland. A threat of an international kind is represented using metonymy. The threat is minimized and made the source of (admittedly bleak) humour, but it is presented in a concise and widely comprehensible manner. Such a parallel also raises the political question of whether it might ever be possible

---

[68] Harold Nicolson, *Why Britain Is at War* (Harmondsworth: Penguin, 1939). Kindle edition, np.

[69] Nicolson, *Why Britain Is at War*, np.

[70] Patrick Hamilton, *Hangover Square* (1941; Harmondsworth: Penguin, 2001), p. 129. See for instance 'The Burglar's Dream', a cartoon by Bernard Partridge that appeared in *Punch*, 20 May 1936, p. 575, where Mussolini appears dressed as a burglar, with a swag bag marked 'Abyssinia'. E. H. Shepard also imagined Hitler and Mussolini as burglars in 'The Burglar's Mate', another *Punch* cartoon, published 13 November 1940, p. 477, which shows Hitler holding Mussolini's ladder while the Italian leader attempts to break into a house named 'The Balkans'. 'Splitting the Swag', a further cartoon by Partridge, published in *Punch*, 5 May 1943, p. 377, illustrates an estimate by the American Board of Economic Warfare of the value of loot taken from occupied territories by the Axis powers, with Hitler as a burglar weighed down by an enormous sack of stolen goods, and Mussolini getting away with only a small potted cactus, labelled 'Tunis'.

to negotiate with such individuals or whether it will be necessary to resort to other types of solution, to somehow fit the punishment to the crime. Framing the dictators as common criminals further underlines the illegitimacy of their actions but appealing to the discourse of domestic criminal law, and the familiar figure of the burglar, or even the gangster,[71] could equally serve as a way of reinforcing the legitimacy of the Allied trials. Considering the defendants accused of executing female Special Operations Executive agents at Natzweiler camp, Anthony Webb commented: 'These men could not have had a fairer trial if they had been charged with some petty misdemeanour instead of a most hideous crime.' Everything, Webb assures his readers, was done 'in accord with the ordinary standards of British justice'.[72] These remarks seem to offer reassurance that, despite the heinous nature of the crimes under consideration, usual, and for a British readership, recognizable judicial standards and procedures will prevail. But other commentators would question precisely whether it was appropriate to deal with Nazis in the same fashion as one might deal with burglars, whether 'ordinary standards' were indeed the correct measure. Writing in November 1944 in the diary she kept for Mass-Observation, the left-wing author Naomi Mitchison comments:

> I can't help thinking of Hang the Kaiser. Revenge may be necessary but I don't like talking about trials and crime, as though this were anything like criminal law. I only hope it will happen soon enough to get counted as one more bloody awful bit of the war, not as anything 'legal'.[73]

[71] Bertolt Brecht's *Der Aufhaltsame Aufsteig des Arturo Ui* (*The Resistible Rise of Arturo Ui*), written in 1941 but not premiered until 1958, draws a parallel between Nazism and Chicago gangsters. As M. E. Humble notes: 'It [...] appears that Brecht adapted the model of the Chicago gangster milieu because he considered that Nazism and gangsterism had in common not only violence and criminality but also a close relation to capitalism.' 'The Stylisation of History in *Der Aufhaltsame Austeig des Arturo Ui*', *Forum for Modern Language Studies* 16.2 (1980): pp. 154–71 (p. 159). The burglar parallel downplays these infrastructural aspects of Hitler and Mussolini's projects. In a 1940 BBC radio broadcast, Labour MP Richard Crossman suggested that young people in Germany had been 'trained to accept the morals of a Chicago gangster as the standard of German civilisation'. Qtd in Siân Nicholas, *The Echo of War: Home Front Propaganda and the Wartime BBC, 1939–45* (Manchester: Manchester University Press, 1996), p. 154. Writing in 1964, Hannah Arendt described the 'organized criminality of the Third Reich' as working in a similar way to that of 'other criminal organizations'. 'Personal Responsibility under Dictatorship', in *Responsibility and Judgment*, edited by Jerome Kohn (New York: Schocken Books, 2003), pp. 17–48 (p. 30).
[72] Anthony M. Webb, 'Introduction', in *Trial of Wolfgang Zeuss and Others (The Natzweiler Trial)*, edited by Anthony M. Webb (London: William Hodge, 1949), pp. 17–31 (p. 31).
[73] Naomi Mitchison, *Among You Taking Notes... ... : The Wartime Diary of Naomi Mitchison 1939—1945*, edited by Dorothy Sheridan (Oxford: Oxford University Press, 1986), p. 299.

Mitchison's placing of 'legal' in quotation marks could imply that she fears that the distinctiveness of the Nazis' actions would be eroded if an attempt were made to address or explain them using existing legal principles. In Mitchison's view, a path has to be steered between vengeance (as represented by the First World War slogan 'Hang the Kaiser', echoed in Churchill's call for summary execution of Nazi leaders) and dignifying the Nazis' actions by implying that they are anything like other sorts of crimes. This leaves in suspense the question of what penalty might be fitting; Mitchison seems to imply that within the context of the war still being in progress, even vengeful reprisals could be considered.

As well as 'criminal law', as Mitchison puts it, being used as a measure of the Nazis' crimes, knowledge of those crimes in turn prompted reflection on domestic judicial procedure. Lizzie Seal and Claire Langhamer have examined the influence that the treatment of Nazi crimes had on how crime more generally, and especially capital crime, was perceived in Britain. The 1938 Criminal Justice Bill had included a proposal to suspend capital punishment for five years, but debate on this issue was placed in abeyance by the outbreak of the war, which led to the postponement of this Bill. When it was revived in 1947–1948, a clause advocating abolition tabled by Labour MP and long-standing opponent of capital punishment Sydney Silverman was voted down in the Lords. In the wake of this, a Royal Commission on Capital Punishment was established under the Chairmanship of Sir Ernest Gowers, and its report, issued in 1953, fed into the reforms around sentencing for murder that were implemented under the Homicide Act of 1957. The Commission was not tasked with specifically considering the abolition of capital punishment, rather with identifying ways in which its use might be modified, and the death sentence remained in place until the 1960s.[74]

Langhamer argues that in the wake of the war, '[a]ttitudes toward capital punishment [in Britain] were embedded in broader attitudes to life and death' which 'had undoubtedly been destabilized during six years of war'.[75] However, as Seal notes, the public appears to have become increasingly attuned to the differences between different types of crime, even different

---

[74] Capital punishment for murder was suspended for five years in 1965, with life imprisonment substituted. The suspension was replaced with abolition in 1969, though the death penalty for treason remained on the statute books until 1998. I return to how war crimes were referenced in debates about abolition in the conclusion.

[75] Claire Langhamer, '"The Live Dynamic Whole of Feeling and Behavior": Capital Punishment and the Politics of Emotion, 1945–1957', *Journal of British Studies* 51(2012): pp. 416–44 (p. 422).

types of war crime, with some coming to believe that the ultimate penalty should be reserved for only the very worst types of crime. Specific causes célèbres became a focal point for disquiet: Seal cites the example of William Joyce, widely known as 'Lord Haw-Haw', who made radio broadcasts from Germany that were designed to damage the morale of the British public, and having, been charged with and tried for treason, was hanged in 1946 despite maintaining that he was not actually of British nationality. 'For some', Seal contends, 'executing Joyce betrayed British values.'[76] Rebecca West, who attended Joyce's trial just prior to going to cover the IMT for the *New Yorker*, suggested in her essay on the case that 'inadequate [newspaper] reports' were partly to blame for the widely held belief among the general public that 'Joyce had not been guilty of any offence against the law', and she goes on to reflect that, where the law is concerned: 'There are always lapses in time when the present and the past are not joined, and it is these which Englishmen such as wished Joyce to live loved to exploit.'[77] What West describes is something like the reverse of the post hoc legislation argument that was raised by critics of war crimes trials: the public, in her view wrongly, felt that the law was out of step with current attitudes. Joyce was tried under legislation that in part dated back to the middle ages, but, as I will show in Chapter 1, the members of the public whom West criticizes were considering Joyce's case not only in the context of, for instance, the 1915 treason trial of Roger Casement, but in the light of other capital trials contemporaneous with Joyce's own, including the Belsen Trial.

A sense, expressed by the correspondents cited by Seal, of the need for some form of proportionality where punishment of criminals is concerned finds an echo in a letter of August 1946 from Hannah Arendt to Karl Jaspers: 'It may well be essential to hang Goring, but it is totally inadequate [...] there is a difference between a man who sets out to murder his old aunt and people who without considering the economic usefulness of their actions ... built factories to produce corpses.'[78] Building 'factories to produce corpses'

---

[76] Lizzie Seal, 'Imagined Communities and the Death Penalty in Britain, 1930–1965', *British Journal of Criminology* 54 (2014): pp. 908–27 (p. 917). I discuss Joyce further in Chapter 1. Notably, surveys carried out by Mass-Observation after the passage of the 1948 Act indicated that 'the abolition or suspension of the death penalty was rejected by between two-thirds and three-quarters of respondents'. Victor Bailey, 'The Shadow of the Gallows: The Death Penalty and the British Labour Government, 1945–51', *Law and History Review* 18.2 (2000): pp. 305–49 (p. 336).

[77] Rebecca West, 'The Revolutionary', in *The Meaning of Treason*, edited by (1949; rev ed London: Reprint Society, 1952), pp. 1–185 (p. 54, p. 58).

[78] Qtd in Robert Eaglestone, *The Broken Voice: Reading Post-Holocaust Literature* (Oxford: Oxford University Press, 2017), p. 31.

is on a different scale to murdering one's aunt, yet they potentially attract the same penalty. Robert Eaglestone interprets this comment as evidence of a desire on Arendt's part not to see the perpetrators demonized, as this 'would offer only a simplistic sort of evil, myth not politics'.[79] The type of punishment demanded might not be measurable against more 'usual' criminality but the crime should nevertheless be reckoned with: executing an individual should not necessarily be seen as a conclusion to the consideration of how 'factories producing corpses' came to exist in the first place.

An illustration of how certain types of discourse can oversimplify or demonize the criminal, placing a block in the path of rational engagement with criminality, can be found in Matthew Grant's examination of the press representation of Neville Heath, hanged for a brutal murder in 1946. Grant notes that both Heath and Nazis including Josef Kramer (Commandant of Belsen from December 1944 until the camp was handed over to the Allies) were often described as 'sadistic', a term that in Grant's view, serves to set Heath, a disgraced Royal Air Force (RAF) pilot, apart from ordinary British servicemen, defusing, in the process, more generalized 'anxiety about the impact of the violence of war' on British society. Using the term 'sadistic', however, reinforces a tendency to 'elide the genocidal violence against European Jews [with] the wider history of Nazi war crimes'.[80] In each case, the criminal is positioned as 'other' and exceptional, a manoeuvre that exposes the extent to which commentators felt they had to reach beyond familiar points of comparison, but which serves to insulate these defendants—in this case both Heath and Kramer—from 'ordinary' criminality and therefore from any closer, more detailed, scrutiny.

In the British domestic context, the Second World War was perceived to have led to an increase in crime. If criminality is viewed as, in many instances, a consequence of disruptions in the social order, then the breaking up of families (through, for instance, evacuation programmes) and the absence from home of parents on active service or other war work can be constructed as potentially deleterious factors. Some commentators believed that the very conduct of the war had led to violence seeming quotidian and to life itself being cheapened. Such views surfaced during parliamentary debates about the potential abolition of capital punishment in 1948,

---

[79] Eaglestone, *The Broken Voice*, p. 32.
[80] Matthew Grant, 'The Trial of Neville Heath, the Popular Press, and the Construction of the Memory of the Second World War in Britain, 1945–1946', *English Historical Review* 133.564 (2018): pp. 1156–77 (p. 1170).

when Viscount Stansgate pointed out the difficulty of making a transition from a situation in which violence is valorized' to one in which it has to be kept in check. Stansgate cited attitudes towards the Commandos, an elite force trained to undertake particularly risky missions on mainland Europe, when describing how, in wartime, 'the moral sense of the people deteriorates and sinks. You cannot have commandos, people smearing themselves with blood and dancing about with bayonets, without degrading the moral sense and reducing respect for human life.'[81] As I have shown elsewhere, though the derring-do of the Commandos, and, for instance, their quasi-legendary training in 'silent killing', did indeed have a high profile in media and literary representations during the war years, such depictions were coloured by concerns relating to the question of how individuals with such training might be reincorporated into civilian society, and indeed, how Special Forces might continue to function in contexts other than war. Notably, a number of post–Second World War crime novels feature ex-Commandos as suspects or indeed culprits: questions about the legality of their wartime actions are refigured as more easily containable and solvable domestic crimes.[82]

Discussing the role of the Special Air Service (SAS) in post-war Palestine, David Charteris points out, 'Special operations by their very nature are conducted in a legal and moral twilight zone.'[83] While the war was underway, the status of Special Forces such as Commandos was acknowledged by Hitler in the so-called Commando Order of autumn 1942, which 'called for the liquidation of any British soldier captured while engaged in commando or sabotage operations.'[84] One consequence of this was that any enemy personnel captured while not in uniform would not be treated as ordinary prisoners of war, and this was why, as I will discuss in Chapter 3, some members of the Special Operations Executive (SOE) were kept in concentration camps rather than prisoner of war camps. The order provided a pretext for some of these prisoners to be executed as spies. The victim status of this group was nevertheless coloured by uneasiness about the nature of the work they may have undertaken.

---

[81] *Hansard* HL debate, vol 156, col 15, June 1947–1948. Accessed 27 August 2020).

[82] See Victoria Stewart, '"Commando Consciousness" and Criminality in Post-Second World War Fiction', *Journal of War and Culture Studies* 10.2 (2017): pp. 165–77.

[83] Qtd in David Cesarani, *Major Farran's Hat: Murder, Scandal and Britain's War against Jewish Terrorism, 1945–1948* (London: Vintage, 2009), p. 218.

[84] Neville Wylie, *Barbed Wire Diplomacy: Britain, Germany, and the Politics of Prisoners of War 1939–1945* (Oxford: Oxford University Press, 2010), p. 137.

These examples show how war can complicate ideas about perpetration and victimhood. Judicial process acts as a preliminary to the punishment of wrong doers but it can form part of a reckoning on behalf of the victims as well. Writing in 1953 in *The Final Solution*, a book which he described as an 'inquest' (that is, a legal inquiry into the cause of a sudden or unexplained death), Gerald Reitlinger reflected: 'In the hour of their liberation the victims of Belsen could not have realised that there was no system of human justice adapted to such immense collective crimes, and that perhaps there would never be.'[85] As I will show in Chapter 1, survivors who gave evidence at the Belsen Trial soon saw that there was, as Devin O. Pendas puts it, a 'conflict between bearing witness and being a witness in the judicial sense',[86] with the court demanding a level of detail and a degree of correlation between witness testimony and earlier statements that took little account of the circumstances in which prisoners had been kept and the traumatic nature of what they had experienced. The idea that 'human justice' might not be adequate raises the question of what could or should have been done instead; alternative, extrajudicial forms of witness testimony, including memoirs, providing the opportunity for survivors to tell their own and others' stories, are a partial answer. Reitlinger's comments are a further reminder that the Belsen Trial was only one in a series of war crimes trials run by the British, and that the focus of the majority of these proceedings was on British victims; even at the Belsen Trial, the sole British survivor of the camp was the first former prisoner to give evidence. This was in part a question, as I have noted, of jurisdictional responsibility, but it reinforces the sense that serving as a proxy for 'human justice' was not the principal motivation for the British trials.

The first chapter of this book, 'Publishing and Publicizing the Belsen Trial', focuses on the influential work of William Hodge & Co, a Scottish legal publishing firm, who, shortly prior to the First World War, had established a series called *Notable Trials*, offering general readers transcripts of trials deemed to be of historical and legal significance, with each volume including an introduction explaining the case's points of interest in lay-person's terms. In the late 1940s, a new subseries, *War Crimes Trials*, was launched. Nine volumes were published between 1948 and 1952, but the subseries ceased publication before several others that had been announced actually

---

[85] Gerald Reitlinger, *The Final Solution: The Attempt to Exterminate the Jews of Europe, 1939–1945* (London: Vallentine Mitchell, 1953), p. 170.

[86] Devin O. Pendas, *The Frankfurt Auschwitz Trial, 1963–1965: Genocide, History, and the Limits of the Law* (Cambridge: Cambridge University Press, 2006), p. 161.

appeared. This chapter situates the volume dealing with the trial of personnel captured at Belsen alongside other contemporary depictions of the trial, such as those that appeared in the popular press, and places it in the context of Hodge & Co's wider project of educating the general public about legal procedure.

James Hodge, who oversaw both the *Notable Trials* and *War Crimes Trials* series, and who edited the trial transcript for the Belsen volume, saw these books as a corrective to what he considered overly sensationalized press coverage of criminal trials. I argue that, where the Belsen Trial was concerned, press reports, despite their deficiencies, were better able to convey a sense of the trial as an event that comprised of more than just the testimony recorded in the transcript. Further, in a number of instances, Hodge omits the testimony of witnesses or makes unacknowledged edits, smoothing over the complexities of the proceedings. Taken together, the Hodge & Co volume and the press coverage reveal the extent to which, both during the proceedings and in later representations of them, resorted to interpretative frames that had emerged in discussions of domestic criminality: as I've noted, rapist and murderer Neville Heath, hanged in 1946, and Josef Kramer, the Commandant of Belsen, were both described in the press as 'sadistic', and the term *beast* was also applied to each of them. This type of language draws on the discourse of degeneration (the late-Victorian fear that man might de-evolve to a savage state), as well as the notion that criminality is inherent. I consider the implications of these attempts to adapt existing understandings of criminality to what were nevertheless recognized to be unprecedented crimes.

Among those who gave evidence at the Belsen Trial were British officers who had been among the first to arrive at the camp in April 1945. Chapter 2, 'Constructing Criminality in the Work of Derrick Sington', focuses on a hitherto under-discussed figure who is significant not least because his experiences at Belsen evidently fuelled his concern with wider issues of the treatment of prisoners and the appropriateness (or, in his view, inappropriateness) of the death penalty. The 1957 book *The Offenders: Society and Atrocious Crime*, which Derrick Sington co-authored with journalist Giles Playfair, included a chapter by Sington arguing that Irma Grese, condemned to death for her actions at Belsen and Auschwitz, should not have been hanged, and suggesting that social pressures could have affected her behaviour. *The Offenders* was published just as the 1957 Homicide Act introduced the defence of diminished responsibility into English and Welsh law, a measure that from Sington's abolitionist perspective did not go far enough.

In the chapter on Grese, Sington revisited his earlier account of Belsen and attempted to contextualize his first, visceral response to what he saw there. Sington's later writing therefore opens up the question of how the aftermath of the war crimes trials intersected with debates in Britain about the potential abolition of capital punishment and judicial and penal reform more generally, as well as reframing both Sington's testimony at the Belsen Trial and his earlier account of the camp.

One of the 'star' witnesses at the Belsen Trial was Channel Islander Harold Le Druillenac. The emphasis placed on his testimony—he was one of the first former inmates of the camp to give evidence—reflects the predominant focus on finding justice for British victims during the British-run trials. My third chapter, 'Memoir, Biography, and Justice', focuses on texts by and about some of the other British prisoners who were held in concentration camps, as opposed to prisoner of war camps, many of them SOE agents captured while working undercover, some of whom, including some women, were executed. Reporting of trials relating to these cases was supplemented during the late 1940s and early 1950s by biographical accounts aimed at a popular readership, including Jerrold Tickell's *Odette* (1949), which describes Odette Sansom's time as a prisoner at Ravensbrück concentration camp, Peter Churchill's *The Spirit in the Cage* (1954), recounting his captivity in Sachsenhausen and Dachau, and R. J. Minney's *Carve Her Name with Pride* (1956), which culminates in an account of Violette Szabo's execution at Dachau. These texts evidence a tendency to deflect attention away from the wider project of which such camps were a part, contributing to an over-simplified description of Nazi personnel and drawing on stereotypes of either German 'national character' or, more broadly, criminal 'types'.

Other examples of this subgenre of agents' biographies do attempt a more nuanced account of both the agents' experiences and the problems, in the wake of the war, of identifying witnesses and constructing coherent narratives of covert activities. The writings of Jean Overton Fuller, including *Madeleine* (1952), her biography of executed agent Noor Inayat Khan, fall into this category. Many of these works were adapted into popular films that often tend towards a further simplification of events that were in any case difficult to research because of the destruction or inaccessibility of much relevant archive material in both Germany and Britain. These texts contributed to a narrowing of public understanding in Britain as to what constituted the crimes of Nazism, and simultaneously engaged in debates about Britishness and British values in the wake of war.

Although many of the representations discussed in this study tend to deflect attention away from the Holocaust and its victims, some British texts from both the war years and the immediate post-war period do incorporate depictions of individuals who have either escaped from the Nazi regime before the outbreak of war or have entered Britain as refugees after surviving the camps. Narratives of crime and criminality are again a crucial means of attempting to organize and understand what is often perceived as a potentially disruptive social presence. Chapter 4, 'Holocaust Survivors and Refugees in 1940s Detective Fiction' examines how, at a period when classic detective fiction was beginning to shift towards the more realistic approach of the police procedural, attempts at incorporating either pre- or post-war refugees into detective narratives often drew on stereotypes, even when the depiction of these individuals was intended to be broadly sympathetic. A comparison between Mitzi, the self-pitying refugee housekeeper in Agatha Christie's *A Murder Is Announced* (1950), and Gerd, a refugee who is a model of forbearance and forgiveness in Ellis Peters's *Fallen into the Pit* (1951), is instructive here.

In many of these novels, events that occurred in Nazi Germany are alluded to only in passing, or via metonymy, with the name of a camp standing for the crimes committed there, and the crimes themselves not described in any detail. The use of this device is related to the economy with which detective fiction in general tends to draw its protagonists, but it implies, as I noted earlier, that readers would be expected to have some sense of the events thus alluded to. These novels for the most part focus on the closed communities that are typically found in interwar detective fiction: the country house, as in G. D. H. and Margaret Cole's *Toper's End* (1942) and Cyril Hare's *An English Murder* (1951); the school, in Gladys Mitchell's *Tom Brown's Body* (1949); even the train compartment, as in Raymond Postgate's *Somebody at the Door* (1943). The presence of refugees and survivors in these communities, and their entanglement with the social disturbance that is concomitant with a crime being committed, provides scope for assessing how new understandings of Britain and its place in Europe were being broached in popular writing at this period.

I will conclude with a consideration of how references to Nazi crimes were brought to bear in debates relating to the potential abolition of capital punishment in Britain in the period between the late 1940s and the trial and execution of Adolf Eichmann in 1961–1962. A particular focus will be the work of Victor Gollancz, founder in 1955 of the National Campaign for the Abolition of Capital Punishment. Having argued in his own writings against what he saw as punitive treatment of German civilians at the end of the war, Gollancz protested against Eichmann's execution at a time when the death penalty was still in force in Britain. Gollancz's interventions show him continuing to grapple with the issue of where the boundaries of responsibility for Nazi crimes might lie and arguing against the continued contemplation of Nazi crimes, with looking away constructed as a means of maintaining 'civilized' values.

These arguments were echoed by Pamela Hansford Johnson in *On Iniquity* (1967), based on her reports from the 1966 trial of Ian Brady and Myra Hindley. Taking place the year after capital punishment was suspended as a preliminary to its abolition, this trial, which centred on the torture and murder of children, prompted discussion about whether imprisonment was sufficient punishment for such crimes, and the question of the appropriateness of certain representations of Nazi crimes being widely and freely available was debated after the nature of Brady's preferred reading matter was made public. I will trace the continuities between these engagements with Nazi crimes and those discussed elsewhere in this book in order to show how, even post-Eichmann, viewing war crimes via the lens of other kinds of criminality continued to provide a strategy for the attempted containment of Nazism's legacy.

1

Publishing and Publicizing
the Belsen Trial

Considering the post–Second World War trials of war criminals from the
perspective of having been Chief Prosecutor for the British at Nuremberg,
Hartley Shawcross drew a comparison with domestic criminality: 'Murder
remains murder, though repeated a million-fold.' But the scale of deaths
being dealt with at proceedings including the IMT was a key point of differentiation: '[T]he mind which is lastingly impressed and shocked by a
single crime staggers and reels at the contemplation of mass criminality.'
Shawcross suggests that the excessive nature of these crimes can prompt
disbelief from those who hear of them, a tendency he attributes, perhaps
generously, to 'subconscious wishfulness', a hope that these things might
not actually be true.[1] For Shawcross, this reinforces the need for an accurate record of war crimes tribunals, which will stand as testimony to what
happened.

Four years earlier, in 1942, Arthur Koestler, the Hungarian-born Jewish author who had left France for England in 1940, described much more
bluntly the difficulties of conveying the scale and nature of violence being
carried out at a distance: 'A dog run over by a car upsets our emotional
balance and digestion; three million Jews killed in Poland cause but a mod-
erate uneasiness. Statistics don't bleed; it is the detail which counts. [...]
[W]e can only focus on little lumps of reality.'[2] Both Shawcross and Koestler

---

[1] Hartley Shawcross, 'Foreword', in *Trial of Wolfgang Zeuss and Others (the Natzweiler Trial)*,
edited by Anthony M. Webb (London: William Hodge, 1949), pp. 13–15 (p. 15).

[2] Arthur Koestler, 'Scum of the Earth—1942', in *The Yogi and the Commissar* (London:
Jonathan Cape, 1960 [1945]), pp. 85–93 (p. 97). Koestler had been in Le Vernet internment
camp in the South of France before arriving in the UK. As well as drawing on his own experiences of incarceration and as a refugee, he wrote several essays and stories influenced by
his meeting with Jan Karski, the Polish courier and resistance worker in London in late 1942.
Karski had brought to Britain information obtained by the Polish underground about the
killing of Jews in German-occupied Poland. He also gave his own testimony, having twice been
smuggled into the Warsaw Ghetto to observe conditions there, and having disguised himself as
a guard to see conditions at a transit camp. This material was the source for Koestler's story,
'The Mixed Transport', *Horizon* 8 (1943): pp. 244–51.

Literature and Justice in Mid-Twentieth-Century Britain. Victoria Stewart, Oxford University Press.
© Victoria Stewart (2023). DOI: 10.1093/oso/9780192858238.003.0002

consider the challenges of apprehending events of an unprecedented scale, but Koestler is more cynical about the impact of statistics. Where Shawcross suggests a listener overwhelmed by the scope of Nazi crimes, Koestler believes that attempting to convey this scope can itself diminish emotional engagement. Shawcross focuses on how the listener might perceive the crimes, and by extension the criminal; Koestler is more concerned that the individual victim might disappear from view. Each, however, indicates the problems of both representing and understanding events which appear to have no meaningful precedent.

Shawcross's comments come in his preface to one in a series of books that intended to present the war crimes tribunals in accessible form to the British public. Scottish legal publisher William Hodge & Co repurposed the format of their existing 'Notable Trials' series, which was an influential and widely referenced source for writers of both factual and fictional accounts of criminal proceedings in the interwar years, and produced a subseries on war crimes trials.[3] Comparing the material offered to readers in the 'War Crimes Trials' volumes to the newspaper reports that the series aimed to supplement and indeed supersede shows that in an attempt to avoid what were perceived as the shortcomings of newspaper reports, Hodge & Co were not always able to circumvent other problems in their framing of the trials.

Caroline Sharples has examined public responses to the war crimes trials, especially those relating to the 'major' war criminals held at Nuremberg, as expressed in a 1946 Mass-Observation survey, and has shown that even the most 'judicious' respondent was liable to 'blur the identity of the Nazis' victims'.[4] Tony Kushner, meanwhile, has made connections between these reactions and attitudes in Britain towards post-war recovery, immigration, and the establishment of the state of Israel.[5] The question posed in this chapter is the slightly different one of how existing conventions for the depiction of legal procedure and criminality might have shaped the presentation and reception of the trials. Donald Bloxham argues that the British war crimes trials were characterized by 'a legal conservatism', not

[3] On the interwar 'Notable Trials' series, see Victoria Stewart, *Crime Writing in Interwar Britain: Fact and Fiction in the Golden Age* (Cambridge: Cambridge University Press, 2017).

[4] Caroline Sharples, 'Holocaust on Trial: Mass Observation and British Media Responses to the Nuremberg Tribunal, 1945–46', in *Britain and the Holocaust: Remembering and Representing War and Genocide*, edited by Caroline Sharples and Olaf Jensen (Basingstoke: Palgrave Macmillan, 2013), pp. 31–50 (p. 45).

[5] Tony Kushner, *The Holocaust and the Liberal Imagination: A Social and Cultural History* (Oxford: Blackwell, 1994).

least because of an emphasis on '"war crimes" as traditionally defined'.[6] My contention is that a certain 'conservatism' can also be perceived in representations of the trials because of how discourse and frames of reference relating to domestic crime (that is, crimes taking place in Britain) were adapted to accommodate and describe war crimes and those accused of them. This meant, among other things, that a differentiation between the events that we now term *the Holocaust* and other war crimes in accounts of trials at this period was not always discernible, and that when it was, the results could be surprising.

I will focus here on *The Belsen Trial*, the volume dedicated to the British-run trial of Josef Kramer and forty-four others that took place at Lüneburg, a town about forty miles to the north of the camp, between 17 September and 17 November 1945. As I outlined in the introduction, these proceedings were established and run by the British military and were rooted in existing British military-legal practice. James Hodge, who edited the trial transcript for this volume, focused on reducing the trial to a manageable *text*, rather than attempting, in the body of the volume, to evoke how the trial unfolded as an *event*. This becomes particularly apparent when the copy of the transcript that was used by Major T. C. M. Winwood, Kramer's defence counsel, is considered. This is made up of a series of clipped together bundles of typescript pages, each representing a single day's proceedings, and it points up the extent to which *The Belsen Trial* inevitably reduces the ongoing record of a process to a completed narrative. The transcript contains a number of moments which indicate that counsel have gone back and consulted the record of earlier days in the trial in order to refresh their memories or reopen points of contention.[7] Hodge's editing removes moments such as these in favour of presenting an account that proceeds day-by-day to the end that the reader will undoubtedly be expecting, and which, in this formal aspect at least, resembles other Hodge & Co volumes that dealt with quite different types of crime.

    [6] Donald Bloxham, 'British War Crimes Trial Policy in Germany, 1945–1957: Implementation and Collapse', *Journal of British Studies* 42.1 (2003): pp. 91–118 (p. 117).
    [7] For instance, in defence counsel Major A. M. Munro's discussion of the word *schlagen* (to beat) in his closing speech, examined further below, the transcript has: 'I would like to illustrate [the potential loss of meaning in translation] by reference to Transcript no, 23 page 7, the cross-examination of [the] accused by my learned friend.' This indicates the written record was not only consulted by counsel as an aide memoire but that it was used in the court room to direct attention to specific moments from proceedings. 'Transcript of the Official Shorthand Notes of the Trial of Josef Kramer and Forty-Four Others', Day 46. http://www.bergenbelsen. co.uk/pages/TrialTranscript/Trial_Day_046.html. Accessed 15 October 2019.

Writing about the Nuremberg IMT, Rebecca West critiqued those proceedings as 'a betrayal of the hopes [they had] engendered. [...] [A]ttended by only a handful of spectators, inadequately reported, constantly misinterpreted, it was an unshapely event [...] It was one of the events which do not become an experience.'[8] By West's reckoning, an event does not succeed in changing how people think or behave in the way that an experience does. Lyndsey Stonebridge reframes these comments by considering 'what turns a legal event into an historical experience', arguing that a sense of justice being felt to be done by all those involved is an important point of differentiation. She sees West as offering a 'glimpse, as it were, of what it meant to respond to genocide in the pre-history of the era of the witness'.[9] As I will show in what follows, a similar claim can be made of the Belsen Trial. A trial is always subsidiary to the crimes that occasion it, but as West points out, and as James Hodge believed, the trial, or rather how the trial is represented, is the main opportunity for those affected either directly or indirectly by the crimes under consideration to grasp how and why those crimes might have been perpetrated. West's event/experience distinction tends then to merge what are, I would argue, intertwined but nevertheless separate questions: the adequacy of the proceedings themselves and the adequacy of how they were mediated to the public.

The Belsen Trial

As I indicated in the introduction, the Lüneberg proceedings, which heard charges against defendants accused of war crimes committed at both Bergen-Belsen and Auschwitz, were just one of many trials established and run by individual Allied nations in the immediate post-war years and did not involve the level of infrastructure and international co-operation required by the IMT at Nuremberg. But, as was the case for the IMT, those running the Belsen Trial had to find a way of applying existing legislation when the nature and scope of the events under scrutiny were only partially grasped. Hearkening back to the images of Belsen that were widely circulated in the British press following the Allies' arrival at the camp, reports of the proceedings were a factor in securing the iconic status of Belsen in British

---

[8] Rebecca West, *A Train of Powder: Six Reports on the Problem of Guilt and Punishment in Our Time* (New York: Viking Press, 1955), p. 246.

[9] Lyndsey Stonebridge, *The Judicial Imagination: Writing after Nuremberg* (Edinburgh: Edinburgh University Press, 2011), p. 26.

understandings of Nazi crimes. A complicating factor at the Lüneberg trial was the linking of Auschwitz and Belsen. This happened because a number of the defendants, including Belsen commandant Josef Kramer, who was redeployed from Auschwitz to Belsen in December 1944, had worked at both camps. The evacuation of Auschwitz prisoners to Belsen began early in 1945, ahead of the Soviet advance, meaning that many of the survivors who gave evidence were able to speak about their experiences of each camp.

While it might have seemed logical, when placing individuals on trial, to consider similar offences alleged to have been committed at both Auschwitz and Belsen, this could imply a false equivalence. Auschwitz was a death camp; Belsen was not; or, as Anita Lasker-Wallfisch, a survivor of Auschwitz and Belsen who gave evidence at Lüneburg, put it in her later memoir: 'Auschwitz was a place where people were *murdered*. In Belsen they *perished*.'[10] Rebecca Wittmann points out that a focus on 'crime complexes', that is, the locations where crimes were committed, could lead to a blurring of issues of individual responsibility, because emphasizing the infrastructure of which the individual was a part could add leverage to an 'obeying orders' defence. Wittmann acknowledges, though, that some German legal commentators at the time of the Frankfurt Auschwitz Trial in 1964–1965 felt that building court proceedings around 'crime complexes' was positive in exposing the workings of Nazi state, helping to illustrate the scope of the camp system.[11]

In his foreword to the first volume in the 'War Crimes' series, the series general editor, Sir David Maxwell Fyfe, appears to anticipate this argument when he suggests: 'It is doubtful whether there will ever be time to write, or whether humanity would have the tenacity and imagination to comprehend, a complete history of the atrocities perpetrated.' He thus positions the published record of the trial as a way of providing 'some idea of what tyranny harnessed to the modern scientific State can mean'.[12] In this analysis, the trial and an account of it have a function as part of the historical record even if they cannot be comprehensive in their scope. By alluding to the 'modern scientific State', Maxwell Fyfe indicates the potential applicability of the lessons learned beyond Nazi Germany. Similarly, Marco Duranti cites Maxwell

[10] Anita Lasker-Wallfisch, *Inherit the Truth 1939–1945* (London: Giles de la Mare, 1996), p.91.

[11] Rebecca Wittmann, *Beyond Justice: The Auschwitz Trial* (Cambridge, MA: Harvard University Press, 2005), p. 258.

[12] David Maxwell Fyfe, 'Foreword', in *The* Peleus *Trial*, edited by John Cameron (London: William Hodge, 1948), pp. xiii–xxi (p. xiii).

Fyfe's reflection that the IMT 'had posed the fundamental question: "What is the duty of a good European?"'[13] However, where the British trials of the late 1940s and their framing by Hodge & Co are concerned, the danger is that the events tried could seem atomized, disconnected from such wider context.

Claire Sharman points out that the terms of the Royal Warrant under which the British trials were established meant that the British 'were able to avoid complex legal questions', but 'the type of war crimes they could try was considerably curtailed'.[14] As the scholar of international law Egon Schwelb wrote in 1946, in comments on the legal grounding for the IMT that are relevant to the earlier trial: 'A connexion with the war [was] presumed in respect of actions committed during the war.'[15] While this might seem self-evident, it raises particular issues in relation to the persecution of Jews and others which began long before the war but accelerated once the conflict was underway. The indictment read at Lüneburg had two charges, one concerning 'violation of the law and usages of war' at Belsen, the other with the same wording, relating to Auschwitz, with named individuals belonging to the Allied nations identified as victims in each charge, and, in addition, 'other Allied nationals whose names are unknown' being mentioned in each.[16] Michael Bryant and Wolfgang Form note that evidence was also admitted of 'crimes by Germans against German and co-belligerent victims' and that while these were 'not technically war crimes [...] because they lacked the diversity of nationality required under the laws of war [...] evidence of these crimes was allowed in order to prove the defendants' involvement in a common plan to commit war crimes on allied victims'.[17] While the fact that different groups of prisoners found themselves in the camps for very different reasons was alluded to during the course of the trial, the wider significance of these differences was not foregrounded.

[13] Marco Duranti, *The Conservative Human Rights Revolution: European Identity, Transnational Politics, and the Origins of the European Convention* (Oxford: Oxford University Press, 2017), p. 141.

[14] Claire Sharman, 'War Crimes Trials Between Occupation and Integration: The Prosecution of Nazi War Criminals in the British Zone of Germany', unpublished PhD thesis (Southampton: University of Southampton, 2007), p. 57.

[15] Egon Schwelb, 'Crimes against Humanity', *The British Yearbook of International Law* 23 (1946): pp. 177–226 (p. 225).

[16] Raymond Phillips, ed., *The Trial of Josef Kramer and Forty-Four Others (the Belsen Trial)* (London: William Hodge, 1949) pp. 4–5.

[17] Michael Bryant and Wolfgang Form, 'Victim Nationality in US and British Military Trials: Hadamar, Dachau, Belsen', in *Justice, Politics and Memory in Europe after the Second World War Landscapes after Battle Volume II*, edited by Suzanne Bardgett, David Cesarani, Jessica Reinisch, and Johannes-Dieter Steinert (London: Vallentine Mitchell 2011), pp. 19–42 (p. 35).

Lawrence Douglas suggests that conceptualizing the Holocaust as a 'war crime' can result in an acceptance of the logic of revisionist historians, 'who have argued that the Nazis reasonably viewed the Jews as military enemies in a time of war'.[18] However, as I discuss further later in this chapter, at Lüneburg, the defence argued that precisely because the persecution of the Jews began prior to the war, it should *not* be seen as a war crime. These issues of definition and classification are important because they point to ongoing debates about the legitimacy of Allied war crimes trials, the IMT, and the later German-run trials to pass judgment on these events. In addition, such points of law intersect with and influence how the proceedings were presented to the public and are further complicated in the British context by their relationship to an existing tradition of crime and courtroom reporting.

Publishing Trials: The Work of William Hodge & Co

The firm of William Hodge & Co was established in Edinburgh in the late nineteenth century and supplied shorthand note-takers to the Scottish courts, as well as having printing and publishing concerns. The company's list initially focused on books with a Scottish interest, and in 1905, Harry Hodge, son of the company's founder William Hodge, initiated a series called 'Notable Scottish Trials'. Each volume began with an explanatory essay, written with a general reader rather than a legal specialist in mind, identifying the main points of legal interest in the case, and the body of the text was a lightly and usually invisibly edited transcript of the trial. The earliest volumes dealt with historical trials with links to the firm's Scottish roots: the 1747 trial of Lord Lovat for treason by the House of Lords during the Jacobite Rebellion was among the first in the series. In 1915, the series was relaunched as 'Notable Trials', from which point English and Welsh cases, and more recent trials, began to be included.

---

[18] Lawrence Douglas, *The Memory of Judgment: Making Law and History in the Trials of the Holocaust* (New Haven: Yale University Press, 2001), p.76. Discussing the Einsatzgruppen Trial, one of the subsequent Nuremberg proceedings, Dick de Mildt notes that the defence argued that despite the Jews not objectively seeming to be a threat, the defendants may have genuinely perceived this to be the case because of their ideological conditioning. De Mildt cites the court's judgment which 'dismissed [this] line of reasoning as nonsensical [...]: "The annihilation of the Jews had nothing to do with the defense of Germany [...] it was entirely foreign to the military issue." *In the Name of the People: Perpetrators of Genocide in the Reflection of Their Post-War Prosecution in West Germany* (The Hague: Martinus Nijhoff, 1996), p. 10.

Of the eighty-one cases that appeared in the series between 1905 and 1960, when publication ceased, sixty-two dealt with murder. The crimes considered in the remainder included fraud, bigamy, and disputed claims to titles, and, along with Lovat's, five other trials for treason, which was, like murder, a capital crime at this period. The importance of having a reliable transcript of proceedings increased after the establishment of the Courts of Criminal Appeal in England (1907) and Scotland (1926), and, for earlier trials, patchy availability of transcripts sometimes meant that the body of the text was in part a narrative summary of proceedings. On occasion, the contentious nature of the trial itself meant that commentary on the case was not especially detailed: the first edition of the trial of Roger Casement, another treason trial, was a case in point.[19]

In his essay for the firm's 1949 catalogue, James H. Hodge, who was editor of the series from the late 1920s until 1960, stressed the series' educative aims: '[Each] book's value to the lawyer, historian, and medical man is beyond dispute, and sensation and human interest abound, but its greatest attribute lies undoubtedly in its interest for the ordinary member of the community.'[20] Although an important characteristic of British justice is that trials are open to the public, Hodge observed that interested individuals were not always able to attend, and needed an alternative to the often partial and occasionally 'lurid' reports provided by the newspapers.[21] From the late 1940s, anthology volumes of the prefatory essays were published in paperback by Penguin, enabling the fruits of Hodge & Co's project to reach an even wider public. The correspondence exchanged by James Hodge and editors at Penguin relating to the selection of trials for the Penguin series illustrates that there was sometimes tension between Hodge's wish to continue this educative project and maintain the historical reach of the series, and what he saw as Penguin's desire to focus on more scandalous cases.[22] Certainly, during the 1920s and 1930s, trials relating to murders that had taken place in a domestic context, while not Hodge & Co's sole focus, were the type of case with which they were most closely associated and which provided the bulk

---

[19] As I explain further below, the Casement volume was one of a number of early arrivals in the series that were later reissued with revised introductory material.

[20] James Hodge, 'Introduction', in *Notable British Trials and War Crimes Trials*, (Edinburgh: William Hodge, 1949), pp. 5–7 (p. 5). Apart from the addition of some comments on the impact of the shortage of newsprint on the reporting of trials and extra paragraphs describing the intentions of the War Crimes subseries, this introduction was the same as that which had appeared in interwar editions of the catalogue.

[21] Hodge, 'Introduction', p. 5.

[22] See Stewart, *Crime Writing in Interwar Britain*, pp. 15–17.

of their source material, and at this period, they often produced volumes within a year or two of the trial in question taking place.

The 'War Crimes Trials' series was therefore presented as a subseries of the established Notable Trials' 'brand' and was underpinned by the same educative principles. Nine 'War Crimes' volumes were published between 1948 and 1952, and as early as 1949, several more had been announced by Hodge & Co as forthcoming.[23] Maxwell Fyfe, who was named as general editor of the series, was Solicitor General in the wartime coalition, and had close involvement in the establishment of the IMT. He was deputy prosecutor to Shawcross for the proceedings but, owing to Shawcross's appointment as Attorney General for the new Labour government, the 'day-to-day direction [of the British team] remained in [Maxwell Fyfe's] hands'.[24] Maxwell Fyfe therefore featured frequently in news reports about the IMT, and his name might well have been familiar to Hodge's readers. By 1948, when he was invited to be general editor of the series, he was both Shadow Minister of Labour and an active defence counsel with involvement in a number of high-profile criminal cases; the following year he would take a central role in the drafting of the European Convention on Human Rights.[25] The editors of the individual 'War Crimes Trials' volumes were all legally qualified, with many having had an involvement in the trials in question, and a roster of prominent legal names provided prefaces, which supplemented the explanatory introductions by volume editors that were usual in the 'Notable Trials' series.

It was evidently deemed appropriate given the nature of the tribunals, the crimes with which they dealt, and the points of law that they raised, that the volumes should have contributions from members of the judiciary and law professors, rather than the crime essayists who were the most usual authors of introductions to the pre–Second World War Notable Trials. In terms of the selection principles that were applied to the 'War Crimes Trials',

---

[23] The volumes published in addition to *Trial of Josef Kramer* were: *The* Peleus *Trial* (1948); *The Gozawa Trial* (1948); *The Hadamar Trial* (1949); *The Natzweiler Trial* (1949); *The Falkenhorst Trial* (1949); *The Velpke Baby Home Trial* (1950); *The 'Double Tenth' Trial* (1951); and *The Dulag Luft Trial* (1952). Those announced but never published were: *The 'Zyklon B' Trial*; *The Justice Trial*; *The Trial of Kesselring*; *The Stalag Luft III Trial*; *The Trial of Arthur Greiser*; and *The Doctors Trial*.

[24] Ann Tusa and John Tusa, *The Nuremberg Trial* (London: Macmillan), p. 95.

[25] The trial of John George Haigh, the so-called Acid Bath Murderer in 1949, a case which ended with Haigh's execution after an unsuccessful attempt at an insanity plea by Maxwell Fyfe, was Maxwell Fyfe's best-known case of the late 1940s and was itself the subject of a 1953 *Notable Trial* volume. For Maxwell Fyfe's involvement in the ECHR, see, Duranti, *The Conservative Human Rights Revolution*.

Hodge notes in the catalogue that the 'object of this series of trials is to present as wide as possible a cross-section of the various crimes committed by minor war criminals against the laws and usages of war and the elementary rights of the human race, during the Second World War'. As with the original series, Hodge stressed the volumes' interest for a wide readership of 'historians, lawyers and all interested in political thought and international affairs'.[26] In this, the projected series differed from the roughly contemporaneous *Law Reports of Trials of War Criminals* (1947–1949), produced by the United Nations War Crimes Commission and published in the UK by HMSO. Rather than containing a full account of the trials, the HMSO volumes restricted themselves to the necessarily narrower remit of the law report as a genre, giving an account of aspects of the cases that had set legal precedents.

Hodge's characterization of the 'War Crimes Trials' as focusing on 'minor war criminals' can be contextualized by the fact that early in the planning of the series, Maxwell Fyfe steered him away from his original idea of publishing the proceedings of the IMT, pointing out that other arrangements were already underway for their publication; to some extent, Hodge made a virtue of necessity.[27] As I have indicated, the trials of 'minor' war criminals often focused on specific locales, the places where the alleged crimes took place, and were usually run by whichever of the Allied powers had occupied the 'crime scene'. The IMT was tasked with dealing with the 'major' war criminals, those who were in overall charge of policy and conduct relating to the war. The later successor trials at Nuremberg, run by the Americans, focused on institutions that formed the infrastructure of the Nazi state, building trials around, for example, the judiciary, the medical profession and banking, and Hodge & Co intended to include some of these in the series.

---

[26] Hodge, 'Introduction', p. 6.
[27] Hodge made initial contact with Maxwell Fyfe via an intermediary, Maxwell Fyfe's fellow M. P. James Scott Reid, and it was in his reply to Reid that Maxwell Fyfe suggested that Hodge & Co should not tackle the Nuremberg Trials, which was the plan initially mooted to Maxwell Fyfe on Hodge's behalf. Letter from David Maxwell Fyfe to J. Scott Reid, 7 June 1946, University of Cambridge, Churchill Archives Centre, KLMR 7/1. Maxwell Fyfe provided a short prefatory note for the first volume to be published (*The Peleus Trial*) but does not appear to have had hands-on involvement in the selection of other cases to be dealt with by the series. In relation to the IMT, Kim Christian Priemel notes, Maxwell Fyfe discussed with Shawcross the need to provide accounts of the proceedings tailored for a variety of audiences. 'Cunning Passages: Historiography's Ways in and out of the Nuremberg Courtroom', *Central European History* 53 (2020): pp. 785–810 (p. 803).

The extent of British involvement in the trials covered by the volumes that did appear in the series was varied. At the Belsen Trial, it was specifically noted in the indictment that one of the known victims at the camp was a British national, Keith Mayor.[28] Meanwhile, at the Velpke Baby Home Trial, held in the spring of 1946, the question of whether a British court had the right to try German nationals for crimes alleged to have been committed against nationals of territory that was, at the time of the crimes, under German occupation, formed part of the defence case. The victims in this case were the children of Polish and Russian forced labourers who had been sent to Germany to work in agriculture or armaments factories, and the British took responsibility for the trial because they were the occupying force of the area where the home was located. Other cases in the series focused more specifically on British interests. The Dulag Luft case, heard in late November and early December 1945, centred on the torture of British prisoners of war in German captivity at Oberursel, and the volume dealing with it was published in 1952.[29] One of the volumes that was announced as forthcoming in the series but never actually appeared would have dealt with the execution of British prisoners of war who were recaptured by the Germans in the wake of their escape from Stalag Luft III, the so-called Great Escape.

The 'Notable Trials' and 'War Crimes Trials' generally did not make money for Hodge & Co, and, as I have noted, publication ceased in 1960, though new Penguin 'Famous Trials' anthology volumes, which did not include any of the war crimes trials, continued to appear until 1964. Aside from financial considerations, another factor in the curtailing of the 'War Crimes' series could have been diminishing public interest in these trials, especially after those directly concerning the fates of British subjects, such as the Natzweiler Trial of May 1946 and the first Stalag Luft III Trial (July–Sept 1947) had been heard.[30] As I will show, the fact that both the Belsen Trial

---

[28] Mayor, whose name is given as 'Meyer' in the indictment was an Able Seaman turned Commando, who was executed at Belsen in early April 1945. The investigation into his death is described by Joseph Quinn in a blogpost for the National Archives, 'The British Sailor Murdered at Bergen-Belsen'. https://blog.nationalarchives.gov.uk/the-british-sailor-murdered-at-bergen-belsen-the-75th-anniversary-of-the-bergen-belsen-trials/. Accessed 9 November 2020.

[29] *Dulag Luft* was the generic name for camps where captured members of the Allied air forces would be taken for interrogation prior to being sent on to other camps (*Dulag* is a contraction of *Durchgangslager*, meaning 'transit camp').

[30] Bloxham, 'British War Crimes Policy', p. 109. The Natzweiler Trial, to which I will return in Chapter 3, dealt with the death of female SOE agents at Natzweiler concentration camp.

and the IMT were protracted proceedings was certainly seen as a reason for the public becoming less engaged in their outcomes.

Although the British-run trials were military courts, with a Judge Advocate General presiding and a panel of judges deciding the verdict, in other respects they unfolded according to common law adversarial principles that would have been familiar to Hodge & Co's readers. The precedents cited were often from previous conflicts, but there were instances when *Archbold Criminal Pleading, Evidence and Practice*, first published in 1822 and still, in updated form, a standard textbook of English and Welsh criminal procedure, was invoked by counsel.[31] One area of divergence from usual English and Welsh criminal law practice was the acceptance of sworn affidavits where witnesses were unable to be present. Usually, statements were only read-in to proceedings when their content was agreed by both prosecution and defence because if the witness was not present, cross-examination could not take place. But the inclusion of such nonagreed material was deemed unavoidable given the circumstances surrounding the gathering of evidence. Many of those who had been interviewed in the summer of 1945 at Belsen were no longer in Germany and could not be compelled to attend the trial. Hearsay evidence was admitted to an extent that would not have usually been permitted in civilian courts. Acknowledgement was made of the fact that the procedures followed would not be familiar to the defendants, even if they had previous court appearances to their names, and so, for instance, defendants were warned that although they had the right to speak in their own defence, a practice not usual in continental law, this would make them liable to being cross-examined. At Lüneberg, the majority did indeed decide to give evidence.

The defendants had these issues explained to them by their counsel, who, with the exception of Lieutenant A. Jedrzejowicz, a Pole who represented six Polish defendants, were British army officers. Winwood, the lead counsel, who represented four defendants including Kramer, described later in a short, unpublished memoir, how he and his fellow officers came to be involved in the trial. Having qualified and worked as a solicitor prior

---

A second trial relating to Stalag Luft III was held in October–November 1948, just as the announcement that there would be no further British war crimes prosecutions was made.

[31] For example, during the *Peleus* trial, which centred on an attack made on the Greek-registered merchant vessel *Peleus* by a German submarine in 1944, the case of the British hospital ship, the *Llandovery Castle*, torpedoed by a German submarine in 1917, was cited as a precedent by the defence. See John Cameron, ed., *The Peleus Trial* (London: William Hodge, 1948), pp. 93–95. *Archbold* was cited in the closing speech for the defendants Oscar Schmitz and Karl Francioh at the Belsen Trial. See Phillips, ed., *The Trial of Josef Kramer*, p. 542.

to the war, Winwood put his name forward when he saw a notice in the British Army on the Rhine headquarters requesting qualified solicitors and barristers to volunteer, without knowing what he might be asked to do. Two months later, he was summoned to report to Celle, and, by his own account, having been the first to arrive, he was simply allocated the first four defendants on the indictment. He and the other counsel were given two weeks to prepare their cases.[32]

Although Shawcross might have argued that the difference between crime in a peacetime context and war crimes, was, where public perception was concerned, largely one of degree, the defendants in the cases covered by the 'War Crimes Trials' series were charged with war crimes, not with murder, and the defence most often mounted on their behalf was one of 'obeying orders'. These were 'minor' war criminals in that they were judged to have knowingly participated in war crimes, even if they had not initiated them. Michael Bryant points out that in the early 1950s, West German Chancellor Konrad Adenauer identified 'Nazi criminality with [...] "true criminals", the "asocials" who filled the ranks of the SA and concentration camp staffs'. Bryant notes that levelling special condemnation at 'the sadistic perpetrator', in line with the historical precedent that violent crimes are treated more harshly than other types of crime, downplays 'an important aspect of the Holocaust—namely, that much of the destruction it wrought was done by dispassionate bureaucrats under orders'.[33] The corollary of this was the difficulty some of those interviewed by Mass-Observation had in assessing what might constitute an 'appropriate' punishment for those on trial at Nuremberg.[34] As I will show, British press coverage of the Belsen Trial also tended to focus on the characterization of individuals and individual behaviour in relation to a pre-existing vocabulary of 'criminality' and horror.

A further tension between sameness and difference pointed up by the co-existence of the original 'Notable Trials' and the 'War Crimes Trials' subseries is illustrated in an advert for Hodge & Co's publications that appeared in the *Times Literary Supplement* in November 1950. The volumes

---

[32] T. C. M. Winwood, 'Over Their Shoulder: Recollections of a British War Crimes Trial in Europe', TSS, 3pp, Winwood P.419, IWM.

[33] Michael Bryant, 'Punishing the Excess: Sadism, Bureaucratized Atrocity, and the US Army Concentration Camp Trials, 1945–47', in *Nazi Crimes and the Law*, edited by Nathan Stoltzfus and Henry Friedlander (Cambridge: German Historical Institute and Cambridge University Press, 2008), pp. 63–85 (p. 66).

[34] Sharples notes that many members of the public were troubled at seeing members of the Armed Forces on trial and, even where German soldiers were concerned, 'clung [...] to the longstanding rhetoric of the "honourable soldier"'. 'Holocaust on Trial', p. 44.

advertised were *The Trial of Peter Griffiths*, edited by George Godwin, and *The Velpke Baby Home Trial*, edited by George Brand, with an introduction by Hersch Lauterpacht, the international law expert who assisted in drafting Shawcross's closing speech for the IMT and was later a judge at the International Court of Justice. The paragraph describing the Griffiths volume provides the essentials of the case:

> On the night of 15th May, 1948, June Anne Devaney, a little girl of three years eleven months, was stolen from her bed in the Queen's Park Hospital, Blackburn, taken into the hospital grounds and brutally killed by dashing her head against a wall. Fingerprints were found on a Winchester bottle in the ward, and the police proceeded to take the fingerprints of all males over sixteen in the Blackburn area—the first time mass fingerprinting had been contemplated in England. Eventually the prints were traced to a young ex-guardsman named Peter Griffiths, who was convicted of the murder at the Lancaster Assizes in October 1948. The defence of schizophrenia makes this an important trial.[35]

While the nature of the defence is highlighted as making this a 'notable' trial, and indeed, unusually, the volume includes an appendix describing current medical thinking on the aetiology of schizophrenia, the use of mass fingerprinting as part of the investigation is also identified as novel in English investigative practice.[36] The fact that this case involved the death of a child made it relatively unusual in the context of the series, hence, perhaps, the precision with which June Devaney's age is given, although this is in line with the stark, legalistic description of the nature of her death; to say that she was 'not quite four' would be to stray into more explicitly emotive territory. This case was not widely covered in the national press, though as was customary, the fact that Griffiths had requested a reprieve from the Home Secretary and had had this request refused was reported.[37] The relative thoroughness with which the case is described in this advert indicates an expectation that readers would not be going to the 'Notable Trials' volumes 'cold'. Even if they had not read newspaper reports about the case, the advert itself identifies

---

[35] Anon, 'Just Published', *Times Literary Supplement*, 17 November 1950, p. 731.

[36] Griffiths was eventually tracked down via fingerprints that he had given in relation to the issuing of ration books. See George Godwin, 'Introduction,' in *The Trial of Peter Griffiths (The Blackburn Baby Murderer)*, edited by George Godwin (London: William Hodge, 1950), pp. 13–65 (p. 44).

[37] See Anon, 'Two Death Sentences to Stand', *The Times*, 11 November 1948, p. 4.

its chief features, creating the expectation that readers would be consulting the book not principally to find out what had happened, but rather to find out how and why, and more specifically, how and why the final verdict was reached.

The succeeding paragraph of the advert, describing the Velpke volume, is couched quite differently:

> In order to obtain the maximum amount of work from their Polish or Russian forced labourers, the Nazis set up a Baby Home in the village of Velpke where babies were forcibly taken from their mothers, usually within a day or two of birth, and placed in the care of a woman with no knowledge of child welfare at all. The children, healthy and well clad when placed in the home, were in a few days starving and covered with sores, and in a very short time they were dead. The accused were charged with the killing of those babies by wilful neglect.[38]

A large portion of this description of the volume is concerned with the historical circumstances which led to the crimes, although the reader is not told where Velpke is located (it is in Lower Saxony). One specific defendant is identified—'a woman with no knowledge of child welfare'—but it is not clear who the rest of the accused might have been, and nor is the verdict of the case indicated. The reader is not told how many children were killed, nor when or for how long the 'home' was in operation. Whereas the defence of schizophrenia is identified as an issue that makes Griffiths's trial noteworthy, in the description of the Velpke case, it is the use of forced labour and the treatment of the labourers and their children that is the point at issue. The context, rather than the individual personalities involved, is brought to the fore. What is highlighted by the juxtaposition of these two cases, both of which of course deal with the deaths of children, is the difficulty of simplifying and summarizing proceedings which involve multiple defendants and multiple victims of different nationalities in specific historical conditions, conditions which in this case had to be addressed as part of the proceedings.

In his introduction to the Velpke volume, Brand uses the Belsen Trial as a reference point, noting that the defence there regarded it as worthwhile to argue that an offence could only be punished as a war crime if it was directly connected with the operations of war [...] [T]he contention that this would

---

[38] Anon, 'Just Published', p. 731.

not have included ill-treatment and killing of internees in Belsen [...] was rejected by the British military court that tried the case.[39]

Indeed, Winwood argued in Kramer's defence: 'It is not a very big step from the laws of Nuremberg to the chimneys of Auschwitz',[40] identifying a continuity between the Nazi racial laws of the early 1930s and the later treatment of Jews and appealing to what would later be termed a functionalist view of the Holocaust in order to suggest that these were not specifically war crimes and should not therefore be considered by that court. By the time of the Velpke trial, a year later and in the wake of the main Nuremberg proceedings, the question of the boundaries of the category of war crime had, according to Brand, been properly established, though the Velpke trial nevertheless included debate on this issue.

The treatment of the Jews, then, is singled out by Brand, but only so that it can serve as a comparator against which other crimes, specifically other war crimes, may be measured. At the same time, the uniform presentation of the books in the 'War Crimes Trials' series, and the range of types of criminal activity covered, could have the effect of de-emphasizing some of these differences. Like the criminal cases with which Hodge & Co more usually dealt, war crimes can be subjected to legal scrutiny and blame can be apportioned for them, with precedent appealed to as a way of making manageable events that might otherwise be considered unprecedented.

The Belsen Trial: Depicting the Defendants

The unusual trial that took place at Lüneburg made an unusual volume for Hodge & Co. The number of defendants and the length of the proceedings meant that even with editing, the book was the longest and most expensive that the company had published. At over 700 pages, it was roughly double the standard size for a *Notable Trial*, and it was priced at thirty shillings, when the usual price per volume in the immediate post-war years was eighteen shillings. For comparison, a Penguin paperback at this period cost 1/6, and this adds point the fact that enough copies of *The Belsen Trial* were sold for James Hodge to identify it later as one of the very few 'Notable Trials' or 'War Crimes Trials' volumes to make a profit.[41] Acknowledging that

[39] George Brand, 'Introduction', in *The Trial of Heinrich Gericke and Others (The Velpke Baby Home Trial)*, edited by George Brand (London: William Hodge, 1950), pp. xvii–liv (p. xxxi).

[40] Phillips, ed., *The Trial of Josef Kramer*, p. 148.

[41] Stewart, *Crime Writing in Interwar Britain*, p. 17.

readers might have difficulty negotiating their way through the material, the publishers included a book mark, attached to the spine with a ribbon, listing the names of the defendants and the names of their defence counsel on one side, with a short glossary of German terms used in the trial and their English translations on the other.

As well as the large number of defendants and witnesses, a further factor that increased the length of the proceedings, originally estimated to be a month in duration but eventually lasting three, was that, unlike at Nuremberg, the technology that would have allowed simultaneous translation was available. Instead, transmission of information between English, German and Polish had to be carried out by the more time-consuming method of consecutive translation, in which speakers had to make frequent pauses while the words they had just said were translated.[42] As Simona Tobia explains, the interpreters involved were by no means specialists in courtroom practice. While 'court interpreting at Nuremberg was internationally recognized as a specific and important job [...] interpreting in [other] trials was [...] one of a number of interpreting duties that interpreters from the Pool [established by the British to support war crimes investigations] might have'.[43] Indeed, the logistical difficulties of courtroom translation when

---

[42] Susan Berk-Seligson describes *consecutive interpreting* as 'perhaps the most difficult of the modes of interpreting'. *The Bilingual Courtroom: Court Interpreters in the Judicial Process* (Chicago: University of Chicago Press, 2002), p. 89. Lieutenant Jedrzejowicz, the Polish officer who acted as defence counsel for six of the defendants, told the court on the fifth day that he would not need a German to Polish translation of witness testimony, but the Judge Advocate pointed out that the linguistic competence of the defendants themselves could not be guaranteed and so a translation would be necessary to ensure they had access to the proceedings: 'the accused must hear the evidence in the language which they could understand. Counsel could not possibly know how to cross-examine except on instructions from the accused whom he represented and his instructions must necessarily be determined by the evidence.' The Judge acknowledged that the suggestion had been made with the intention of 'endeavouring to shorten proceedings' but affirmed that it would be 'wrong in law' not to provide a translation. *Law Reports of Trials of War Criminals Selected and Prepared by the United Nations War Crimes Commission Volume II: The Belsen Trial* (London: HMSO, 1947), p. 145. Like much of the discussion of procedural matters, these exchanges are omitted from *The Trial of Josef Kramer*. Describing his preparations for the trial in his memoir, Winwood notes that he refused the offer of a German to English translator as he felt his German was good enough. There was some discussion towards the end of the trial of potential deficiencies in the translation. In his closing speech, Major Munro (for the defence) commented on 'the difficulties of translation, where the word "schlagen" could mean anything from a single blow up to a beating.' Phillips, ed., *Trial of Josef Kramer*, p. 528. The Hodge volume gives a summary rather than a word-for-word transcription of this speech, which the full transcript reveals contains further ruminations from Munro on the semantics of *to beat*.

[43] Simona Tobia, 'Questioning the Nazis: Languages and Effectiveness in British War Crime Investigations and Trials in Germany, 1945–48', *Journal of War and Culture Studies* 3.1 (2010): pp. 123–36 (p. 128).

more than two languages and large numbers of defendants were involved were one of the spurs for the development of the much more sophisticated system, based on a model that had been tried at the League of Nations and using microphones, headphones, and a team of interpreters working between each language, which was employed at Nuremberg.[44]

Responding to criticisms of the duration of the trial, Raymond Phillips, in his introduction to the volume, suggests that such complaints were made 'by a public whose interest was in a spectacular example of retribution rather than a minute assessment of the evidence.'[45] Another issue affecting public perceptions of the trial and especially its length could have been that it was unusual for a trial to have such a large number of defendants, and at this period even murder trials in Britain were dispatched with what would now seem like indecent haste. The trial of Peter Griffiths, mentioned earlier, lasted a not-untypical two days.

Comparing selected press coverage of the trial to its presentation in the Hodge & Co volume is one way of testing James Hodge's claim that his series avoids the sensationalizing of crime to which newspaper reports are prone, as well as his hope that the books would prove of use to future historians. Before considering examples of how witness evidence was presented in the newspapers and in the Hodge volume, the representation of the defendants warrants attention. Press reporting of criminal trials in Britain had long centred on the appearance and demeanour of the accused, and in this regard Josef Kramer and Irma Grese came to be seen as figures who embodied the type of criminality under scrutiny. Considering the SS defendants as a group, Phillips remarks: 'it is strange to consider that such ordinary-looking persons could be guilty of such cruelty. If they bore the mark of the beast on

---

[44] As Jesus Baigorri-Jalon points out, despite simultaneous interpretation having been tried out at the League of Nations, 'there were no interpreters with [meaningful] experience in simultaneous interpreting [available to work at Nuremberg] for the simple reason that this mode did not exist as such'. *From Paris to Nuremberg: The Birth of Conference Interpreting*, trans. Holly Mikkelsen and Barry Slaughter-Olsen (Amsterdam: John Benjamins, 2014), p. 218. The recollections of Alfred Steer, head of the languages division at the IMT, and Peter Uiberall, who worked there as an interpreter, show the extent to which the system used at Nuremberg had to be developed on the hoof. Aside from the various technological issues that needed to be ironed out, there was a presumption that competence in languages was in and of itself a qualification to act as an interpreter, and, indeed, that being able to translate documents implied competence in interpreting speech. See Hilary Gaskin, *Eyewitnesses at Nuremberg* (London: Arms and Armour, 1990), pp. 38–39, pp. 42–48.

[45] Phillips, 'Introduction', in *The Trial of Josef Kramer*, pp. xxi–xlv (p. xlv). Although Phillips is named on the title page as the volume editor, he points out in his acknowledgements that the task of editing the transcript for publication fell to James Hodge (p. v).

their faces it was not easy to discern at the trial.'[46] Other faces in the dock, he suggested, 'seemed to contain all the generally accepted characteristics of the debased criminal type'.[47] Phillips refers here to the Kapos among the defendants, some of whom were in the camp system in the first place after being found guilty of misdemeanours such as robbery or assault. His comments attest to the persistence, especially in popular discourse, of a watered-down version of mid- and late-nineteenth-century ideas, stemming originally from the work of the Italian criminologist Cesare Lombroso, about how criminality might be reflected in appearance. In 1881, British researcher Francis Galton developed the technique of composite photography as a way of visually identifying 'types', including the 'criminal type'. The lower and/or criminal classes were viewed in such typologies as throwbacks to a less developed phase of human evolution, although, as Stephen Arata points out, at the fin de siècle, an excess of 'refinement', or decadence, as supposedly displayed by 'cultured aesthetes', was also seen as symptomatic of degeneration.[48] The anxieties produced by such ideas, especially in their popularized and simplified forms, were therefore diffuse and multidirectional.

In terms of early academic criminology and the development of methods for dealing with criminals, in Britain at least Lombroso's ideas did not generally find favour.[49] But while criminology grappled with issues of whether criminality was an inbred tendency in order to assess whether rehabilitation was a viable prospect, in popular culture, the legacy of an over-simplified version of Lombrosian and Galtonian precepts had a long life, and the idea that an individual's appearance might betray their personality and, specifically, their criminality persisted—even, to some extent, still persists. Indeed, in the press and in popular literature, reference might be made to supposed criminal attributes whether the defendant in question seemed to match or defy them. If the defendant did not 'look' typically criminal, this could be taken as a sign their duplicity or cunning.

This determined adherence to the notion that criminality can be read from appearance is demonstrated in the newspaper coverage of the trial of Neville Heath, which I mentioned in the introduction, and which took

---

[46] Phillips, 'Introduction', pp. xliii.

[47] Phillips, 'Introduction', pp. xliii.

[48] Stephen D. Arata, 'The Sedulous Ape: Atavism, Professionalism, and Stevenson's "Jekyll and Hyde"', *Criticism* 37.2 (1995): pp. 233–59 (p. 235).

[49] David Garland points to the critique of Lombroso in Charles Goring's *The English Convict* (1913). 'British Criminology before 1935', *The British Journal of Criminology* 28.2 (1988): pp. 1–17 (p. 11).

place a year after the Belsen Trial. Heath raped and murdered two women, subjecting them to extreme sexual violence, and his terrible crimes were seen as being at odds with his neat appearance, military bearing in the dock, and reportedly suave manners when at liberty.[50] Rather than serving to undermine the idea that character can be read from appearance, the apparent normality of Heath's looks was offered as evidence of how dangerous and deceptive an individual he was. What never really became clear during the trial was what went on inside Heath's head, as opposed to what could be read from his demeanour. An attempt at mounting an insanity defence failed because Heath had evidently known what he was doing and known that it was wrong, this being the test for criminal responsibility at the period.[51] A large part of the threat embodied by Heath was seen to lie in his ability to 'pass' as respectable. It is not simply that his face did not betray the stereotypical marks of criminality: neither did his clothes nor his ability to be accepted in middle-class social circles.

The treatment of Heath helps to contextualize Phillips's comments about the Belsen defendants, especially the distinction he makes between the 'ordinary-looking' SS and the 'debased' Kapos. Here a divide is drawn between those of whom criminality might be expected, and those who, one would hope, might rise above it. While many Kapos undoubtedly did commit vicious acts of violence against their fellow prisoners, the way they were often described implies a direct equation between habitual criminality and an inherent lack of moral decency.[52] Criminality is thus constructed as a personality trait rather than as a form of behaviour with socio-cultural causes. Lasker-Wallfisch seems to recognize this when, reflecting on the experience of giving evidence at Lüneburg, she comments: 'I thought it entirely wrong that [the Kapos] should be tried alongside the people whose system had turned them into the animals they had become.'[53] Primo Levi elaborates a more complex typology for the Kapo, suggesting that while this role was one for which individuals were chosen, this choice was made based on the Nazi perception of a 'potential collaborator', and he qualifies this by observing that some individuals 'spontaneously aspired to power' and did so because

[50] See for instance, Guy Ramsey, 'Heath, man-about-town at 15, played lone wolf to the end', *Daily Mail*, 27 September 1946, p. 4
[51] For further discussion of how Heath was depicted in the press, see Victoria Stewart, 'The Criminal Type in Mid-Twentieth Century Britain: Hamilton, Gorse and Heath', *Open Library of Humanities*, 5.1 (2019). https://olh.openlibhums.org/articles/10.16995/olh.472/. Accessed 4 August 2022.
[52] I discuss the representation of Kapos further in Chapter 2.
[53] Lasker-Wallfisch, *Inherit the Truth*, p. 124.

they were 'sadists'.[54] Both Lasker-Wallfisch and Levi agree, then, that where the Kapos were concerned, questions of responsibility were more complex and more fine-grained than the categories constructed by either popular culture or the judicial system allowed.

Like all Hodge volumes, *The Belsen Trial* included photographs of the defendants. As well as a frontispiece depicting the prisoners in the dock, each wearing a number for identification purposes, several plates were taken up by 'mug-shot' style individual images.[55] Readers could therefore draw their own conclusions about whether the appearance of the defendants betrayed their criminality. At the time of the trial, some of the newspapers distinguished between different categories of defendant in the same way that Phillips does. The *Manchester Guardian* newspaper was in partial agreement with Phillips's view of the SS defendants as 'ordinary-looking', describing Kramer as the 'most nearly normal' of the defendants in appearance. The popular press, however, tended to take a different approach. *The Daily Express* referred to the defendants as the 'Belsen Gang', emphasizing their corporate responsibility and pointing towards the discourse of organized crime.[56] Kramer, though, was widely singled out as a special case, and was frequently dubbed the 'Beast of Belsen', a nickname that Sharples notes had been in use since shortly after the opening up of the camp.[57] According to the *Daily Mirror*, a 'crescent-shaped scar [seared] across his pale, brutish face': contrary to Phillips, the *Mirror* discerned the mark of the beast.[58]

[54] Primo Levi, 'The Grey Zone', in *The Drowned and the Saved*, trans. Raymond Rosenthal (London: Abacus, 1989), pp. 22–51 (pp. 31–32).

[55] The volume also includes photographs taken by soldiers and journalists on arrival at Belsen and at Auschwitz. It is beyond the scope of this chapter to discuss these in detail, but many had already been published in the press or in news magazines. Some are analysed by Barbie Zelizer in *Remembering to Forget: Holocaust Memory through the Camera's Eye* (Chicago: University of Chicago Press, 1998) and by Hannah Caven, 'Horror in Our Time: Images of the Concentration Camps in the British Media, 1945', *Historical Journal of Film, Radio and Television* 21.3 (2001): pp. 205–53.

[56] Vincent Evans, 'The Belsen Gang Stops Smiling', *Daily Express*, 19 September 1945, p. 4.

[57] Caroline Sharples, '"Where, Exactly, Is Auschwitz?" British Confrontation with the Holocaust through the Medium of the "Belsen" Trial', in *The Palgrave Handbook of Britain and the Holocaust*, edited by Tom Lawson and Andy Pearce (Basingstoke: Palgrave, 2020), pp. 181–200 (p. 186).

[58] Harry Ashbrook, 'Belsen Blonde on Her High Horse', *Daily Mirror*, 17 September 1945, p. 8. *The Daily Express*'s front-page photograph of Kramer, under armed guard and wearing leg irons, published on 21 April 1945, bore the caption: 'The Shackled Monster of Belsen'. The alliteration of the phrase 'Beast of Belsen' is likely to have been part of the reason that this label stuck; similarly, Peter Manuel, hanged in 1958 after committing a series of rapes and murders across Scotland was referred to as the 'Beast of Birkenshaw'. Both these labels echo the idea condensed in the title of Emile Zola's novel *La bête humaine* (1890), sometimes translated as 'The Beast in Man', that in some cases civilisation cannot completely subdue primal urges.

Though there were divergent views as to whether Kramer looked 'normal' or 'beastly', the equation of appearance with criminality was still a key reference point for depictions of him in the press. The contradictions of the Nazi regime—a surface of order and civility concealing depraved behaviour—are variously read from his body.

The use of terms such as *beast*, and, more generally, the othering of the defendants is something that the Lüneburg tribunal had in common with other post–Second World War trials. In her discussion of the 1963–1965 Frankfurt Auschwitz trial Wittmann observes that because this was conducted under the German civil code rather than international law, both the proceedings, and the press coverage of them, focused on 'excess perpetrators'. This meant in effect that a single markedly brutal instance of killing or torturing an individual might be treated more harshly than the 'routine' killing carried out at the gas chambers. Press coverage 'capitalized on the legal emphasis on excessive cruelty and individual sadistic behaviour'.[59] Devin O. Pendas points to the alienation of observers or readers that can result from this focus on extremes of atrocity, and, in particular, to how this might have assisted the German press and public in distancing themselves from the events thus described: '[T]he press accounts of the Auschwitz trial perhaps unintentionally displaced attention from the Holocaust as a historical process with continued implications for German society onto Auschwitz as an infernal, largely incomprehensible netherworld, populated by "monsters", "demons", or devils.'[60] While the stakes were different for the British press and public in the 1940s, it is nevertheless notable that this archetypal vocabulary was discernible at the Belsen Trial and in discourse surrounding it.

This is illustrated in a cartoon that appeared in the *Daily Express* on 18 September 1945. A diminutive 'Tommy', armed but with informal bearing, leads an enormous, top-heavy, almost ape-like individual, with the characteristically low brow of Kramer, into a courtroom, the caption reading: 'Must come strange to you, this idea of giving people a chance to defend themselves.'[61] Considering the IMT, Lawrence Douglas argues that characterizing Nazi crimes as 'crimes of atavism, horrific deeds committed in an orgy of barbarism' was necessary so that Western democratic values,

---

[59] Wittmann, *Beyond Justice*, p. 179.

[60] Devin O. Pendas, '"I Didn't Know What Auschwitz Was": The Frankfurt Auschwitz Trial and the German Press, 1963–1965', *Yale Journal of Law and the Humanities* 12. 2 (2000): pp. 397–446 (p. 422).

[61] 'Giles', cartoon, *Daily Express*, 19 September 1945, p. 2.

specifically in this instance the rule of law, could be asserted.[62] As Douglas points out, a different view of the relationship between atrocities and civilization is put forward by scholars including Zygmunt Bauman, who emphasize that the Holocaust emerged from a highly civilized Western nation thus problematizing the dichotomy between civilization and barbarism that labelling these crimes as atavistic attempts to impose.[63] For Douglas, labelling Nazism as atavistic was therefore a strategic claim, one which helped to shore up the court's own legitimacy as the arbiter of civilized values. The depiction of Kramer in the *Daily Express* cartoon can be seen as a way of reminding British readers that the values represented by the 'Tommy'—lack of awe in the face of this 'beast' and a common-sense assertion of the right to a fair trial—are those shared by the country at large and indeed the Allies. This acts as a riposte both to suggestions that the defendants should have been summarily executed and to any questions about the legitimacy of the court proceedings. More problematically, it suggests that the prisoners at the camps where Kramer was stationed were there only because of the failure of due process, rather than having been targeted because of their identities. Further, the caricaturing of Kramer as a 'beast' has a similar genealogy to the caricaturing of the Jews as animalistic or less evolved.[64]

Douglas describes the brief appearance Kramer makes in the film that was shown during the Nuremberg Trial, much of which had previously been screened at the Belsen Trial:

> The camera focuses briefly on the face of Josef Kramer, the former commandant of Belsen, whose unusually brutal appearance—small eyes cast to the side; thick neck; beefy cheeks beribboned with, to all appearance, dueling scars—makes him a helpful exemplar of the kind of person responsible for such crimes. Yet notwithstanding its brief focus upon this specimen of evil, the film fails to clarify more specific question of legal responsibility.[65]

---

[62] Douglas, *The Memory of Judgment*, p. 84.

[63] Douglas, *The Memory of Judgment*, p. 87.

[64] Other images of Kramer published in the newspapers reinforced the sense that might had been overcome by right: the *News Chronicle* pictured him seated, with manacled hands and downcast eyes, a pose that emphasizes his heavy brow, with a British soldier of relatively slight build standing guard over him. Anon, 'This Is the Killer of Belsen Camp', 20 April 1945, p. 1.

[65] Douglas, *The Memory of Judgment*, p. 37. The material screened at the Belsen Trial was a short film of conditions at Belsen made by the Army Film and Photographic Unit, and Russian footage of Auschwitz.

Douglas is evidently attempting to ventriloquize the way in which telling details of Kramer's appearance, as shown in the film, might have been read by the court. It is not just that Kramer's eyes are 'cast to the side', suggesting duplicity, but that his eyes are 'small', an anthropometric marker of dishonesty; a 'thick' neck implies not just physical stature but a tendency towards the use of brute force. The one unexpected association here is Douglas's suggestion that Kramer's facial scars could be read as the result of having been in a duel. Duelling, a practice associated with elites, university students, and honour codes, seems at odds with both the indicators Douglas marshals here as pointing towards 'brutality' and with what is actually known about Kramer: the world of university fraternities was not one within which he moved.[66] But by including this apparently out of kilter detail, Douglas provides further evidence of how degenerationist discourse works in both directions, Not only have the brutes been put in charge, but the supposed elites have become debased.

Given that he was the commandant of Belsen when it was reached by the British, it was unsurprising that Kramer became a focal point for coverage of the trial. Irma Grese was another defendant who attracted a good deal of press attention. I will discuss Grese further in the next chapter, but it should be noted that while Kramer was labelled the 'Beast of Belsen', the most frequent epithet assigned to Grese was 'blonde'. The soubriquet 'Belsen Blonde' seems to have drawn on the equation of 'blonde' with glamour and sensuality, emphasizing the mismatch between the cultural expectations generated by her appearance and her actual behaviour. Even where this term, with its specific cultural freight is not employed, Grese's apparent vanity as regards her appearance is noted. For instance, covering the opening days of the trial, the *Guardian* noted that she, and several other female defendants, had their 'fair hair neatly arranged in swept-up coiffures'.[67] When the court was shown a film as evidence of the conditions at the camp, the *Express* juxtaposed its description of images, which would have been familiar to many readers, of a

---

[66] Kramer left school at fourteen and began to train as an electrician before working in a department store, but was unemployed for most of the later 1920s, and began salaried work for the SS in 1934. See Tom Segev, *Soldiers of Evil: The Commandants of the Nazi Concentration Camps*, trans. Haim Watzman (New York: McGraw-Hill, 1987), p. 48.

[67] Anon, '13000 People Died in Six Weeks at Belsen', *Manchester Guardian* 18 September 1945, p. 5. It is striking that in their 'mug-shots', all the female defendants have 'done' their hair, almost all pinning it back and curling it in a style characteristic of the period. This could signal the persistence of cultural expectations relating to female appearance even in these most exiguous circumstances, but equally could be seen as an attempt by these women to retain a small shred of agency as regards self-presentation in what they evidently knew was a parlous situation.

bulldozer pushing bodies into a mass grave with an evocation of Grese, 'the 21-year-old blonde SS woman' adjusting 'her still neat ringlets'.[68] Grese did wear her hair curled, but the choice of the word 'ringlets', more usually associated with children, adds a macabre tone to this description, coupling with the indication of her age not to act as any kind of mitigation for Grese but to invite the reader to condemn her further for her behaviour. Her gender and her youth are both presented as adding to the seriousness of her actions.

The Belsen Trial: In the Courtroom and Beyond

As Bloxham notes, despite the interest generated by Grese, there was a 'dramatic decline' in press coverage of the trial in Britain once Kramer had given his evidence at the start of the defence case. Popular papers such as the *Daily Mirror* and *Daily Express* frequently erred on the side of 'local colour', including comments such as those already quoted relating to the demeanour of the accused, rather than prioritizing reporting the evidence presented. Bloxham describes British press coverage as 'capricious',[69] though it should be noted that, owing to continuing paper rationing and production issues, at this period space in British newspapers was at a premium, with some, such as the *Express*, consisting of only four pages at the time of the trial. Nevertheless, it is certainly the case that, like the trial itself, British newspaper coverage was largely skewed towards a British angle. Kushner points out that 'it was especially the evidence of the British liberators [...] or the few British victims of the camp that predominated'.[70] Indeed, the first witnesses for the prosecution were British army officers (including, as I discuss in Chapter 2, Derrick Sington) who had taken charge at Belsen in April 1945, and the first former prisoner to testify, on the opening day of the trial, was Harold Le Druillenac, a Channel Islander who was the only known British survivor of Belsen. Bloxham observes that Le Druillenac testified at several trials, describing him as 'something of a star witness for the British'.[71] Newspaper reports, necessarily, echoed the structure of the trial itself in foregrounding the British aspects of the case, but for all their shortcomings, they were at

---

[68] Anon, 'Briton Ate Grass in Belsen Camp', *Daily Express*, 18 September 1945, p. 4. I discuss the treatment of Grese further in the next chapter.

[69] Donald Bloxham, *Genocide on Trial: War Crimes Trials and the Formation of Holocaust History and Memory* (Oxford: Oxford University Press, 2001), p. 99.

[70] Kushner, 'The Memory of Belsen', p. 190.

[71] Bloxham, *Genocide on Trial*, p. 99.

times better able than the transcript contained in the Hodge & Co volume to convey the impact of the trial as it played out in the courtroom.

For example, on the ninth day of the trial, the court heard the evidence of Abraham Glinowieski, who was a prisoner in Auschwitz between 1942 and the end of 1944, and who, after moving between other camps, arrived at Belsen in early 1945. Like other former prisoners, Glinowieski was asked which of the defendants he could identify: 'I recognize No. 1, Kramer; No. 9. Grese; No 11, Hilde (Lobauer); No. 3, Weingartner; No. 48, Stanislawa (Starostka).'[72] Asked what he knew about Weingartner, Glinowieski described how the guard had severely beaten his brother. The transcript of his testimony in the Hodge volume continues:

> [My brother] could not stand during roll-call so we took him to hospital, to which I later went and spoke to the doctor, offering the latter a reward for looking after my brother when he got better. I was not allowed to see my brother. Later on he died.
>
> (At this point the witness broke down.)[73]

The text resumes with the opening of the next day of the trial, during which Glinowieski eventually continued giving evidence, with no allusion being made to the events of the previous day. In the *Manchester Guardian*'s report, Glinowieski is identified as Jewish. His testimony relating to his brother is summarized:

> He offered the doctor a reward to cure his brother, but later learned that he had died. At this stage witness broke down and wept in the silent court, while Kramer bared his teeth in a grimace more like a derisive grin than anything else. So overcome was the witness that the president of the Court, General Bernay, ordered the proceedings suspended.[74]

The report resituates Glinowieski's break-down within its context. While the switch in attention to Kramer and his reaction might seem, inappropriately, to divert the reader from considering the impact on the witness of having to recall his brother's death, it is a reminder of what is stripped away when

[72] Phillips, ed., *The Trial of Josef Kramer*, p. 103. The bracketed surnames in this quotation are editorial insertions made by Hodge.

[73] Phillips, ed., *Trial of Josef Kramer*, p. 104.

[74] Anon, 'Reports of Threats against the Belsen Witnesses', *Manchester Guardian*, 27 September 1945, p. 5. The *Manchester Guardian* gives the witness's name as Glinowiełcski.

the transcript alone is considered. The witness is not merely testifying: he is testifying in the presence of those responsible not only for his own suffering but for the death of a loved one.[75]

The *Guardian* correspondent includes the comments made by a 'Russian observer' while leaving the courtroom: '"To us it seems more like a game than a trial. Anyone who was on the staff at either Belsen or Auschwitz should be shot on the spot". In the heat of the moment one was inclined to agree with him, but it is not as simple as that in any respect.'[76] The reporter goes on to comment that, despite the harrowing nature of Glinowieski's evidence, other prisoners identified guards who, in their view, had not committed the crimes of which they were accused. This report then, while admitting the strong emotions experienced by both those giving evidence and those hearing it, warns against translating these emotions into the knee-jerk, blanket response advocated by the nameless Russian. It underscores the implication of the *Daily Express* cartoon, that allowing a fair trial even to those accused of heinous crimes, is one way of guaranteeing the reassertion of 'civilised values'.

If in this example the newspaper report supplements the evidence, in at least one other case, the newspapers gave coverage to evidence that Hodge saw fit to omit completely. Phillips explains some of the editorial principles behind the volume in its introduction, explaining that the 'question and answer of the examination in chief has been turned into the form of a connected statement', as was the practice with volumes in the 'Notable Trials' series. He continues: 'Short passages in the evidence have been omitted where they are either mere repetition or do not contribute more or less directly to the matter in issue', and notes that: 'The evidence of certain witnesses has been omitted altogether', though no rationale is given for these omissions.[77] Evidently editorial judgements have been made about

---

[75] For another, rather different example of the need to look beyond the transcript for reactions to material presented in court, see Douglas, *The Memory of Judgment*, pp. 23–27, where he discusses the showing of 'Nazi Concentration Camps' at Nuremberg.

[76] Anon, 'Reports of Threats', *Manchester Guardian*, 27 September 1945, p. 5.

[77] Phillips, 'Introduction', p. xxxvii. The expression 'examination in chief' refers to the questioning of defence witnesses by the defence counsel and prosecution witnesses by the prosecution counsel, as opposed to cross examination, which involves the counsel questioning witnesses called by the other side. Although Phillips is named as volume editor, he mentions in the 'acknowledgements' that Hodge took responsibility for 'the bulk of the work' in 'the condensation and preparation of the trial.' *The Belsen Trial*, p. v. The affidavits that were read to the court are included at the end of the volume in an appendix, which is proceeded by a note that is likely to have been written by Hodge, and which outlines the decisions taken in the presentation of the material, and which give some indication of the editorial principles applied

the relative importance of particular witness testimony, and reducing the trial to manageable proportions has taken precedence over, for instance, the rhetorical force that might arise from repeated evidence on certain points at issue.

One of those whose words were not included in the volume was Anita Lasker, who, as Anita Lasker-Wallfisch, included some harsh words about the trial together with a full transcript of her own evidence in *Inherit the Truth*.[78] As I have noted, she felt that the Kapos ought to have been tried separately and expressed anger that the trial seemed to provide 'a wonderful opportunity for a lot of young barristers to display their ability to defend criminals'.[79] Hodge's omission is interesting not least because Lasker's testimony was widely reported in the British newspapers. Interest in her was piqued by the fact that she played the cello in the camp orchestra at Auschwitz, and her uncle, resident in the United States, was a chess champion and therefore a minor celebrity of sorts. This 'human interest' angle comes to the fore in the presentation of the *Daily Express* report relating to the day on which Lasker testified. The headline reads: 'The death music of Auschwitz: Orchestra Played for Gas Chamber Parade'. Lasker is described as a 'pretty nineteen-year-old', and her hope of joining her uncle in America and continuing her music studies is mentioned.[80] But while Lasker's story is foregrounded in this article, slightly more than half of its column inches are taken up with an account of evidence given earlier in the day by Dr Charles Bendel, a Rumanian Jew who was a survivor of the Auschwitz *Sonderkommando* (the 'special squad', charged with operating the crematorium). The *Manchester Guardian*'s article covering the same day of proceedings also dealt in detail with Bendel's harrowing evidence and included only a very brief account of Lasker's testimony which was described as adding a 'touch of the macabre' at the end of what had been, according to the reporter, a day of unequalled 'ghastliness'.[81] Rather than constructing Lasker's story as providing a spark of hope, the *Guardian* emphasizes

---

to the volume as a whole: 'The first deposition [...] has been given in full to show the method of attestation, but in order to economise in space and for fluent reading the remainder of the depositions are produced without the [...] preliminaries. [...] Where any objection has been raised by the Defence to a paragraph, or any part thereof, of any deposition, that section has been deleted.' Phillips, ed., *Trial of Josef Kramer*, p. 654.

[78] Lasker-Wallfisch, *Inherit the Truth*. Her account of the trial is at pp. 124–30, and the transcript of her evidence at pp. 157–63.

[79] Lasker-Wallfisch, *Inherit the Truth*, p.127.

[80] Vincent Evans, 'The Death Music of Auschwitz', *Daily Express*, 2 October 1945, p. 4.

[81] Anon, 'Doctor Describes Routine of Gas Chambers', *Manchester Guardian*, 2 October 1945, p. 6.

the utter disjunctiveness of her story in the light of the evidence proceeding it, and by extension emphasizes the cynicism that underpinned the very existence of the Auschwitz orchestra.

Hodge's decision to omit Lasker's testimony could equally have been influenced by the nature of the preceding evidence; in view of the newspapers' treatment of Lasker, it is worth noting that they, like Hodge, gave no consideration to the evidence of two other female witness, Geria Zylberdukatan and Syncha Zamoski, who, like Lasker, testified at the end of the seventeenth day of the trial. Hodge did however include comments made in his closing speech by Major Cranfield, who was representing Irma Grese among others. Cranfield questioned the reliability of some of the prosecution witnesses, characterizing them as a 'procession of young women', and doubting that their testimony could be trusted: 'I do not think that it is unnatural or surprising that those young Jewesses should be vindictive towards their former warders, or to seek to avenge themselves on them.'[82] The slippage here from 'young women' to 'young Jewesses' associates these witnesses with a stereotype of Old Testament vengefulness, a primitive emotion that apparently has no place in the courtroom.

This trial did at least give some survivors a chance to describe what they had seen and experienced at both Belsen and Auschwitz, though defence counsel were not slow to identify apparent contradictions in witness testimony, or, like Cranfield, to undermine its reliability. For example, during testimony relating to the gathering of witness affidavits, one of the Judges Advocate commented that: 'especially in the case of the Jewish witnesses, [...] the dates and sometimes the years differ between what they have apparently said in the affidavit and what they say here. Do you know whether the Jews have a different calendar or anything of that kind?'[83] Marking the passage of time would be difficult for any prisoner in the parlous situation of the camps, but this explanation does not seem to have occurred to the court.

The Hodge & Co volume also attempts to mitigate the extent of the victim-blaming that was indulged in by Winwood, who, in his opening speech for the defence, made the following comments about the prisoners in the camps:

> The type of internee who came to these concentration camps was a very low type and I would go so far as to say that by the time we get to Auschwitz and Belsen, the vast majority of the inhabitants of the concentration camp

---

[82] Phillips, ed., *The Trial of Josef Kramer*, p. 244.
[83] Phillips, ed., *The Trial of Josef Kramer*, p. 116.

were the dregs of the Ghettos of Middle Europe. There were people who had very little idea of how to behave in their ordinary life and they had very little idea of doing what they were told, and the control of these internees was a great problem.[84]

Offence taken at these comments, especially the phrase 'dregs of the Ghettos', was such that Winwood was obliged to issue a retraction in his closing speech.[85] Here, whilst expressing 'regret' if any of his words caused 'pain to that race which has suffered so much in Nazi Germany', he nevertheless maintained: 'the Court will appreciate that I have been acting only as a mouthpiece of the accused whom I represent and that I have expressed no personal view of my own at all.'[86] Both the original comment and his apology are omitted from the Hodge volume, where Winwood's remarks in his opening, quoted above, are edited to read: 'The type of internees who came to these concentration camps was low and had very little idea of doing what they were told, so that the control of these internees was a great problem.'[87] The substance of his comments therefore remains, and Hodge retains an allusion made to Winwood's remarks by Colonel Backhouse, the lead prosecuting counsel, who, in closing, follows the logic of Winwood's claim to be speaking for his client rather than himself by attributing the phrase 'dregs of the Ghettos' directly to Kramer: 'It has been suggested by Kramer that the persons who were in those camps were the dregs of the ghettos. That is manifestly untrue from the evidence.'[88]

Hodge's editing of this contentious section of the transcript, which, unlike his omission of the testimony of Lasker and others, is invisible to the reader, could be an attempt on his part to honour the request made by the Jewish World Council to strike Winwood's remarks from the record. But although these offensive words are, in their original form and context, absent from the Hodge & Co volume, Winwood's implication that prisoners somehow contributed to conditions in the camps is nevertheless still clearly discernible when Winwood refers to the 'type of internee who came to concentration camps' as 'low', and in his suggestion, in relation to his claim that Kramer

[84] http://www.bergenbelsen.co.uk/pages/TrialTranscript/Trial_Day_019.html#Day019_WinwoodAddress. Accessed 4 August 2022.

[85] See Sharman, 'War Crimes Trials', pp. 68–70.

[86] http://www.bergenbelsen.co.uk/pages/TrialTranscript/Trial_Day_046.html. Accessed 4 August 2022.

[87] Phillips, ed., *The Trial of Josef Kramer*, p. 149. Winwood's use of the verb *came* is also problematic, implying a degree of agency or choice on the part of the camp inmates.

[88] Phillips, ed., *The Trial of Josef Kramer*, p. 599.

attempted to improve sanitation arrangements at Belsen, that 'amongst the prisoners were people who naturally performed their natural functions where they felt inclined'.[89] An alternative approach would have been for Hodge to include both the original comment and Winwood's apology, as did the newspaper reports,[90] but in choosing to make these post hoc excisions from the transcript, Hodge omits any reference to the events external to the court room that brought about Winwood's retraction.

Comparing war crimes trials to other kinds of criminal proceedings, Dick de Mildt comments: 'Criminal proceedings do not focus on abstract historical events, but on particular human individuals who stand accused of having violated specific laws. [...] Generally [court proceedings require] no specific historical knowledge outside the defendant's personal biography.'[91] Placing Nazi crimes on trial, however, required, as de Mildt notes, precisely such historical contextualization. While the early life and career of each defendant was outlined to the court, this information was significant mainly insofar as it placed the individual as a part of the camp system. But the camp system was itself not completely understood at this period, and indeed the trial was functioning as a means of starting to explain its workings, not because of some over-arching educative purpose that the court had ascribed to itself, but as a necessary preliminary to beginning to grasp what had been done there.

Hodge & Co was not without experience in the production of 'Notable Trials' volumes that covered crimes with an explicitly political aspect, and these were not restricted to the historical treason trials that appeared in the early years of the series. The 1945 treason trial of William Joyce, who had made broadcasts to England from Nazi Germany, appeared as a Notable Trial in 1946, and Hodge was keen for the introduction to this trial, by barrister J. W. Hall, to be included in the Penguin series, noting that the issues of nationality and citizenship on which the case hinged were pertinent to readers.[92] He may have been mindful, when making this recommendation to Penguin, that the original volume on Joyce had been another of Hodge & Co's bestsellers, a sign of the widespread public interest the man who

[89] Phillips, ed., *The Trial of Josef Kramer*, p. 149, p. 154
[90] See Anon, 'Kramer in the Box', *The Times*, 9 October 1945, p. 3, which quotes the reference to 'the dregs of the ghettoes', and Anon, 'Final Stages in Belsen Trial', 9 November 1945, p. 3, which reports his apology.
[91] De Mildt, *In the Name of the People*, p. 40.
[92] James Hodge, letter to A. S. G. Glover, 11 December 1952, University of Bristol, Penguin Books Archive, DM 1107/338. Hall's introduction was included in *Famous Trials 4* (Harmondsworth: Penguin, 1954), alongside four murder cases.

entered public consciousness during the war years under the soubriquet 'Lord Haw-Haw' and whose trial opened the same day as the Belsen proceedings, a coincidence that was commented on in newspaper coverage.[93] As I noted in the introduction, Lizzie Seal has argued that some members of the public expressed the view that it was wrong for Joyce to receive the same punishment as, for instance, Kramer, given the very different nature of Joyce's crimes, and Seal further suggests that the perception of disproportionality in sentencing was one of the factors causing shifts in attitudes to capital punishment at this period.[94]

This sentiment finds an echo in Hall's introduction, where he avers that:

> Joyce's crime, detestable though it was [was not] deserving of the same punishment as the mass murders and torture of prisoners of which the Belsen criminals were convicted [...]. I have found [...] a very considerable feeling, shared by lawyers and laymen, servicemen and civilians, that [...] the decision was wrong [...]. The feeling is not so much that Joyce, having been convicted, should have been reprieved, but that he should not have been convicted.[95]

This is a relatively rare example of a Notable Trials' preface dealing with a contemporary trial that critiques the legal basis of proceedings. Drawing a distinction between Joyce's trial and many of the others in the series, Hall notes that Joyce's is a case of 'almost wholly of legal interest. The reader will find none of that conflict of evidence on crucial matters of fact [...] which lend a fascination of their own to many murder trials.'[96] From this

---

[93] The front page of the *Daily Express* for Monday 17th September 1945 has a photograph of the Lüneburg court room, with a group of British officers receiving a briefing, captioned 'Court No. 1—Ready for Silent Witness' (an allusion to the film that would be screened as part of the prosecution evidence). Towards the bottom of the page, a photograph of members of the public intending to sleep on the pavement outside the Old Bailey in the hope of being in the public gallery for the Joyce trial, is captioned 'Court No. 2—Midnight queue for Joyce trial.' Also on 17 September, the *News Chronicle* used the same photographs, in a story headlined 'Kramer of Belsen is on Trial Today', embedding the Old Bailey photograph just below the Lüneburg image. In each case, even though it is presented with minimal context, the Old Bailey photograph invites the reader to consider the eccentricity of the members of the public depicted; the photograph from inside the court room—itself an unusual sight for the British public—and its inclusion of about twenty-five servicemen, emphasizes the weightiness of the proceedings that were about to start.

[94] Lizzie Seal, 'Imagined Communities and the Death Penalty in Britain, 1930–1965', *British Journal of Criminology* 54 (2014): pp. 908–27 (p. 917).

[95] J. W. Hall, 'Introduction', in *Trial of William Joyce* (London: William Hodge, 1946), pp. 1–36 (pp. 35–36).

[96] Hall, 'Introduction', p. 16.

perspective, it is interesting that Hall emphasizes that both professionals and the public share his view about the verdict, as though to indicate that his opinion is not a capricious one and that the issues raised by the trial hit home with the public, despite the trial's lack of obvious drama. His comments contrast with Rebecca West's observation that those who argued for Joyce's reprieve did not respect the law and wished it 'to be purely arbitrary'.[97] While West argues that the law is both an 'eternal truth' and a 'solution [to] temporal problems',[98] Hall emphasizes that that the law is practised and applied in a specific socio-historical context.

Joyce's broadcasts were aimed at the listening public in Britain, but the inclusion of 'servicemen' on Hall's list of those who considered Joyce's sentence to be inappropriate, suggests that those who undertook active service in the war would have a form of authority when it came to the question of the comparability between Joyce's actions and those of, for instance, the Belsen defendants. While Joyce was charged with treason, not war crimes, his punishment was the same as Kramer's and Grese's. As Hall points out, although after the Belsen Trial 'Kramer [...] and ten others were executed, others were sentenced to varying terms of imprisonment', the punishment, implicitly, being tailored to fit the crime.[99] The laws relating to treason are presented by Hall as outdated and not used in a sufficiently nuanced way, while the legislative basis for the Belsen verdicts is deemed sound. Further, the case against Joyce hinged on what was widely seen to be a technicality— the question of whether he held, and had the right to hold, a British passport at the time of the crimes—but one which, as both Hall and James Hodge, pointed out, was to increase in importance as Europe was reshaped in the wake of the war.[100] In this regard, it was not difficult for Hall to emphasize the wider relevance of the case even for those who had never actually heard Joyce's broadcasts.

It is possible that having the *War Crimes* series under development encouraged Hodge & Co to engage with Joyce's case, which, as I have indicated, was not typical of the kind of crime covered by the series in the interwar years, though, as I have noted, they had previously dealt with trials for treason. No new 'Notable Trials' appeared during the period 1939–1945, and the Joyce volume was the first to be published when the series resumed

---

[97] Rebecca West, 'The Revolutionary', in *The Meaning of Treason* (1949; rev ed. London: Reprint Society, 1952), pp. 1–185 (p. 57).

[98] West, 'The Revolutionary', p. 57.

[99] Hall, 'Introduction', p. 35.

[100] Hall, 'Introduction', pp. 20–29, pp. 32–33.

in 1946. Later, H. Montgomery Hyde produced a completely new standalone volume on the trial of Roger Casement, and this appeared in 'Notable Trials' in 1960 and as a Penguin 'Famous Trial' in 1964. Hyde's account ranged far beyond the trial itself to cover recently released information about Casement's controversial diaries. The trial proceedings, presented as a summary rather than a transcript, occupy about ten percent of the volume's pages.[101] This atypical volume underlines further the limits of what could be achieved within the usual format of the 'Notable Trials', and reinforces the tension between offering entertainment for lovers of crime and educating the public that had existed from the inception of the series.

In his comparative study of war crimes trials, Lawrence Douglas notes that although the prosecutors at Nuremberg where not 'primarily occupied with trying the defendants for the extermination of the Jews in Europe', these actions were 'explored and condemned' during the proceedings. By contrast, the trial of Adolf Eichmann in Jerusalem in 1961 'seemed to *create* the Holocaust'.[102] Douglas explains that while the Nuremberg Trial eschewed the use of personal testimony by survivors of the camps, preferring documentary evidence, the Eichmann trial deliberately set out to give the survivors a voice. The Belsen Trial also gave selected survivors a voice, but the manner in which their testimony was communicated to the public in different genres varied greatly. In the context of the Hodge & Co series, this trial was acknowledged as different, at least in its scale, but it was one among many other trials, and, when read as part of the sequence of 'War Crimes Trials', its role in exposing not just the scale but the scope of the Nazis activities is diminished. The focus remains on the legal, rather than humanitarian or even historical lessons that the trial might provide, not least because of choices made at the editing stage.

Lasker-Wallfisch's recovery of her own testimony from the trial transcript housed at the Imperial War Museum and her inclusion of it, together with facsimile reproductions of newspaper reports of her evidence, in an appendix to her memoir, can be seen in this context as a way of correcting Hodge & Co's omissions without expressing unreserved approval of how the trial itself was conducted. This intervention, by a survivor who felt that

[101] H. Montgomery Hyde, 'The Trial', in *Famous Trials 9: Roger Casement* (Harmondsworth: Penguin, 1964), pp. 85–114. Including appendices, the book runs to 226 pages.
[102] Douglas, *The Memory of Judgment*, p. 6.

the trial had not been adequate as a means of providing justice for what happened at Belsen and Auschwitz, underlines that if later trials 'seemed to *create* the Holocaust', this did not happen *ab initio*. Survivors were speaking in the immediate aftermath of the war, but the implications of what they were saying were not always being heard or understood.

2

Constructing Criminality in the Work of Derrick Sington

After the arrival of Allied soldiers at Bergen-Belsen in April 1945 and the initiation of relief efforts there, those who had been responsible for running the camp were taken into custody, even before arrangements had begun for their trial.[1] The writings of Derrick Sington provide a particularly striking example of the challenges of representing what it was like for a British soldier to be at Belsen at this period, when caring for survivors was coupled with attempts at identifying perpetrators. His work shows how the legacy of having been at the camp could linger, not just as a difficult memory but as a challenge to presumptions about criminality and justice. Sington, a Captain in the Intelligence Corps, was among the first British servicemen to enter Belsen in April 1945. His unit had been supporting advancing Allied troops by using a loudspeaker van to make announcements about curfews and issue warnings about looting, as well as distributing propaganda, to the local population in and around Celle and Osnabrück and was requested to join the advance into Belsen on 15 April. Once there, the loudspeaker van was used to communicate with the remaining prisoners, but the unit also gave more general assistance with the relief operation.[2]

Sington gave evidence at the Lüneburg Trial, and it is possible that by that time he had already started work on *Belsen Uncovered*, the book about his experiences that was published by Gerald Duckworth & Co in 1947. With a focus on attempts at self-management by the inmates who were in the camp when the British arrived, this work foregrounds the connection between war crimes, criminality, and the restoration of order at Belsen. Sington shows

[1] As Raymond Phillips notes, 'The procedure governing the trial was [...] laid down by the Regulations for the Trial of War Criminals made under the Royal Warrant of 14th June 1945.' 'Introduction', in Raymond Phillips, ed., *The Trial of Josef Kramer and Forty-Four Others* (London: William Hodge, 1949), pp. xxii–xlv (p. xxxi).

[2] Information from 'Monthly report (in lieu of war diary) of 14th Amplifier Unit and 19 Leaflet Unit for month April 1945', WO 171/8142: 14 Amplifier Unit, National Archives. The report is signed by Sington.

Literature and Justice in Mid-Twentieth-Century Britain. Victoria Stewart, Oxford University Press.
© Victoria Stewart (2023). DOI: 10.1093/oso/9780192858238.003.0003

how, apparently at least in part because of the influence of the Allied forces, acts of vengeance gave way to more organized forms of justice.

Ten years later, in the context of an ongoing series of articles and longer works on penal reform, Sington reconsidered his Belsen experience, prepared by this point to write in a more explicitly autobiographical fashion, and, importantly, to offer a critique of the Belsen Trial. Neither preparations for the trial nor the proceedings themselves are described explicitly in *Belsen Uncovered*. Sington only considers these later in the chapter on Irma Grese which was included in *The Offenders: Society and the Atrocious Crime* (1957), a book he co-authored with Giles Playfair, and which formed part of their effort to publicize issues of criminal justice reform and to support the abolition of capital punishment in the 1950s and 1960s.[3]

The opening of this chapter on Grese describes in some detail Sington's own subject position and provides a good deal of personal context that is not included in *Belsen Uncovered*.[4] Sington reveals to the reader that he is a 'half-Jew [...] My own forebears on my father's side had been Jewish business people in Germany', and this adds point to the description that follows of a Nazi rally he attended during a summer vacation visit to Germany in 1928 or 1929, while he was still an undergraduate: 'I was suddenly intensely aware of [...] a quality of irrational hatred in the world of which I had hardly suspected the possibility.'[5] It is striking that Sington omits to mention in *Belsen Uncovered* either that he has Jewish heritage or how he came by his evident proficiency in German. While he does make it clear in *Belsen Uncovered* that he is writing about what he saw, the main focus of the book is not the impact of his experiences on himself, but the situations and individuals he encountered at the camp. To use Aimee Bunting and Tony Kushner's term, Sington

---

[3] See also Giles Playfair and Derrick Sington, 'Clinic for Murderers', *Picture Post*, 3 December 1956, pp. 21–24. In addition, Sington took part in a discussion of 'The Psychopath' on the BBC's 'Lifeline' television programme, broadcast on 22 May 1958, alongside a QC. From the late-1950s until the mid-1960s Sington reviewed books and wrote articles relating to criminal justice for publications including *The New Statesman*, the *Guardian*, and *Encounter*. A second book jointly written with Playfair, *Crime, Punishment and Cure* (1965) develops in particular the authors' argument in favour of the abolition of prisons, drawing on comparisons between penal systems in Britain and Europe.

[4] It is possible that the dust jacket of *Belsen Uncovered* provided the reader with some details of Sington's background: I have been unable to locate a copy of the book with its jacket. This itself is signal of the fact that at this period dust jackets were often seen by both libraries and private individuals, as disposable, and an author might not have presumed that information included there would be accessible to future readers.

[5] Giles Playfair and Derrick Sington, *The Offenders: Society and the Atrocious Crime* (London: Secker & Warburg, 1957), p. 148.

was a 'co-present' whose understanding of what he had seen evolved and was revisited in different contexts over the succeeding years.

At the heart of Sington's engagement with the issues of crime and its punishment that arose from having been at Belsen is this double bind: any attempt at promoting 'civilized' values in a place from which these appear to have been evacuated relies on measuring behaviour against what would 'normally' be expected. But though this is understandable given the conditions pertaining at Belsen in April 1945, it can lead to a smoothing over of the specificities of the Nazis' victimization of the Jews. Sington's relative lack of consideration of the Jews as victims in *Belsen Uncovered* is both complicated and partially explained by the omission of detailed reference to his own subject position; while written in the first-person, the book is at times much closer to anthropology than it is to autobiography.[6] Further, the acknowledgements to *Belsen Uncovered* conclude with the following: 'I must here thank my perfect secretary, Gertrude Neumann, herself a Belsen prisoner, not only for all her help but for much invaluable, first-hand information of conditions in the concentration camps.'[7] It is necessary to look beyond Sington's own published writings to discover that the person referred to here would later become Sington's wife. Gertrude Sington was a Czech Jew and had been a prisoner at Theresienstadt, Neugraben, and Auschwitz before being sent to Belsen, where she and Sington met. As well as helping him with *Belsen Uncovered*, she assisted in the collection of affidavits prior to the Belsen Trial.[8] This information comes from two articles published in the later 1960s, shortly before Derrick Sington's death, which describe the difficulties Gertrude Sington was facing in her compensation claim against the German government. They detail that her first husband died in Auschwitz and that she was left unable to have children after being obliged to have an abortion while in Theresienstadt.[9]

---

[6] In piecing together Sington's early life and background, I have drawn on both his published work and the material, including several versions of his CV, contained in his BBC files. L1/1,640/1 and L1/1,640/2 Sington, Derrick Adolphus, BBC Written Archives, Caversham. Sington's father owned a textiles firm and Sington worked there after graduating from Oxford. He may have picked up the German language at home, but as part of his work for the firm, he spent a year living in Germany, with time in Munich, Freiburg, Augsberg, and Dresden in 1930–1931.

[7] Derrick Sington, *Belsen Uncovered* (London: Duckworth, 1946), p. 7.

[8] A number of the affidavits taken at Belsen that are now held at the National Archives, WO 209/1698, identify her at the translator.

[9] See Terence Prittie, 'A Victim of Nazism Still Awaits her Compensation', *Manchester Guardian*, 2 November 1965, p. 12 and 'Nazi Concentration Camp Victim Is Still Denied Justice', *Manchester Guardian*, 23 January 1967, p. 3.

Though Sington becomes less circumspect about his own identity position in *The Offenders*, he never seems to have written about what happened to his wife (to whom *The Offenders* is dedicated), other than indirectly, as when he acknowledges that she shared her 'first-hand information' about the camps with him. It might seem paradoxical that he should eventually choose to tell the story of Grese, a perpetrator, rather than sharing the experiences of a former prisoner, but choosing to remain silent on this topic is, from another perspective, completely understandable and can be taken as a signal not of evasion or reticence, but of respect. What happened to her is *her* story, to share or not, and, unlike Grese's, not to be used to inform a wider argument. As I will show, a concern to allow survivors to speak rather than speaking for them has an effect on both the content and structure of *Belsen Uncovered*.

The generic uncertainty of this text reflects on a structural level both the challenge of being at Belsen, even as an observer or co-present rather than an inmate, and the challenge of writing about it. Usual forms seem inadequate to the task of representing these events, but at the same time, where both formal devices and social, cultural, and legal frames of reference are concerned, the lure of the familiar is strong. In the context of its place as an early account of the aftermath of what would later be termed the Holocaust, the preoccupation with the restoration of order and the consideration of criminality that emerge in *Belsen Uncovered* and are developed in Sington's later writings prove to be both powerful organizing tropes and blind spots in Sington's work.

Writing about Belsen

Sington and Patrick Crichton-Stuart, the editor who worked with him at Duckworth, evidently saw *Belsen Uncovered* as a book with topical currency. It gives an account of the period between April and October 1945 together with limited reflections on the wider legacy of the camp and its place within the Nazi regime. Sington's narrative ends when he leaves the camp, but as he points out, at least eight thousand former inmates remained there over the winter of 1945–1946.[10] As I have noted, Sington may well already have started writing *Belsen Uncovered* in mid-September 1945 when he was called as a prosecution witness at the Lüneburg Trial. The foreword to

[10] Sington, *Belsen Uncovered*, p. 206.

the published text is dated December 1945, and correspondence between Sington and Crichton-Stuart reveals that the completed manuscript was submitted for military censorship on 9 December 1945 and having been approved was sent on to Crichton-Stuart, in order for production to begin, on 18 January 1946. It is apparent from their letters that Sington and Crichton-Stuart were known to each other before Sington started work on the book, and indeed the book was written at Crichton-Stuart's prompting.[11] Crichton-Stuart, who was part-owner of Duckworth as well as an active commissioning editor, evidently believed at an early stage that there was a market for a book about Belsen, albeit that the exigencies of the publishing industry in the immediate post-war period, including paper shortages and difficulties with production and distribution, delayed publication by what Sington saw to be crucial months.

The book has a publication date of 1946 on its copyright page, but did not in fact appear until 20 February 1947, a fact which caused Sington some anxiety. Having corrected the galley proofs in mid-May 1946, he returned the page proofs to Crichton-Stuart in mid-July. In November he contacted Crichton-Stuart again, expressing his concern about how long it was taking for the book to appear. He had heard that Victor Gollancz had '2 KZ books' coming out, and was worried about the potential impact of these competitor volumes on the reception of his own work.[12] In a further letter, in February 1947, he again mentioned the Gollancz publications and reminded Crichton-Stuart that the 'last big KZ trials' were likely to end soon.[13] Sington could be referring here to the US-led Subsequent Nuremberg proceedings;

---

[11] Crichton-Stuart was called-up in October 1939 and, like Sington, served in the Intelligence Corps; it is possible that the two met during the war, but their time as undergraduates at Oxford overlapped, so the acquaintance could have gone back further. Information about the writing and commissioning of the book is drawn from the Gerald Duckworth & Co Archives, Senate House.

[12] All that Sington tells Crichton-Stuart about these books is that one of them is 'by an Austrian, the son of Otto Bauer, and the other by a German.' MSS letter, 20 November 1946, MS 959/1/196, Gerald Duckworth & Co Archives, Senate House. Otto Bauer (1881–1938) was a prominent Austrian Marxist. He had no children of his own, though his wife Helena had two children from her first marriage to Max Landau, including a son, Zbigniew. I can find no trace of him having published a 'KZ' book either with Gollancz or another publisher. See John Haag, 'Bauer, Helene, (1871–1942)'. Women in World History: A Biographical Encyclopedia, Encyclopedia.com. Accessed 15 June 2018. There are a number of potential candidates for the other book, by 'a German', depending on how capaciously Sington was using the expression 'KZ'. One strong possibility is Ernst Wiechert's *The Forest of the Dead*, published by Gollancz in 1947, which deals with the four months the author spent in Buchenwald in 1938, after speaking in support of Martin Niemöller.

[13] Derrick Sington to Patrick Crichton-Stuart, MSS letter, 1 February 1947. MS 959/1/205. Gerald Duckworth & Co Archives, Senate House.

the 'Doctors Trial', largely concerned with mistreatment of concentration camp inmates, began in August 1947, and the proceedings as a whole did not conclude until the autumn of 1948. The Poles and Russians conducted a trial of former personnel from Sachsenhausen camp in autumn of 1947 in Berlin, and this trial could have been in Sington's mind.

Whichever specific proceedings he meant, Sington's comments certainly indicate that he saw a relationship between the war crimes trials, which he believed were keeping Nazi crimes in the public eye, and *Belsen Uncovered*. He did not want the book to miss its 'moment', and this concern reflects his perception of the potentially fickle nature of the reading public and the reportage aspects of the work, its attempt at capturing a very specific period in the history of the camp. From a publisher's perspective, the fact that other works on the same or a related topic were likely to be appearing would not be a disincentive to publish. Up to a certain point, the existence of rival publications with a similar focus demonstrates the existence of a potential readership, though as David Cesarani argues, a moment was reached in the later 1940s when 'the market' for books about 'Jewish suffering and resistance under Nazi domination' became 'saturated'.[14] Sington's perspective on the currency of his work could be further coloured by the fact that, unlike Crichton-Stuart, who had been discharged from the army and was back at Duckworth's London offices by October 1945, Sington was still serving in Germany, initially in Hamburg as a publications officer, doing work relating to censorship. In early 1946, he was appointed as managing editor at *Die Welt*, the newspaper that had been established in the British Zone by the Control Commission, with the first issue appearing on 2 April 1946. He would remain in Germany until 1950.

Sington's use of the expression 'KZ' when describing both the topic of Gollancz's rumoured forthcoming publications and, by extension, that of his own book, is striking. The letters are the contraction for the German word *Konzentrationslager*, and their appearance in Sington's letter to Crichton-Stuart indicates an awareness on his part of the distinctiveness of this particular aspect of his war experience. He has not just written a war book, but a 'KZ' book. From a contemporary perspective, as a metonymy for the Holocaust, this terminology has its problems, focusing in narrowly as it does on the camps, and indeed, a particular type of camp. It reflects

---

[14] David Cesarani, 'A New Look at Some Old Memoirs', in *Justice, Politics and Memory in Europe after the Second World War: Landscapes after Battle Volume 2*, edited by Suzanne Bardgett, David Cesarani, Jessica Reinisch, and Johannes-Dieter Steinert (London: Vallentine Mitchell, 2011), pp. 121–68 (p. 161).

the extent to which, as Cesarani has argued, during 1945–1946, '[r]eports and newsreels [in Britain] tended to focus exclusively on the concentration camps in the West, reinforcing the impression that this was the *locus classicus* of Nazi crimes'.[15] Sington certainly conceived of his project as, principally, an account of what he saw and heard at Belsen, in the belief that an eye-witness record would be of value, though, as I will show, there is some attempt in *Belsen Uncovered* to contextualize the camp within the workings of the Nazi regime and to describe the earlier lives of at least some of those incarcerated there. The use of the expression 'KZ' offers a glimpse of a moment when, for Sington at least, it did seem that there was, if not an emerging genre, then at least a meaningful cluster of texts relating specifically to the concentration camps, and, from Sington's perspective, a work by someone who had not been an inmate at the camp could be included in this category.

Despite the fact that Sington made reference to other related publications when writing to Crichton-Stuart, it is apparent that, so far as the actual structure and approach taken in *Belsen Uncovered* were concerned, there were few if any models on which the author could draw.[16] Sington's book is a memoir, but one in which the first-person narrator, while willing at times to describe his feelings, tells us little about himself, save that he is a British army officer. As the title indicates, the focus of the book is on revealing what was found when the camp was 'discovered' by the Allies. There are consonances between this approach and the testimony that Sington gave at the Belsen Trial. The third prosecution witness to be called, Sington was asked to recount what he saw on first arriving at the camp and was questioned about his interactions with prisoners and guards, including Josef Kramer. The book has a plates section, reproducing images similar in nature to those that would have been familiar to readers from coverage in newspapers and illustrated magazines, and it includes a fold-out plan of

[15] David Cesarani, 'Great Britain', in *The World Reacts to the Holocaust*, edited by David S. Wyman (Baltimore: Johns Hopkins University Press, 1996), pp. 599–641 (p.611).

[16] Patrick Gordon Walker's *The Lid Lifts* was published by Victor Gollancz in 1945 and includes a chapter on the author's visit to Belsen, as well as reflections on how war criminals and Germans more generally might be treated, but these sections together comprise about a quarter of a book that is less than one-hundred pages long. As the diaries on which he drew when writing *The Lid Lifts* reveal, Walker met Sington while at Belsen, but Sington is not named in *The Lid Lifts* which reproduces the diaries in edited form at this point, and *Belsen Uncovered* makes no mention of Walker's visit to the camp. See Patrick Gordon Walker, *Political Diaries 1932–1971*, edited by Robert Pearce (London: The Historians' Press, 1991), p. 144 (p. 148). Sington is described as having 'done a magnificent job of work' (p. 144).

the camp, these marking it for the reader as an evidence-based account.[17] The foreword describes the book as 'a story of personal experiences', and Sington goes on to admit that he doubts whether 'any book on liberated Belsen could pretend to completeness'.[18] This disclaimer indicates Sington's awareness of the potential limitations of his perspective, indeed of any single perspective, and this is an issue that he grapples with throughout the narrative.

Following the foreword, the main text of *Belsen Uncovered* opens with a short passage of direct speech, dropping the reader in *medias res*:

'If we agree to by-pass this place, Belsen, the Germans are talking about giving us the bridge at Winsen', said the lieutenant. We were studying the operations map outside the divisional commander's caravan.

It was April 12th, the hedges were sprouting and dust was rising on the roads, as in Normandy.

'What's Belsen?' I asked.

'It's a concentration camp. Typhus is apparently rife there, and Himmler has sent a personal representative to talk about sealing the place off.'

'Sounds a bit odd.'

'H'm, does, doesn't it?'[19]

The approach to Belsen is situated in relation to the narrator's and the lieutenant's earlier progress; it is a continuation of ongoing military manoeuvres from west to east across Europe. There is a passing appeal to the trope of spring as a time of renewal in the 'sprouting' hedges, though the 'dust [...] rising on the roads' is mildly ominous. The manner in which Belsen itself is spoken about here, with the lieutenant referring to 'this place Belsen' and thus indicating its relative unfamiliarity, and Sington completely innocent of what 'Belsen' might be, both reinforces the sense that those who advanced on the camp were indeed unprepared for what they would find there, and serves as a reminder that anyone reading this book, either in 1947 or now, is very likely to know at least roughly what to expect. Much later in *Belsen Uncovered*, Sington mentions that in November 1944 he had been at Vught,

---

[17] The plan was reproduced, with an acknowledgement to Sington, in Hodge & Co's volume on the trial. Phillips, 'Acknowledgements', *Trial of Josef Kramer*, p. v.

[18] Sington, *Belsen Uncovered*, p. 7.

[19] Sington, *Belsen Uncovered*, p. 9.

the only concentration camp established in the Netherlands, and although there too he saw 'the aftermath of massacre and crime', Vught had been evacuated prior to the Allies' arrival in September 1944, and the scale and scope of what Sington could have seen there was evidently an inadequate preparation for what he and his fellow servicemen encountered at Belsen.[20] The question, 'What's Belsen?' is the question that *Belsen Uncovered* attempts to address but it is one that, by the time he writes this scene, Sington knows he will never be able to answer fully. He momentarily recreates the sense of not knowing, of being, to a degree, innocent, but he does so from a position of having been at the camp, and part of the challenge that he sets himself is to recreate for the reader the initial shock of arriving at Belsen when he lacked any meaningful idea of what he would see there.

An agreement for Belsen to be surrendered to the Allies was signed on 13 April, the day after Sington, by his own account, first heard of the camp. Two days later, Allied personnel, Sington among them, entered the camp and in *Belsen Uncovered* he describes the impression the camp made upon him. He recalls that the wooden gate to the main compound reminded him 'of the entrance to a zoo', and continues:

Once through the gate this resemblance was strengthened [...] we came into a smell of ordure—like the smell of a monkey-house. [...] I had tried to visualise the interior of a concentration camp but I had not imagined it like this. Nor had I imagined the strange simian throng, who crowded to the barbed wire fences [...] with their shaven heads and their obscene striped penitentiary suits, which were so dehumanising.[21]

Shortly after, he describes the prisoners in their 'broad-striped garments' as like 'prancing zebras'.[22] The reference to the 'smell of a monkey-house' seems to prompt or pre-empt the description of the prisoners as 'simian'. The use of this word to describe the prisoners is highly problematic and the absurdity of the phrase 'prancing zebras' seems even more out of kilter

---

[20] Sington, *Belsen Uncovered*, p. 183. This is emphasized in *The Offenders*, where Sington mentions having seen 'an abandoned concentration camp at Vught' six months before arriving at Belsen 'into the midst of deliberate inhumanity', implying a contrast between the two places. He goes on to remind the reader that although 'Sachsenhausen, Dachau and Buchenwald had been minutely described in the British press by refugees who had suffered in them and escaped from Germany', the scope of the camp system was not realized in spring 1945, and '[h]ardly anyone in the British forces had heard of Belsen'. Playfair and Sington, *The Offenders*, p. 149.

[21] Sington, *Belsen Uncovered*, p. 15, p. 16.

[22] Sington, *Belsen Uncovered*, p. 17.

with the situation. As Mark Celinscak notes, this is not the only occasion when Sington resorts to 'zoomorphic language', imagery which attributes 'animal characteristics to humans or their behaviour'.[23] Drawing out the moralistic implications of zoomorphism, Celinscak continues that Sington 'initially viewed the behaviour of camp-inmates as [similar to that of] low-level animals, inferior to the rational, strong, and healthy Allied soldier'.[24] Sington, as Celinscak points out, was not alone in drawing such parallels which Celinscak sees as a form of defence mechanism, a way for soldiers to assert that it was not 'possible that this could also happen to them'.[25] Celinscak concludes that falling back on this type of language is a sign of the incommensurability of what those arriving at the camp were seeing; one might have expected greater compassion or sensitivity. But this, of course, is not the full extent of Sington's description of the camp. It is a recreation of how alienated he felt on arrival, how he 'initially' felt, as Celinscak has it, and it precedes a text in which the prisoners *do* become individuated and humanized, or rather, are able to reassert the humanity that has been ground down and effaced by their dire circumstances. Even in this early passage, Sington suggests that it is the inmates' uniforms that are 'dehumanising', that is, that they have been dehumanized or made simian by the conditions in which they have been forced to exist. Undoubtedly, this imagery tends to reinforce the power imbalance between the prisoners and Allied soldiers that is further implied by the word 'liberation', but in Sington's case there is an attempt to emphasize not that this is how the prisoners inherently *are*, but rather, how they have *become* because of their treatment by their captors.[26]

Later, in his account of his first evening at Belsen, Sington describes soldiers urging a group of women to return to their huts, at which: 'Three

---

[23] Mark Celinscak, *Distance from the Belsen Heap: Allied Forces and the Liberation of a Nazi Concentration Camp* (Toronto: University of Toronto Press, 2015), p. 64.

[24] Celinscak, *Distance from the Belsen Heap*, p. 63

[25] Celinscak, *Distance from the Belsen Heap*, p. 68.

[26] Later in *Belsen Uncovered*, Sington quotes a female French political prisoner's comment on the effect of having her hair shaved off: 'They have made monkeys of us' (p. 66). In the account of Belsen published in *Horizon*, Alan Moorehead describes prisoners as 'animals', but in revising this essay for inclusion in his book *Eclipse*, he qualifies this passage to read 'enforced animals'. See 'Glimpses of Germany II - Belsen', *Horizon*, 12.67 (July 1945), 26–35 (p. 30) and *Eclipse* (1945; London: Granta, 2000), p. 254. Similarly, Henry Standish, reporting from Belsen, asserted that: 'Human beings have been reduced to the status of animals.' Anon, 'The Living Dead of Belsen', *News Chronicle*, 21 April 1945, p. 1. Use of such imagery was not confined to descriptions of concentration camps: after visiting a Displaced Persons camp in Germany, Stephen Spender commented: 'The [former] slave labourers, in their vast herds in Germany, look like human animals who have been put in a foreign zoo.' *European Witness* (London: Hamish Hamilton, 1946), p. 77.

white-faced, bright-eyed women called out: "Good-night, boys!" It was like some fantastic closing-time.'[27] It is difficult to know whether Sington, with this reference to the end of the evening at a public house, is implying that the women were propositioning the soldiers, or whether he is simply remarking on the women's use of the colloquial word *boys*. In either case, the word *fantastic* is important here, underlining as it does Sington's recognition of the disjunctive nature of the parallel that the women's words brought to his mind. In the context of both these comments and his use of zoomorphic imagery, it is notable that, reflecting on what had been achieved by the end of the first full day at the camp, Sington remarks on a change in the prisoners' behaviour that he attributes to the change in their treatment: 'That terrible scene of smoking muzzles, and stampede and cries [...] seemed already a vanished nightmare. The food had arrived and would continue to arrive. We had seen smiling faces, and human beings responsive to the reasoning human voice.'[28] The women, then, have rapidly been 're-humanised'. There is of course still a power imbalance here, with the Allied forces embodying—or rather, enunciating—reason, a faculty that has, temporarily, been lost sight of by the camp population.

Sington's objectification of those he sees on first arriving at Belsen is further countered by a later effort to give narrative agency to at least one former inmate of the camp. Chapter 6, 'How We Lived at Belsen: A Retrospect', which comes half-way through *Belsen Uncovered*, and, at forty-four pages, constitutes about a fifth of the book as a whole, is authored not by Sington but by Rudolf Küstermeier, who evidently stayed in touch with Sington after both left Belsen, because in March 1946 he was appointed editor at *Die Welt*.[29] Küstermeier's contribution is a way of contextualizing the conditions that Sington sees at the camp, providing an 'insider' perspective. The choice of author for this chapter is notable. As Sington describes in his introduction to this chapter, Küstermeier was arrested in 1934 and sentenced to ten-years' hard labour for his part in the underground newspaper *Der Rote Stosstrupp* ('Red Strike Troops', named after the underground left-wing organization of the same name), and, after several years spent mainly in Brandenburg prison, was moved to Sachsenhausen in 1943. He arrived at Belsen in early 1945. As Sington notes in introducing the chapter, Küstermeier was one of 'the tiny group of German political prisoners' at Belsen and it seems likely

[27] Sington, *Belsen Uncovered*, p. 24.
[28] Sington, *Belsen Uncovered*, p. 41.
[29] Ben Witter, 'Verhöre im Plauderton', *Der Zeit*, 26 March 1988, pp. 13–14.

that he was chosen to write the chapter partly because of his facility with English. He also impressed Sington as an example of 'a German who showed that in Germany too there were at least a few decent men, of great moral and political courage, who proved ready to face anything rather than compromise with Hitler's tyranny'.[30] Küstermeier is compared here to those who did 'compromise', the fellow-travellers who were complicit or who took active roles in supporting the Nazi regime, and is thus constructed as a 'good German' rather than solely as a voice representing the inmates of Belsen. At this point, therefore, the text swerves away from the more difficult question of how to incorporate the stories of those who were in the camp not because of their brave actions against the regime or their politics but because of their perceived racial and/or cultural identity.

This is not to imply that having political convictions made surviving incarceration any easier, but Küstermeier's narrative, like the narrative within which it is embedded, shows a tendency to categorize camp inmates without considering the wider significance of the differences between them. Describing the types of people he encountered at Belsen, Küstermeier notes:

> I do not know what grades of humanity I did not at one time or another meet in the camp. Some of them were criminals, who would have been imprisoned in any country and under any government [...] There were prisoners of war and foreign civilian workers who had been accused of idleness or disobedience, or of having taken part in anti-German plots and propaganda; Jews who had survived the liquidations in other camps because they had been robust workers; Poles who had fought in the Warsaw rising, Yugoslav and Slovak partisans. There were resistance workers from all the German occupied countries, and German communists, socialist, pacifists and liberals. Finally, there were religious believers of every denomination.[31]

This list underlines the impact on the already bad conditions at Belsen of the movement there, ahead of the Russian advance, of prisoners from camps further east. The paragraph focuses on framing the reasons for prisoners' incarceration in relation to active measures they have taken against the Nazis; they have fought, resisted, asserted their religious beliefs. The Jewish prisoners seem anomalous. They have survived 'liquidations' (a term which

---

[30] Sington, *Belsen Uncovered*, p. 99.
[31] Sington, *Belsen Uncovered*, pp. 116–17.

is itself a euphemism) because they are 'robust workers' who can therefore be productively exploited by the regime and, as they have been named separately, it is difficult to know whether they are included among the 'religious believers of every denomination'. Küstermeier signals that the Jews are a group who were treated in a particular way, but he does not allow that there could be overlaps between these different categories (that Jews could also be Poles or Germans, for instance) nor does he foreground that many of the Jews were brought into the camps in the first place precisely because they were Jews, and that, to this extent, the camp system cannot simply be seen as an enlarged prison, designed to contain and punish enemies of the regime for supposedly subversive actions.

However, just as Küstermeier's account is Sington's way of giving voice to at least one of the survivors, so Küstermeier himself does try, later in the chapter, to individuate some of the prisoners with whom he came into contact while he was helping out at the camp infirmary and, indeed, to tell their stories. He encounters a 'lad of seventeen, a French Jew', who was taken with eight members of his family to Auschwitz: 'There the two men and three of the boys had been killed; and when the Russians were drawing near, the three remaining boys had been marched away in one of the unending processions which at that time were trekking from the Eastern camps towards the West'. The 'French youth' and his brother arrive at Sachsenhausen, where the brother dies: 'And now the last of the eight Frenchmen lay in Belsen reduced to skin and bone by chronic diarrhoea'.[32] Though the young man is identified as Jewish at the start of this account, by the end, this aspect of his identity is not foregrounded. His fate—death from typhus—is shared by many others, and indeed Küstermeier goes on to describe his contact with 'another Frenchman', and a 'German communist' who come to similar ends.[33] A survivor therefore tells the stories of some of those who did not survive the camps, but he does not do this in a neutral or objective fashion.

Just after a moving account of the death of the 'German communist', who is unnamed but described as a poet and 'German idealist, a successor to the great romantic poets who had lived a century or more before', Küstermeier gives a less sympathetic description of the patient in the next bed, an 'old Jew', whose nationality is not specified.[34] According to Küstermeier, this man

[32] Sington, *Belsen Uncovered*, p. 124.
[33] Sington, *Belsen Uncovered*, p. 126, p. 127.
[34] Sington, *Belsen Uncovered*, p. 126.

is 'one of a big group [of Jews] who had once been rich and comfortable. Some of them had bank deposits in London or Zurich and jewellery buried in the soil of Poland, Hungary or Rumania. But what good was their wealth to them now?'[35] Küstermeier reflects on a number of occasions when he was offered material rewards to provide extra rations to such individuals but reaches a cautionary conclusion: 'These poor old men had to learn the worthlessness of money, influence, and a name. All of them died.'[36] While this could be taken as a story about how death did not discriminate in the camps, it reinforces the stereotype of the greedy, materialistic Jew. Notably, Küstermeier does not specify the nationality of any of the individuals who tried to barter with him: they are just 'old Jews'. The young, passive French Jew, the last to die in his family, is constructed as a much more immediately sympathetic figure albeit that he, too, embodies a stereotype, and those prisoners who, like Küstermeier himself, are able to articulate their anti-Nazi convictions are deemed especially worthy of memorializing. The 'old Jews', meanwhile, learnt a salutary lesson. Some victims, then, are more deserving of the reader's sympathy than others, and, by extension, some are more worthy of having justice done on their behalf.

Seeking Justice at Belsen and Lüneburg

Küstermeier's account ends with the arrival of the Allies at Belsen, and while he sketches the chaos that initially ensued, he does not dwell, as the other chapters in *Belsen Uncovered* and Sington's trial evidence both do, on how relations between different groups that had pertained while the camp was under Nazi control affected the situation there later. Questioned at the trial, Sington described how, on first entering the camp, he saw some prisoners attacking others: 'A number of them [...] started running about, striking various inmates with flat pieces of wood. These people, I found out, were inmates who were given special disciplinary powers over the others. They had various names, such as "Lagerältester, Blockältester, Stellvertreter and Kapo".'[37] There is some blurriness in these comments as to

[35] Sington, *Belsen Uncovered*, p. 126–27.
[36] Sington, *Belsen Uncovered*, p. 127.
[37] Phillips, ed., *Trial of Josef Kramer*, p. 48. Elie A. Cohen describes the different responsibilities of these functionaries in *Human Behaviour in the Concentration Camp*, trans. M. H. Braaksma (London: Jonathan Cape, 1954), pp. 23–24.

who was hitting whom, but it becomes evident that what Sington saw were prisoner-functionaries attacking other prisoners.

He describes the same scene, and his initial confusion about what he was seeing, in *Belsen Uncovered*, where he adds: 'I did not know then that they were hut-leaders "keeping order".[38] A number of those on trial at Lüneburg were Kapos or belonged to other categories of prisoner-functionary,[39] and Sington was cross-examined about their role, being asked whether he took them to be members of the camp's staff:

> No. They were definitely internees and prisoners nominated and exploited by the camp staff. I was told that a large number were professional criminals, thieves or murderers, who were being used in this particular way. [...] I understand there were certain bonuses, for instance, in the distribution of food an unscrupulous Blockältester could very often improve his own conditions of living.[40]

Sington's comments here are perhaps more sympathetic than some accounts of the behaviour of prisoner-functionaries. Although he describes them as 'professional criminals', he sees the Kapos as having been 'used' or 'exploited' by the Nazis in the running of the camps. Similarly, in *Belsen Uncovered*, he describes how the Nazi 'system of indirect administration [...] succeeded in setting race against race, nation against nation, and class against class'. He gives an example: 'a primitive type of Czech or Slovak girl would be put in charge of refined Polish women, and the wrongs she wreaked upon them would arouse a generalised hatred of all Czechs.'[41] Sington acknowledges that 'primitiveness' or 'refinement' are not racially specific, as, just prior to these comments, he refers to the reverse of this situation, in which 'an illiterate, insensitive and characterless Polish woman would be made overseer of a hut full of Czech women, many of them girls of breeding and education.'[42] But it is notable that in each of these examples he refers to Eastern European women, not, for instance, to Dutch or French women, and he does not appear to dispute the notion that an individual of whatever nationality could be inherently 'primitive' in their behaviour.

    [38] Sington, *Belsen Uncovered*, p. 17.
    [39] See Primo Levi, 'The Grey Zone', in *The Drowned and the Saved*, trans. Raymond Rosenthal (London: Abacus, 1989), pp. 22–51 (p. 29) for the popularization of the term *Kapo*.
    [40] Phillips, ed., *Trial of Josef Kramer*, p. 52.
    [41] Sington, *Belsen Uncovered*, p. 71.
    [42] Sington, *Belsen Uncovered*, p. 71.

Aside from the question of potential racial stereotyping, there is certainly a presumption in much of the commentary on the prisoner-functionaries as a group that those imprisoned for criminal activity and who wore a green triangle were liable to be more open to the inducements available for, essentially, doing the regime's work by keeping order. Eugen Kogon, a political prisoner in Buchenwald for six years, explained the system in this way in *The Theory and Practice of Hell*, first published in 1950: 'Nearly all the [green triangle prisoners] were the dregs of society [... .] There were many SS officers who preferred to deal with the convicts, sometimes to the exclusion of all other categories, and who assigned them to all the important prisoner functions.'[43] He continues that the system of triangles was not an infallible means of identification: 'Time and again the greens, or criminals, included men with whom it was possible to work—who showed staunch loyalty, indeed— whereas many a red, or political prisoner, should of rights have worn the green triangle.'[44] Nevertheless, Kogon felt that:

The 'shiftless elements' or 'asocials' and the convicts underwent the least change in the camp. The reason must be sought in certain individuals and social resemblances to the SS. They too were men who had gone down in the social scale, who were of limited education, who were predominantly guided by instinct, who lacked convictions arrived at as the result of mental effort.[45]

This analysis relies on a presumption that all green triangle prisoners were indeed guilty of the crimes for which they had been imprisoned, and that as a group they had an inherent tendency to brutality, even though not all of them would necessarily have been found guilty of crimes of violence. This is not of course to say that prisoner-functionaries did not increase the misery of other prisoners' lives, more to note that they did so in circumstances that were not of their own making and that the different categories were a control mechanism, not an infallible guide to identity or personality. As Wolfgang

[43] Eugen Kogon, *The Theory and Practice of Hell: The German Concentration Camps and the System Behind Them*, trans. Heinz Norden (1950; New York: Berkley, 1982), p. 30. Kogon was a former prisoner of Buchenwald, and his book was originally written as a report for the US Army Psychological Warfare Unit, who assisted him in publishing his work. Kogon features in Christopher Burney's account of his time in Buchenwald, *The Dungeon Democracy* (1945), under the name Emil Kalman, and Kogon's characterization of the different groups of prisoners echoes Burney's.
[44] Kogon, *The Theory and Practice of Hell*, p. 36
[45] Kogon, *The Theory and Practice of Hell*, p. 306.

Sofsky notes, the 'labels used by the SS matched existing stereotypes in the social environment [...] the prisoners attributed criminal, asocial, or solidaristic behaviour, almost as a matter of course, to the respective categories. Whoever unexpectedly did not fit this framework was only an exception that confirmed the rule.'[46] The use of 'red' and 'green' prisoners as functionaries reinforced these perceptions of the characteristics of different categories as well as serving as a means of divide and rule: 'By making a small number of victims into its accomplices, the regime blurred the boundary between personnel and inmates.'[47] This in turn caused difficulties when the time came to apportion responsibility for conditions in the camp.

In *Belsen Uncovered*, Sington describes how, on his first full day in the camp, he saw 'seven murdered men' who had been 'savaged to death [...] The faces had been ferociously beaten or stamped upon' so that they were 'quite unrecognisable'. He is told that these are 'Unpopular Capos and Block Seniors, who beat the other prisoners and stole their food, and made life a misery.'[48] Sington passes no judgement on this episode of summary justice, moving on to describe an encounter with a 'little Jewish boy' who is starving and kisses Sington's hand when Sington gives him some sweets. The brutal deaths of the seven 'anonymous' functionaries are only of passing interest to Sington, whose focus turns immediately to those who are still living or clinging to life, though implicitly he is evoking what the prisoners may have witnessed or experienced for them to have been prompted to attack the Kapos. There could also be an element of displacement in the description of the Jewish boy. Just after that encounter, Sington hears rifle shots, and goes to investigate, admitting: 'My nerves were on edge now.'[49] This is one of the few moments when the reader glimpses the emotional stresses that Sington (and other Allied soldiers) were under at this time. The juxtaposition of the two incidents—seeing the consequences of revenge and offering some comfort to a small boy—emphasizes the difficulties of beginning to make sense of the situation at the camp and helps to explain why Sington is keen to underline how order began to be restored. From this perspective, the

---

[46] Wolfgang Sofsky, *The Order of Terror: The Concentration Camp*, trans. William Templer (Princeton: Princeton University Press, 1997), p. 132.

[47] Sofsky, *The Order of Terror*, p. 139. As Michael J. Bazyler and Julia Y. Scheppach explain, there were Jewish Kapos, some of whom were prosecuted in Israel for crimes against humanity. 'The Strange and Curious History of the Law Used to Prosecute Adolf Eichmann', *Loyola of Los Angeles International and Comparative Law Review* 34.3 (2021): pp. 417–61.

[48] Sington, *Belsen Uncovered*, p. 31.

[49] Sington, *Belsen Uncovered*, p. 31.

two incidents are not just connected by contiguity; those who would add to the suffering of a small child deserve some form of punishment.

A few days later, a Dutch prisoner reports that a group of Russian prisoners have obtained revolvers and are 'planning to take their revenge on at least five Block Seniors'. Sington takes the matter to a senior officer, Captain Farmer, and they both acknowledge the importance of forestalling a 'minor civil war' in the camp: 'We decided to follow a twofold policy of disarming the illegally-armed Russians, and trying to discover who were the worst criminals and oppressors among the Block Seniors, and arresting them forthwith.'[50] The British here attempt to intervene and replace a process of summary justice—the shooting of the Kapos by the Russians—with more formalized judicial procedure. The phrase *civil war*, ascribed here by Sington to Captain Farmer, is used by Sington again shortly after and indicates a particular conception of the camp 'community'. Although the camp contains individuals from a whole range of nationalities, the notion of 'civil war' implies that it is nevertheless, at some level, a coherent grouping, albeit one with divided loyalties, and that part of the role of the Allied military is to establish and keep the peace within it.

The prisoner-functionaries are difficult figures for Sington to encompass because, as Sofsky argues, they trouble the binary between prisoners and guards. They act in accordance with the roles assigned to them by the guards, and in many cases are not slow to behave in ways that increase the difficulty of the other inmates' already parlous situation. Identifying them as criminal elements of the prisoner community and arresting them, is one way of dealing with them, but Sington's judgements about their behaviour are always shadowed by the fact that they were, by one measure, criminals before they came to the camps, and that being in the camps is seen to have fostered or rewarded their existing 'criminal tendencies'.

In his trial testimony, Sington alludes to this 'peace-keeping' effort and to the assistance given with it by the International Committee, which he discusses at greater length in *Belsen Uncovered*. The International Committee was a self-selected group of prisoners of different nationalities, which is described to Sington by a fellow officer as claiming to express 'the public opinion of the prisoners in the camp'.[51] Sington finds the committee members reluctant to name publicly prisoners who they believe to have behaved criminally in the camp but they comply with Sington's suggestion

---

[50] Sington, *Belsen Uncovered*, p. 75.
[51] Sington, *Belsen Uncovered*, p. 75.

that they should submit written accusations to him in confidence.[52] At the trial, he explained the International Committee's role in producing 'accusations against such people [prisoner-functionaries] who had behaved in this brutal manner'.[53] The International Committee, and Sington's discussion of his negotiations with it, illustrate that even amidst the starvation and chaos of the final days of the war, the prisoners in the camp began to organize themselves into a kind of semi-autonomous society or a self-policing community. This, however, went alongside a continuing resort to what Elie A. Cohen calls 'unorganized justice'. Cohen uses this term to describe a system of justice practised within the camps which supplements the 'organized administration of justice' as represented by the guards and the prisoner-functionaries. A principle of 'unorganized justice', according to Cohen, might be that stealing from fellow prisoners is not tolerated even though other kinds of theft, known as 'organizing', are deemed acceptable.[54] Part of the task of Sington and others was to enable a shift from 'unorganized' to 'organized' justice, but the complexities of the camp as a social structure, illustrated by the International Committee's initial reluctance to name names, made this a far from straightforward procedure, a fact compounded by the form taken by the eventual trial proceedings.

Where issues of criminality are concerned, then, in *Belsen Uncovered* Sington appears to be more interested in how crime was treated within the camp, as an indication of how quickly recognizable norms of behaviour were re-established, than in describing the trial preparations (and, once identified as a witness, he would not have been permitted to be involved in these preparations). Although *Belsen Uncovered* does not describe in detail the interviewing of survivors or the production of affidavits prior to the trial, in the context of discussing the varied assistance offered to the British relief effort by former prisoners, and the central role played by interpreters, Sington notes that 'the majority of the witnesses called by the War Crimes Investigation Team were found and cross-examined by two Czech Jewish girls'.[55] Nor does he give any special attention to the female guards,

[52] Sington, *Belsen Uncovered*, p. 77.
[53] Phillips, ed., *Trial of Josef Kramer*, pp. 52–53.
[54] Elie A. Cohen, *Human Behaviour in the Concentration Camp*, p. 150.
[55] Sington, *Belsen Uncovered*, p. 154. Given Gertrude Neumann's involvement in the translation of affidavits, mentioned earlier, it is possible that, although his description of the work involved is not quite accurate, Sington's future wife is one of the 'Czech girls' he alludes to here. The establishment and work of the Investigation Team is described in A. T. Williams, *A Passing Fury: Searching for Justice at the End of World War II* (London: Jonathan Cape, 2006), pp. 92–134.

who appear not to have attracted his particular notice. Even at the trial, though he reports that there were approximately fifty-five male SS personnel and twelve or fifteen females at the camp, he adds that the women: 'were not guards but were supposed to be the administrative staff'.[56] However, he does describe how, at least partly in order to fend off potential revenge attacks, the British implemented the policy of arresting Kapos accused of ill-treating fellow prisoners.[57] One notable case discussed in some detail in *Belsen Uncovered* is that of Erich Zoddel.

Zoddel first comes to Sington's attention after a woman is shot and killed, and it is initially believed that Zoddel, who was with her and appears to have sustained a minor injury during the incident, was the intended target. The shooting is therefore thought to be a failed revenge attack. But Zoddel is arrested for beating other prisoners, and while he is in custody, further evidence about the shooting emerges and he is put on trial for murder at a British-run court in Celle in August 1945 and found guilty. He was therefore already under a death sentence when he was tried at Lüneburg. Sington's description of Zoddel is striking for its deployment of discourse that reads the Kapo's behaviour and character traits from his appearance. According to Sington, Zoddel is: 'A short man with round shoulders, low forehead and beady eyes. His nose was flattened like a boxer's or perhaps it had been ravaged by syphilis.'[58] Shortly after, Sington learns more about Zoddel's 'depraved and bestial' character when he interviews him about the allegations of brutality being levelled by other prisoners, remarking on Zoddel's 'ape's face and beady eyes', and, twice in rapid succession, his 'ugly' face.[59]

For Sington to fall back on deducing personality from appearance is particularly striking given that in *Belsen Uncovered* he generally preserves an unemotional, distanced tone, even when evoking, for instance, the piles of corpses he sees in the camp. Shortly before describing Zoddel in this way, Sington gives pen-portraits of the Russians who reported Zoddel to him: 'Michailovski was a stocky man with thick lips and curly hair. [...] With his lined face, burly frame and muscular arms, [Ustinov] looked more like a blacksmith than an Army officer.'[60] Through these descriptions of their appearance, the Russians are allied with brawn, rather than brains. There

[56] Phillips, ed., *Trial of Josef Kramer*, p. 51.
[57] Sington, *Belsen Uncovered*, p. 75.
[58] Sington, *Belsen Uncovered*, p. 78.
[59] Sington, *Belsen Uncovered*, p. 82
[60] Sington, *Belsen Uncovered*, p. 78.

is also judgement here, but it is more implicit than in the description of Zoddel, and the Russians prove themselves trustworthy, in Sington's eyes, by reporting the bad behaviour of one of their own countrymen before mentioning Zoddel. Their reporting of a Russian assures Sington that they are 'not merely exponents of a vendetta against another nationality group'.[61] Sington, then, quickly learns how to negotiate his way between the different groups in the camp, but his judgements are based at least in part on existing presumptions about national character and, as his written account presents it, the relationship between character and appearance. On one level, this is no more than one might expect; Sington displays the prejudices of his time. But questions of identity and identification were to become crucial in the judicial process that soon followed.

At the Lüneburg Trial, three affidavits were read into evidence in which former prisoners, having identified Zoddel from a photograph, though none of them previously knew his full name, asserted that they had either seen him beating others or had themselves been beaten by him. The problems of using photographs in this way were raised in court by Captain Phillips, one of the defence counsel, who cross-examined Lieutenant-Colonel Champion, a British officer who had been involved in collecting the affidavits. Phillips asked whether there was a 'general rule' that 'photographs of people who were obviously not connected' to Belsen were shown to potential witnesses, to which Champion replied that: 'the only innocent side of the thing would be that in any photographs they did identify there would be other people or [...] they would be given four or more [photographs] out of which to make their selection'.[62] More usually, it was not accepted practice under English law to show potential witnesses a photograph of a suspect prior to asking them to attend an identity parade, and when photographs were used to establish an individual's identity, pictures of individuals known to be innocent—in Phillip's words, 'obviously not connected'—would be included alongside the suspect's as a failsafe. By the same logic, showing a witness a photograph and then asking them later to identify an individual in court could be deemed problematic, as the witness's memory of the photograph, rather than their memory of having previously seen the individual in the flesh, could be what prompted an identification.[63]

---

[61] Sington, *Belsen Uncovered*, p. 78.

[62] Phillips, ed., *Trial of Josef Kramer*, p. 115.

[63] The case law on this matter referred to in England and Wales throughout the 1940s and 1950s was an Appeal Court ruling from 1925, in the case of *R v Ferguson and Dwyer* 2 KB

Zoddel denied the detail of the accusations against him, saying, for instance, that he never wore a green triangle, which was one of the identificatory details given by the prosecution witness Benec Zuckermann. When Abram Glinowieksi returned to continue giving evidence after breaking down while describing his brother's death, he recounted hearing about and seeing a prisoner-functionary called Erich, and a man referred to as Zoddel, but he did not identify Zoddel among the prisoners in court.[64] Evidence shortly followed from Champion, who described the procedure used to try to identify suspects, and a photograph was offered to the Judge Advocate to compare with Zoddel himself.[65] These issues around the identification of Zoddel are outlined in the closing speech for the defence given by Captain Corbally, Zoddel's defence counsel, who argued that if Zoddel had indeed been a prisoner-functionary, there would have been a good deal more evidence against him. Corbally goes so far as to suggest that Glinowieski, among others, was 'actuated by motives of spite and revenge and almost a racial hatred'.[66]

These comments about a potential racial motivation to the witnesses' accusations compound the sense, for a present-day reader, that Zoddel's defence seems to be clutching at straws, both in claiming a revenge motive, and in quibbling about identification evidence, although the latter is a fundamental aspect of trial procedure and identification of the accused was particularly difficult given the circumstances in which witnesses would have encountered the defendants at Auschwitz and Belsen, to say nothing of how the evidence was collected. Indeed, one of those on trial at Lüneburg, Oscar Schmitz, claimed that he had been arrested by the British because he was wearing an SS uniform but that he had stolen this to wear because he had no other clothes, and that he was a prisoner, not a guard. He told the court that since his arrest he had 'repeatedly tried to establish [his] true identity'.[67] There was little or no evidence to counter his story that, a petty thief, he had been moved from prison in Germany to Mauthausen, then to Nordhausen, and eventually to Belsen, always as a prisoner, never as a Kapo or guard, and he was found not guilty. In the context of the trial the reliability

799. The defendants' convictions for burglary were overturned because of problems in the way photographs were used to jog the memories of witnesses who later identified the men in court.
[64] Phillips, ed., *Trial of Josef Kramer*, pp. 106–07.
[65] Phillips, ed., *Trial of Josef Kramer*, p. 110.
[66] Phillips, ed., *Trial of Josef Kramer*, p. 558.
[67] Phillips, ed., *Trial of Josef Kramer*, p. 290.

of identification using photographs is brought into question, overlaid as it is by presumptions related to race, gender, and class. From the perspective of usual legal procedure, it is unsurprising that the defence attacked what they saw to be a weak point in the prosecution case. The defence demanded 'normal' levels of evidence-gathering in an exceedingly abnormal situation, and, further, undermined the reliability of witnesses—camp survivors—in much the same way that they might question an account of a traffic accident or a street fight given by a passer-by. This is an approach that, from the perspective of the defence, was validated by the format of the trial, notwithstanding its other highly unusual features and context. No concessions were made to the witnesses, even when this amounted to what would now be called victim-blaming,

Grese on Trial

When Sington wrote about Irma Grese in the mid-1950s, he did so in the knowledge that readers' perceptions of her could be influenced by memories of how she had been depicted in the British press at the time of the trial. As I showed in Chapter 1, and as Sington recognizes in his chapter on Grese in *The Offenders*, photography, important as evidence at the trial, played a key role in newspaper reports, not least because photographs of defendants taken inside the courtroom were a novelty in the British context. Where Kramer was depicted in cartoons as a threatening ape, and in photographs was often shown shackled, a tamed 'beast', the female defendants were measured against what were deemed to constitute 'proper' forms of femininity. As Susannah Heschel points out, 'The largest number of women tried at one time [for Second World War war crimes] occurred at the Belsen Trial [...] Of the twenty-one women, sixteen were SS *Angehörige* and five were Kapos.'[68] Heschel suggests that the fact that across all the proceedings relating to the camps, 'only a handful of women were tried' can itself be explained by gender expectations: 'women's cruelty is surprising, while men's is expected; women are [supposedly] basically innocent by nature,

[68] Susannah Heschel, 'Does Atrocity Have a Gender? Feminist Interpretations of Women in the SS', in *Lessons and Legacies VI: New Currents in Holocaust Research*, edited by Jeffry M. Diefendorf (Evanston: Northwestern University Press, 2004), pp. 300–21 (p. 304). The term *Angehörige* translates as '*associates*' or '*members*', though as Heschel notes, that women were 'not SS members, but part of the SS staff' (p. 302).

so an act of cruelty is viewed as abnormal."[69] Among the Allies, there was an inability to believe that women could be responsible for committing atrocities, while the aversion to prosecuting women in post-war Germany reflected a 'desire to rehabilitate [Germany's] men by asserting the normalcy of its women'.[70] Where female defendants' self-presentation in court is concerned, the performative aspect of femininity becomes particularly pronounced. The depictions of Grese in the popular press took their bearings from implicit shared standards of femininity, inflected, in the British press, with racial overtones, with Grese measured as lacking whether she complied with expected feminine paradigms or not. A consideration of these representations is important in contextualizing Sington's later account of Grese's life and death.

As I noted in Chapter 1, Grese was referred to in newspapers as the 'beastess' or more commonly the 'Belsen Blonde',[71] with blondness standing for femininity and at times being contrasted with other aspects of her appearance. Thus the *Daily Mirror* described her as the 'blonde, harsh-faced girl of 21 [who Kramer] placed in charge of his women slaves'.[72] 'Blonde', is on the surface a neutral or, in the context of the time, a positive designation, though to describe a woman as 'a blonde' (as in 'Belsen Blonde') summons images of potentially predatory femmes fatales, or what Lisa Downing, in a different context, calls 'debased cultural ideals'.[73] Certainly, these negative connotations are reinforced by the epithet 'harsh-faced'. 'Blonde' evokes the notion of the Aryan ideal, and racial characteristics were also attributed to Grese.[74] Grese's appearance came in for particular criticism on the day the court visited the site of the camp, when, as the *Daily Express* put it in their

[69] Heschel, 'Does Atrocity Have a Gender?', p. 304, p. 305.

[70] Heschel, 'Does Atrocity Have a Gender?', p. 318.

[71] Harry Ashbrook, 'Belsen Blonde Is on Her High Horse', *Daily Mirror*, 17 September 1945, p. 8.

[72] Harry Ashbrook, 'Block 18—Men Died in 12 Days', *Daily Mirror*, 18 September 1945, 8.

[73] Lisa Downing, *The Subject of Murder: Gender, Exceptionality, and the Modern Killer* (Chicago: Chicago University Press, 2013), p. 109. Downing is here considering the treatment in the press of Myra Hindley, who was tried alongside Ian Brady in 1966 for the so-called Moors Murders. Hindley carried a photograph of Irma Grese in her purse and Brady's apparent fascination with Nazism was a focus for analyses of the trial that saw it as emblematic of Britain's post-war moral decline. See Pamela Hansford Johnson, *On Iniquity: Some Personal Reflections Arising out of the Moors Murders Trial* (London: Macmillan, 1967). I discuss this further in the conclusion.

[74] For instance, writing as the trial drew to an end, the Marchioness of Huntly, who reported throughout the proceedings, notes that when she stood up, Grese revealed 'the typical German figure, rather broad-hipped with heavy legs'. Marchioness of Huntly, 'Close-up of Belsen Beasts', *Aberdeen Journal*, 15 December 1945, p. 2. Mary Pamela Gordon, Marchioness of Huntly, was the daughter of newspaper magnate Viscount Kemsley and a Director of the *Aberdeen Journal*

headline: 'Irma put on her silk stockings.' While most of the female prisoners wore 'darned [...] lisle stockings [...] with heavy shoes or jackboots [...] Irma Grese, the "blonde beastess", wore silk stockings, which looked new, and a pair of thin court shoes'.[75] The silk stockings, a rare luxury, are seen as a tasteless indulgence, and, implicitly, a cynical attempt on Grese's part to distance herself from her role at the camp, as signified by the 'jackboots' mentioned here.

The idea that Grese could be using self-presentation as a way of both attempting to project a positive image and to confuse the witnesses was raised during her evidence. Grese herself admitted when cross-examined by Backhouse that she had altered her hair style. Backhouse asks: 'In her affidavit [...] Dunklemann said you had your hair up at the back?' to which Grese responded: 'I did not wear my hair in that way at all. I had a sort of drum of pigtails, and that was quite low on the neck.' Backhouse asked her to confirm that her current way of wearing her hair was 'something new' and she told him that it 'originated in the prison in Celle'. When he pointed out that it is hard to 'recognize people when you come and look at them in the dock if they have changed their hair style completely', she retorted: 'The face is always the same'.[76] Backhouse was suggesting that changing their hair styles was a way for the female defendants to attempt to mislead witnesses and avoid being identified. Grese asserted that, on the contrary, the face is the key factor where identification is concerned, and that this does not change. It was in Grese's interest to affirm the continuity in her own appearance, notwithstanding supposedly minor alterations she might have made, because this could have helped further undermine witnesses who were unable to identify her positively. But from the perspective of the public reception of the trial in Britain, this counted for little, because in the British newspapers, all aspects of her appearance were given a negative interpretation: her hair was too well-cared for, too fancy, and her smart shoes and stockings an affront.[77]

By the time Grese took the stand, then, her demeanour in court and on the visit to the site of the camp had already been subjected to close scrutiny.

from 1940–1959. Adrian Smith, 'Berry, (James) Comer, First Viscount Kemsley (1883–1968), newspaper proprietor', http://www.oxforddnb.com.

[75] Anon, 'Irma Put on Her Silk Stockings', Daily Express, 22 September 1945, p. 4.

[76] Phillips, ed., Trial of Josef Kramer, p. 258.

[77] On 10 October 1945, The Daily Mail juxtaposed on its front page a photograph of Grese taken before the war with one that was taken during the proceedings, commenting on how her appearance had in fact changed: 'her eyes [are] darker and sunken, her jaw more set' (p. 1). The implication is that her actions have had a deleterious effect on her appearance.

On launching his defence of Grese and three others—Hilde Lohbauer, Ilse Lothe, and Josef Klippel—Major Cranfield pointed out that although Grese was charged with murder, some allegations about her behaviour only emerged when Dora Szafran was examined in court. Having identified Grese at the start of her evidence, Szafran described seeing Juana Bormann setting her dog on prisoners, gave an account the process of selection, and then was asked whether she had seen other prisoners being beaten:

> I have seen Grese [beat prisoners] in Auschwitz, and about a fortnight before the British troops liberated Belsen I saw her beat a girl in the camp. She had a pistol, but she was using a riding-crop. The beatings were very severe. If they were not the cause of death they were not called severe in the camp.[78]

Under cross-examination by Cranfield, she elaborated this account: 'I remember now, it was in the kitchen [...] She beat the girl with a riding-whip made of leather.'[79] She maintained this even when Cranfield told her that Grese did not carry a whip in Belsen, and, towards the end of his cross-examination, Cranfield asked her why she did not include this incident in her written statement. Szafran responded: 'I am able now to add many things to my descriptions, and not everything I told at that time was written down.'[80] Cranfield implied that having spent time together outside the courtroom, the prosecution witnesses could have colluded in concocting stories about the defendants. This line of questioning was an attempt by Cranfield to further undermine the methods used to gather evidence prior to the trial and to critique the wider context in which the trial took place: witnesses would usually be warned not to discuss the case with each other outside the courtroom and would not be permitted to make additional accusations while giving evidence. Later, Cranfield combined this attack on the prosecution's procedure with a version of the 'obeying orders' defence while simultaneously minimizing of the awfulness of conditions at the camp.

As Cranfield's examination of Szafran illustrates, the defence expressed unease about the perceived discrepancies between the affidavits compiled prior to the trial and the live evidence, and the use of photographs as a form of identification was also scrutinized. After Grese gave evidence, the defence made a formal objection to the admission of affidavits and raised the issue

---

[78] Phillips, ed., *Trial of Josef Kramer*, p. 85.
[79] Phillips, ed., *Trial of Josef Kramer*, p. 87.
[80] Phillips, ed., *Trial of Josef Kramer*, p. 87.

of discrepancies between live and written evidence, mentioning that at least one witness was not able to identify Grese in court. This was deemed by the prosecution to be an attempt at gaming the system, although in his summing up, C. L. Stirling, the Judge Advocate, also warned against over-reliance on this evidence: 'I agree with the defending officers that [the affidavits] are dangerous material. We all know how people will tell you things in the smoke-room and how they would quickly retract them if they had to appear in a court and be cross-examined.'[81] Stirling's comparison between the gathering of affidavits at Belsen and the smoking room of a club or officers' mess is a highly dissonant one. It raises the suspicion that the testimony of survivors could be no more reliable than gossip, a shaggy-dog story or an anecdote told to amuse friends. This is another moment when the disjunction between the court proceedings and the events on which they are intended to adjudicate comes sharply into focus.

Stirling expressed what seem like highly idealistic expectations in relation to witness testimony: 'We all feel, I am sure, very sorry for these unfortunate people [...] But you have to remember that the law likes to have, if it can get them, what it calls "credible witnesses". That is a witness who has no personal interest, who is calm and collected, and who is free from any sort of bias.' Stirling emphasized that he did not doubt that the witnesses had 'been through terrible things' but warned that this might precisely lead to them allowing their feelings 'to rather elaborate or tint their evidence'.[82] Emotion is liable to move an account further from the truth, and a rational, reasonable, and consistent account is the most credible. In this analysis, emotion has its own truth, but this does not belong in the courtroom, no more than vengeance does.

Sington's Account of Grese

The idea that the eventual execution of Grese, Kramer and other defendants was itself an emotional rather than rational response to their crimes is one that was taken up by Sington just over ten years after the trial. In the intervening time, Sington had developed the view that where crime was not the consequence of mental illness, it was a product of the social circumstances and upbringing of the defendant, and that criminals should therefore be given medical treatment if necessary and helped to rehabilitate rather than

[81] Phillips, ed., *Trial of Josef Kramer*, p. 633.
[82] Phillips, ed., *Trial of Josef Kramer*, p. 634.

receiving punishment. Sington's professional life was not connected to the criminal justice system. After leaving his post with the Control Commission in 1950 he worked as a freelance journalist, writing for newspapers including the *Manchester Guardian* on South East Asian matters, before, in 1952, taking up the Manchester-based post of Foreign Subeditor and Leader Writer for the *Guardian*. In 1954, he returned to the BBC, where he had worked for the Monitoring Service in the early years of the war,[83] as Far East Service Talks Assistant. During this period, he had a parallel career, pursued in his own time, as a campaigner for prison reform. He volunteered as a prison visitor and, together with his co-author Giles Playfair, a former barrister later better known as a journalist and theatre historian, who had worked at the BBC during Sington's first spell there in the early 1940s, investigated prison conditions in Britain and abroad, arguing for the complete abolition of both capital punishment and prisons. Playfair and Sington's book *The Offenders* gave Sington the opportunity to revisit his wartime experiences, with the chapter on Irma Grese including long sections that are written by him in the first-person.

This chapter forms one in a series of case-studies intended to cast doubt on the efficacy of current penal practice in Britain and the United States. The first four chapters are examples of how murderers have been dealt with in Britain, Europe, and the USA. Neville Heath was hanged in 1946 for rape and murder, and the authors believe him to have been mentally disturbed, but his condition did not fit with the narrow legal definition of insanity that was in place at the time, nor did the court hear evidence about his early life, which the authors offer as important support for their claim that Heath was a psychopath. As a counter to the case of Heath, they consider Rudi Brettinger, who received treatment in an American psychiatric hospital rather than imprisonment after being found guilty of armed robbery, and the authors believe this will forestall further, more serious crimes on his part. The case of Joseph Redenbaugh is offered to support the argument against whole life terms of imprisonment, which the authors see as purely retributive: Playfair visits Redenbaugh in prison in Minnesota and argues that, based on what he says in interview, Redenbaugh has completely reformed since his youthful involvement in a robbery and murder. In the authors' view, the most progressive approach to murder is that taken in Sweden, and the case of Aake Horsten is cited as an example of how treatment in a special clinic might

---

[83] Sington could have stayed at the Monitoring Service for the duration because his job was a reserved occupation, but he requested to be released so that he could undertake active service.

enable a murderer who has been judged insane to recover sufficiently to be reincorporated into society. The closing paragraph of this chapter acts as a bridge to the chapter on Grese. It is noted that one of the patients at a similar clinic in the Netherlands is a man who collaborated with the Nazis and worked as a camp guard during the Occupation: 'In Holland, apparently, it has now come to be realised that the proper approach even to so-called crimes against humanity is the curative one.'[84] The chapter on Grese is followed by one dealing with the Rosenbergs, executed for espionage, and these chapters are connected because the political beliefs of the defendants are seen to have led to their crimes.

Some reviews of the book felt that linking together such varied cases was not necessarily helpful. Kenneth Younger, in *The Observer*, noted that the two types of case dealt with—those committed through illness or maladjustment and those committed for ideological reasons—are 'wholly different' from each other, while Gordon Rose's *Manchester Guardian* review critiqued the 'case-study' approach with reference to earlier examples of what would now be termed *true crime* writing aimed at a popular audience: 'The book is [...] in great danger of condemnation as merely another of those volumes which make money by collecting together meaty details of famous cases.'[85] Certainly the 'true crime' anthology was a genre that had flourished in the interwar years. The volumes alluded to by Rose often dealt with either unsolved crimes or those that presented particular challenges to the investigators. Edgar Lustgarten, a prominent true crime author and television presenter in 1950s and 1960s Britain, partly followed Playfair and Sington's lead in his 1968 essay collection *The Business of Murder*, in which he considers killers for whom murder is 'an habitual occupation', rather than those who commit their crimes 'on impulse, in rage or under great temptation.'[86] Like Playfair and Sington, he includes chapters on both Grese and Neville Heath. The underlying issue here is whether focusing on 'unusual' or notorious crimes is the best way to draw conclusions about how criminals as a group should be treated, and Rose's use of the word *meaty* indicates that he at least considers such anthologies to have a disreputable aura. While he

---

[84] Giles Playfair and Derrick Sington, *The Offenders: Society and the Atrocious Crime* (London: Secker & Warburg, 1957), p. 146. See also Giles Playfair and Derrick Sington, 'Clinic for Murderers'. This article includes a number of photographs of the clinic and its patients, their faces concealed, by Slim Hewitt.

[85] Kenneth Younger, 'Minds Diseased', *The Observer*, 3 November 1957, p. 15; Gordon Rose, 'Crime and Society', *Manchester Guardian*, 8 November 1957, p. 6.

[86] Edgar Lustgarten, *The Business of Murder* (New York: Scribners, 1968), p. 8.

focuses on cynical authors making money from such cases, the corollary of this is that some readers of Playfair and Sington's book might focus in on such 'meaty details' without giving proper consideration to the wider questions that the cases are intended to illustrate. In this regard, it is notable that Rose underlines the value of the concluding chapter in which Playfair and Sington summarize their conclusions in relation to current debates about the abolition of the death penalty in Britain.

Indeed, the book was published at a key juncture in these debates. In an appendix, the authors discuss the provisions of the Homicide Act (1957), which would have been making its way into law during the period of the book's research and composition. As Playfair and Sington note, among other provisions, the Act divided murder into two categories, capital and noncapital, reclassified as manslaughter some offences that would previously have been tried as murder, and introduced the concept of diminished responsibility into English and Welsh law. The authors consider this to be 'a compromise measure forced on a staunchly retentionist Government by a minority of dissidents in its own ranks',[87] criticizing diminished responsibility as an unhelpfully blurry category and asserting that the Act illustrated the danger of considering abolition in isolation from other aspects of penal reform.

While the early chapters of The Offenders outline measures that might be taken to prevent the escalation of antisocial behaviour into more serious crime, the case of Grese involves, as the reviewers indicate, different considerations. Sington's description in The Offenders of his own background and upbringing, as well as his revisiting of his memories of being at Belsen and giving evidence at the trial, is also pertinent to his analysis of Grese's behaviour in the chapter because he stresses that while in an English court, 'adverse childhood influences' would be taken into account prior to the passing of a sentence, the effect on Grese of growing up in Nazi Germany was not considered at the Belsen Trial.[88] Her early experiences will have affected her attitudes, just as his own have affected his.

Before examining Grese's case in detail, Sington again recounts his arrival at the camp, focusing on the 'unconcern' of Kramer and the other officers, and reflecting that, in April 1945, 'a rational interpretation of the conduct of the Belsen warders was not to the foreground of my mind [...] I did not then see the attitude of these warders as perhaps a symptom of human

---

[87] Playfair and Sington, The Offenders, p. 266.
[88] Playfair and Sington, The Offenders, p. 180.

demoralisation [...] nor as perhaps a challenge to attempt the reconditioning of people utterly corrupted by a terrible system.'[89] Sington seems to use the word *demoralization* as meaning the state of having one's moral standards eroded (rather than in the sense of having one's morale lowered) and his comments about the guards having been corrupted by 'a terrible system' do not engage with the fact that this system was itself man-made, and indeed relied on individuals' willingness to co-operate. But Sington goes further, citing what he remembers about his own sentiments at this period as evidence of the consequences of engaging emotively, rather than in a 'rational' way, with the situation, noting that he felt 'no compunction' when he saw the guards being subjected to retribution:

> Once when an SS man jumped from a burial lorry, and running for it, was shot down by escorting British troops, I remember experiencing a feeling of satisfaction. The feeling was not very different probably from that which German concentration camp guards experienced when they saw a Jew shot who had strayed from a working party.[90]

This is a bold and indeed troubling comparison on Sington's part, implying as it does that the British engaged in acts of vengeance at Belsen. The parallel he makes between his own feelings and those he attributes to 'German concentration camp guards' further suggests that he, and the other British soldiers in Belsen at this point, were, like those guards, ideologically motivated. There is an echo here of the concerns expressed by some members of the public in Britain about putting German army officers on trial, a suggestion that, as I argued in the introduction, raised the question of what British soldiers might have done in the heat of war.[91]

Sington's self-inculpatory reflections chime with the sense, conveyed both here and in other chapters of *The Offenders*, that contingency, not destiny, produces criminality. He also takes the opportunity to comment on how evidence was gathered prior to the trial; as I have noted, *Belsen Uncovered*

[89] Playfair and Sington, *The Offenders*, p. 153. In fact, sentiments of this kind are to be found in *Belsen Uncovered*, when Sington wonders why Kramer and his fellow officers stayed at the camp rather than trying to make their escape and puts this down to their 'utter ignorance of all western standards and codes of behaviour [... .] [T]heir sense of wickedness had been dulled by years of brutish crime' (p. 25).

[90] Playfair and Sington, *The Offenders*, p. 154.

[91] See Caroline Sharples, 'Holocaust on Trial: Mass Observation and British Media Responses to the Nuremberg Tribunal, 1945–46', in *Britain and the Holocaust: Remembering and Representing War and Genocide*, edited by Caroline Sharples and Olaf Jensen (Basingstoke: Palgrave Macmillan, 2013), pp. 31–50.

is largely silent on this issue. The move from 'unorganized' to 'organized' justice is described in this way:

> The first British troops [...] were told at once by the inmates about terrible experiences at the hands of German SS guards. [...] Individual tormentors were named and very soon the camp was alive with denunciations. A small legal unit arrived to investigate allegations. They soon arranged to photograph individually all the SS personnel and the photographs were displayed in one of the huts for identification purposes. Evidence was then collected from any man or woman who cared to relate what he or she had endured or seen others endure at the hands of these people.[92]

Sington does see a clear differentiation between what was happening before the arrival of the legal unit, and what happened afterwards. 'Denunciations' are reframed, in the next sentence, as 'allegations', which have to be supported by 'evidence', but the phrase *cared to relate* implies a lack of systematization to the process. The SS personnel can be identified from photographs, but the accusations come from 'any man or woman'. Sington asserts later that during the preparations for the trial 'a serious effort had been made to observe standards in selecting witnesses such as would have prevailed in a criminal investigation in Britain' in the knowledge that 'the case [...] would have to stand up in a court that would be adhering pretty closely to normal English legal procedure'.[93] However, there are aspects of the legal proceedings at Lüneburg, including the court's eventual sentences, that Sington believes were not so far removed from 'rough justice' as the Allies might have wanted to maintain.

While allowing that attempts were made to conduct 'the assize at Lüneburg' fairly, Sington attacks the proceedings on a number of grounds, including the fact that, although run according to 'English legal procedure' (hence his use of the word *assize*), it was prosecuting offences against international law.[94] He argues that a regulation that essentially disallowed a defence of 'obeying orders' which had been introduced into British military law in 1944, was applied retroactively, and he believes that it is difficult to

---

[92] Playfair and Sington, *The Offenders*, p. 155.

[93] Playfair and Sington, *The Offenders*, p. 161.

[94] Playfair and Sington, *The Offenders*, p. 156. *Assize* was the term used at the time for courts in England and Wales where jury trials were heard. Since reforms and reorganization in the early 1970s, these have been known as Crown Courts.

challenge the notion that this was victor's justice.[95] Notwithstanding these problems, Sington asserts that the court, so far as it was able, 'apportioned reprobation that had been earned', but he nevertheless feels that the ultimate sentences of the court, and specifically its use of capital sentences, undermined any sense in which the court could be seen as attempting to 'prevent a recurrence of such inhumanity'.[96] While capital punishment might ostensibly be used either as a deterrent to others or as retribution, in the context of this trial, Sington rejects the idea that it ever could be a deterrent and he reframes retribution in negative terms, seeing the executions as, 'a response to the clamour for revenge that was sounding all through Allied countries at the time'.[97] This further reinforces the argument that is threaded throughout the book's chapters: presenting capital punishment as a deterrent is only ever a smoke-screen for its real purpose, which is to satisfy feelings of vengefulness.

These comments on the trial serve as a frame within which Sington presents Grese to the reader. Having briefly mentioned her continuing adherence to Nazi ideology during her initial interrogation, he spends a section of the chapter describing her demeanour in court, recalling his own perceptions of her as well as alluding to how she was depicted in the British press. She initially appears to be the 'most alert and spirited-looking of the women' and is notable for being 'by any standards, a pretty girl [...] blonde, with fair ringlets [... .] She might have been a handsome young nurse, a secretary, or even the head prefect of a girls' school'.[98] Whereas in *Belsen Uncovered*, Erich Zoddel's appearance is seen by Sington as an indicator of his criminal propensities, Grese, initially at least, seems to challenge the reading of negative personality traits from appearance. But Sington's initial impressions are soon qualified. He notes that other observers believed Grese to resemble 'a tyrannical young queen in the age of absolutism', and comments that during the proceedings: 'She looked and behaved in fact like the classical Nazi woman. And yet perhaps it had something of the quality of

[95] Playfair and Sington, *The Offenders*, p. 157.

[96] Playfair and Sington, *The Offenders*, p. 158.

[97] Playfair and Sington, *The Offenders*, p. 158. As Mark A. Drumbl has pointed out more recently, it is difficult if not impossible to measure the effectiveness of deterrent measures where war crimes are concerned as 'we simply cannot know how much worse atrocity would have been [...] in the absence of judicial institutions'. In Drumbl's analysis, the deterrent approach is underpinned by a presumption that perpetrators might 'make some kind of cost-benefit analysis and thereby control their behavior'. *Atrocity, Punishment, and International Law* (New York: Cambridge University Press, 2007), p. 17.

[98] Playfair and Sington, *The Offenders*, p. 159.

a mask, this arrogant consciously ruthless bearing.'[99] That Grese's arrogant appearance might be a mask, unlike Zoddel's brutality, which is engraved on his features, fits with Sington's argument that she has been trained into one way of thinking and behaving and could potentially have been re-educated towards a different set of values. He points to the moments at which Grese showed emotion, noting for instance that she cried when her sister was giving evidence in her defence, and is at pains to emphasize her relative youth. Thus while the newspaper reports deployed feminine stereotypes to underline Grese's monstrousness even as she was on the surface complying with cultural expectations of femininity, Sington sees her displays of emotion as evidence that her brutality, as signalled by her 'arrogant' demeanour, is itself a performance, and positions her display of emotion as the truth. The infantilization involved in this manoeuvre is itself an appeal to a stereotype of female vulnerability.

Sington draws a particularly striking comparison when attempting to analyse Grese's appearance in the dock:

> We once asked a German Jewish woman who had been prosecuted for high treason in a Nazi court when she was twenty-one (exactly the age at which Irma Grese was tried) to describe her own feelings and behaviour at her trial. She said she had found the situation 'romantic and thrilling'; it had been her first experience of a court; and she had felt 'like an actress before an audience'. 'But', she added, 'I hardly visualised what lay before me.' So it was, almost certainly, with Irma Grese in September 1945.[100]

To consider being in court 'romantic' is presented here as naïve and immature, qualities that Sington is keen to ascribe to Grese. But this comparison relies on an implicit equivalence between an anti-Nazi and a Nazi. Though he does not elaborate on the detail of the case, one might presume that the charge of 'high treason' levelled against a twenty-one-year-old woman by a Nazi court is a trumped up one. It serves Sington's wider purpose to draw what might seem like an unlikely comparison because he wants to focus the reader's attention on aspects of Grese's background that were not scrutinized in court but which he feels ought to have been taken into account. In order to do this, it is necessary for him to resituate Grese, to distance her from both her fellow defendants and from epithets such as

[99] Playfair and Sington, *The Offenders*, p. 159.
[100] Playfair and Sington, *The Offenders*, p. 160.

'beastess', to an extent to normalize her.[101] Youthful idealism, no matter what its ideological shading, is the keynote here and the detail of how these ideals might have been expressed in action are not dwelt on at this point.

Sington does outline the evidence presented against Grese in court, noting that: 'The evidence of cruelty on her part was considerable; and she herself had provided some corroboration of it.' His concern is not so much with the court's unsurprising verdict of 'Guilty', but with how Grese was subsequently dealt with, or rather not dealt with:

> A magistrate or judge in peace-time and under normal conditions would, after a girl of twenty-one had been convicted, ask for a report on her background, her family life and her circumstances. [...] But defeated Germany in 1945 was hardly a theatre in which to expect crime to be treated objectively or in a spirit of healing.[102]

The second half of the chapter thus attempts to make good this deficiency: 'We have, therefore, endeavoured to play the part—too long after the event—of social workers reporting on her childhood, upbringing and earlier environment.'[103] The argument here is a circular one. In 'normal' circumstances, Grese would not have been sentenced without her background being taken into account, but the circumstances in which her crimes were committed were precisely not normal. The analysis of Grese's early life is framed as being no more than any defendant might expect but this inevitably shifts focus away from questions of individual agency towards a more deterministic view of behaviour. In the account that follows, Grese's youth and the over-riding influence of being raised in a culture of Nazism are emphasized as drivers of her behaviour. For example, citing Helene Grese's evidence that she and her sister wanted to join the Bund Deutscher Mädel (League of German Girls) but were forbidden to do so by their father, the authors comment that in a small village like theirs, 'the influence of BDM members, even on "outsiders", if they were receptive, would obviously be strong.'[104] Irma Grese is thus constructed as, essentially, a victim of ideology, though the fact that

---

[101] In relation to the use of the epithet *beastess*, Sington notes that some sections of the press used the term *beast* to refer to Neville Heath, and argues that in both cases, this language expresses a 'primeval revenge instinct'. Playfair and Sington, *The Offenders* (London: Secker & Warburg, 1957), p. 178.

[102] Playfair and Sington, *The Offenders*, p. 164.

[103] Playfair and Sington, *The Offenders*, p. 165.

[104] Playfair and Sington, *The Offenders*, p. 166.

her sister, subject presumably to the same influences, took a different path, is not dwelt on.

In its closing pages, the chapter quotes the description of a gas chamber 'selection' that was part of Stirling's summing up, with all the horror that entails, but in the remarks that follow, Grese's youth and lack of agency are again underlined, with the reader being reminded that Stirling did not detail

> the punishment that could be meted out to an SS wardress who refused to take part [...] what he also failed to allude to—and it is an aspect that would have been taken into account by any London magistrate dealing with a twenty-one-year-old delinquent—was the long history of adverse childhood influences in National Socialist Germany.[105]

To see a continuity between the kinds of crime most usually sentenced at magistrates' courts and those of which Grese was accused might appear odd: the two types of offence seem to be on completely different scales.[106] But the authors' point is that if personal history and circumstances are going to be taken into account for crimes like shoplifting, then there is all the more reason to consider the precise circumstances, including social forces, that have led to involvement in war crimes. As Mark Drumbl has noted, one important difference between war crimes and 'ordinary crime' is that 'ordinary crime tends to be deviant in the times and places it is committed' whereas the 'extraordinary acts of criminality that collectively lead to mass atrocity' are 'a product of conformity and collective action, not delinquency'.[107] The danger of Playfair and Sington's approach that as a consequence of attempting to steer away from discourse that depicts war criminals as 'bestial' and impossible to incorporate into existing descriptive frameworks, they endorse by default an 'obeying orders' defence.

---

[105] Playfair and Sington, *The Offenders*, p. 180.

[106] Magistrates' courts in England and Wales try and sentence crimes liable to attract penalties of sixth-months' imprisonment or less, as well as dealing with youth crime and family-related matters such as child protection and adoption. At the period when Sington was writing, magistrates, who are volunteers without legal training, would have been likely to be embedded in the local community where the cases were being heard. Even relatively small towns had their own courts, and defendants would frequently be known either personally or by reputation to the members of the bench. Considering how Kapos should be dealt with, Christopher Burney draws a similar comparison: 'As a metaphorical magistrate, I would recommend them to a long course in a metaphorical approved school.' *The Dungeon Democracy* (1945), in *Solitary Confinement and the Dungeon Democracy* (London: Macmillan, 1984), pp. 137–248 (p. 179).

[107] Drumbl, *Atrocity, Punishment, and International Law*, p. 8.

The framing of Grese's story is partly dictated by its place in the wider argument of *The Offenders*, hence the statement that the execution of Grese, 'like all the other executions for war crimes—seems to have been useless as well as barbaric.'[108] Sington's experiences reporting on the Korean War are alluded to here in a dismissal of the idea that capital punishment could have a deterrent effect; the execution of Nazi war criminals has done little to dissuade others from committing war crimes.[109] Further, the chapter includes a description of a visit to the site where the remains of Grese and the other executed prisoners were eventually interred, and reports that it has become a place of pilgrimage: 'There is not much doubt that this strip of hillside outside Hamelin is raising up a legend. Not a healthy or constructive legend but one which is concerned largely with the callous side of the British occupation.'[110] The alternative suggested is a programme along the lines of the one instituted at Wilton Park, which ran from 1946 until 1948. This has parallels in the approaches outlined in other chapters of Playfair and Sington's book, where, in relation to antisocial behaviour, mental illness, and ideology as causes of violent crime, re-education and reconditioning is advocated.[111] The shortcomings of de-Nazification, the question not only of whether re-education is possible or measurable or whether former Nazis could ever be reincorporated into democratic society, issues which would increasingly be debated in Germany during the 1960s, are beyond the authors' remit.[112]

---

[108] Playfair and Sington, *The Offenders*, p. 183.

[109] Sington refers to the 'Chinese guards' treatment of British prisoners of war in Korea in 1950' (p. 183), but as Grace Huxford notes, although '[t]wenty-five Royal Marines were captured in November 1950', the first Chinese offensive did not take place until January 1951, resulting in the capture of a further eighty officers and other ranks. The Chinese People's Volunteers took responsibility for all prisoners from early 1951. Grace Huxford, *The Korean War in Britain: Citizenship, Selfhood and Forgetting* (Manchester: Manchester University Press, 2018), p. 100. The bulk of British prisoners were taken in April 1951 following the Imjin River offensive. In the British Official History of the Korean War, Anthony Farrar-Hockley, who was himself taken prisoner during the conflict, asserts that the Chinese treated their captives more humanely than did the North Koreans. *The British Part in the Korean War: Volume II an Honourable Discharge* (London: HMSO, 1995), p. 266. It is odd that Sington is not more specific in his claims at this point in his argument, and that he does not note one of the most distinctive aspects of the treatment of prisoners of war in Korea: the attempts made to convert them to Communism. During 1950–1952, Sington was based in Singapore but travelled to Burma, Hong Kong, and Malaya as a war reporter.

[110] Playfair and Sington, *The Offenders*, p. 184.

[111] In *The Offenders*, it is suggested that the Rosenbergs 'should have been committed to some kind of treatment or education centre' but '[n]o such centre existed, of course, nor does it exist in America today.' A parallel is drawn not to de-Nazification but to 'education centres for Communist rebels' established in 'Malaya and Singapore in 1950–52.' Playfair and Sington, *The Offenders*, p. 212, p. 212 n. 1.

[112] Sington's work overseeing *Die Welt* was also part of the effort to reinstate democratic values in Germany. He does not seem to have ever written about the time he spent in Germany in the immediate post-war years. Notably, *Belsen Uncovered* was included in the British government's Selected Book Scheme, which identified texts deemed to 'promote democratic and

Sington's post-war writing on criminal justice attempts to classify instances of criminal behaviour as either a response to a particular social-political or sociocultural set of circumstances, in which case the criminal can be educated away from their criminality, or as stemming from mental illness, and therefore warranting treatment. But in attempting to fit Irma Grese and other war criminals into the former category, Sington relies on underlying but unstated norms of what constitutes a fair and just society. He also disallows or at least downplays the role of individual agency or even expediency in decisions relating to criminal acts. Sington's own concealment, or at least omission, of details of his background in his earlier writing is notable in this regard. His decision, in *Belsen Uncovered*, not to mention that his father was Jewish could have been designed to prevent distracting the reader from the real focus of the text, the condition of the prisoners and their attempts to constitute themselves into a functioning social unit. His later revelation of his own subject position seems, by contrast, to be designed to give force to his argument: even he, a person of Jewish heritage who glimpsed the rise of Nazism and saw its awful aftermath, feels that Grese was treated too harshly. His tactical deployment of biographical information about himself mirrors his exploration of Grese's own background. Sington's sense, expressed in his letters to Crichton-Stuart, that *Belsen Uncovered* should be published as soon as possible after the events it described took place, can be contrasted with the longer perspective that characterizes his reflections on Grese. Not only is he writing ten years after the trial, but he is drawing not just on the events of the war but on her earlier history—and his own. Justice delayed is justice denied, the saying goes. For Sington, the extraordinary conditions that pertained at the end of the war did not allow for the proper thinking through of the consequences of dealing with war criminals in a precipitate fashion. Sington does not dwell, in either *Belsen Uncovered* or *The Offenders*, on the part his own trial testimony might have played in the verdict that was released, but it is clear that for him, the attempt to understand what Belsen was could not be adequately addressed either by the trial at Lüneburg or by his own attempts at revisiting those proceedings.

humanitarian' attitudes and thus appropriate for circulation in defeated Germany. Rhys W. Williams, '"The Selections of the Committee Are Not in Accord with the Requirements of Germany": Contemporary English Literature and the Selected Book Scheme in the British Zone of Germany (1945–1950)', in *The Cultural Legacy of the British Occupation in Germany: The London Symposium*, edited by Alan Bance (Stuttgart: Verlag Heinz-Dieter Heinz, 1997), pp. 110–38 (p. 111).

3

Memoir, Biography, and Justice

Between 1964 and 1967, Airey Neave, the Conservative MP for Abingdon in Oxfordshire, campaigned on behalf of a number of former prisoners of Sachsenhausen concentration camp, in the hope that they would receive a share of the £1,000,000 compensation that the West German government had released for the benefit of British citizens who had been victims of Nazi crimes. The claimants included prisoners who had been recaptured following the so-called Great Escape from Stalag Luft III Sagan in March 1944, and the Special Operations Executive agent Peter Churchill, all of whom had been held at Sachsenhausen's Sonderlager (special camp). According to Churchill's own account in his autobiography *Spirit in the Cage* (1954), after arriving and being taken past the 'machine-gun-turreted and electrically-wired walls' of the camp, the new arrivals were led to a 'pine-tree studded enclosure'. In comparison to the rest of the complex, and in the light of Churchill having spent the previous ten months at the notorious Fresnes prison in Paris, it seemed 'a haven [...] the next best thing to an RAF camp'.[1] Separated off from the main camp, the Sonderlager was nevertheless within its precincts, and guarded, as was the whole of Sachsenhausen, by the SS. After fractious discussions in Parliament, with Neave losing few opportunities to attack the Labour administration, and with his authority to speak on behalf of the claimants shored up by his own wartime experience as a prisoner in, and high-profile escapee from, the notorious Colditz camp, the government agreed to compensate the former captives.[2]

The compensation claim, as a legal procedure, is very different in focus and intent from the other legal engagements with the impact of Nazism that had taken place immediately after the war. At war crimes trials, victims

[1] Peter Churchill, *The Spirit in the Cage* (London: Hodder & Stoughton, 1954), p. 125 (p. 126, p. 144).
[2] This incident is explored in detail in Glen O'Hara, 'The Parliamentary Commissioner for Administration, the Foreign Office, and the Sachsenhausen Case, 1964–1968', *Historical Journal* 53.3 (2010): pp. 771–81. Neave described his experiences, including his escapes and his later involvement in the Nuremberg Trials, in *They Have Their Exits* (1953). A later volume, *Saturday at M. I. 9* (1969) focused on his work, in the final two years of the war, organizing escape lines from occupied Europe for Allied servicemen.

Literature and Justice in Mid-Twentieth-Century Britain. Victoria Stewart, Oxford University Press.
© Victoria Stewart (2023). DOI: 10.1093/oso/9780192858238.003.0004

gave evidence in the hope that judicial punishment would be meted out to perpetrators. Though victims may have welcomed the opportunity to describe and make more widely known what they had experienced, any 'compensation' would come indirectly, in the form of seeing the perpetrator penalized for their crimes. In financial compensation cases, victims gave accounts of their experiences in the specific hope that they might receive some recognition and material recompense for suffering they had undergone. The offer of money to a particular group was a means of acknowledging responsibility beyond the boundaries of any judicial proceedings that might be ongoing against individuals.

The debate about the Sachsenhausen case can indeed seem, as one of the government ministers involved observed at the time, 'a bit legalistic', with the term *legalistic* here implying that an adherence to the letter of the law is taking precedence over the consideration of the merits of individual cases.[3] If 'having been in a concentration camp' was the criterion for receiving compensation, then attempting to establish the exact boundaries of any particular camp described in this way was indeed important. But from the former prisoners' point of view, even if their conditions were distinct from those endured by other inmates, they were nevertheless also quite different from those that pertained in prisoner-of-war camps. From this perspective, the precise status of satellite camps or compounds was not believed to be of central importance. Though the West German government had acknowledged the wrongs of Nazism, the former SOE agents and other ex-prisoners whose cases were taken up by Neave were faced unexpectedly with questions being raised by the British government about the extent and nature of their victimhood.

This was partly a consequence of compensation being conceived of as distinct from reparations, the latter being defined by Susanna Schrafstetter as 'payment of war damages by the losing party to the winners'.[4] This shift from economic reparations being paid by the defeated nation to compensation 'for "injury" sustained by individuals and their descendants'

---

[3] George Brown, who became Foreign Secretary, with responsibility for the case, in August 1966, quoted in O'Hara, 'The Parliamentary Commissioner', p.774.

[4] Susanna Schrafstetter, '"Gentlemen, the Cheese is All Gone!" British POWs, the "Great Escape" and the Anglo-German Agreement for Compensation to Victims of Nazism', *Contemporary European History* 17.1 (2008): pp. 23–43 (p. 26). In West Germany, compensation claims were dealt with separately from restitution claims, which related to the reclamation of appropriated property.

is characterized by Nicole L. Immler as a post–Second World War phenomenon.[5] The situation that arose in Britain in the early 1960s illustrates the 'fundamental tension' that Immler identifies between 'official efforts and subjective experience that is inherent to the nature of compensation itself'.[6] That Peter Churchill's autobiography was effectively used in evidence against him seems a particularly unfortunate aspect of the Sachsenhausen case, given the cultural currency accorded to such memoirs and biographies of SOE agents in the late 1940s and early 1950s.[7] But it underlines the double bind of compensation: the recompense it offers is symbolic, in that there is little pretence that experiences can have a precise monetary value or that money can right the wrong, but the processes of administering such schemes involves discriminating between individual life-stories to establish who is, and who is not, worthy of receiving a pay-out.[8]

One of the goals for the British government in the war crimes trials they oversaw was to seek justice on behalf of those, who, like Churchill, had undertaken secret work on continental Europe and had been mistreated after being captured, and the administration of later compensation claims therefore supplemented these earlier efforts. Some agents were tortured while in Nazi captivity, and some were executed, ostensibly for espionage. This treatment was a consequence of the fact that SOE agents were a distinct category of both combatant and prisoner. As I mentioned in the introduction, working undercover in occupied Europe in the wake of Hitler's 1942 Commando Order, these agents did not have the relative protection offered

---

[5] Nicole L. Immler, '"Too Little, Too late?" Compensation and Family Memory: Negotiating Austria's Holocaust Past', *Memory Studies* 5.3 (2012): pp. 270–81 (p. 271).

[6] Immler, '"Too Little, Too Late?"', p. 271.

[7] As I mentioned in the Introduction, when looking back from the vantage point of the early 1980s, Ken Worpole included Bruce Marshall's *The White Rabbit* (1952), W. Stanley Moss's *Ill Met by Moonlight* (1956), and Anne-Marie Walters's *Moondrop to Gascony* (1951), all of which recount experiences of SOE agents, in the list of what he deemed to have been the twenty most-popular texts about the Second World War during the 1950s. *Dockers & Detectives: Popular Reading; Popular Writing* (London: Verso, 1983), p. 51.

[8] Tony Kushner notes that Harold Le Druillenac, the former Belsen inmate who gave evidence at the Belsen Trial, received 'one of the largest awards, totaling £1835'. 'The Holocaust in the British Imagination: The Official Mind and Beyond, 1945 to the Present', *Holocaust Studies* 23.3 (2017): pp. 364–84 (p.376). In the German context, the Roma and Sinti faced particular challenges in claiming compensation. As Julia von dem Knesebeck explains, 'Initially, cases where the National Socialist justification for imprisoning Roma had been their criminality or "asociality", claims by Roma for compensation were rejected on the grounds that they had not been victims of racial persecution. [...] That indiscriminate ascription of characteristics such as criminality and "asociality" to an ethnic group was a form of racial persecution in itself was not considered.' *The Roma Struggle for Compensation in Post-War Germany* (Hatfield: University of Hertfordshire Press, 2011), p. 10.

by a uniform and were deemed to be carrying out espionage when captured in the field; the same applied to prison camp escapees who were wearing civilian clothes when recaptured.[9] Some SOE agents, such as F. F. E. Yeo-Thomas, retained a British 'cover' identity when in captivity though towards the end of the war he found it necessary to claim that he was French.[10] As I will show, this caused problems when Yeo-Thomas finally made contact with Allied forces and needed to reassert his actual identity. Peter Churchill benefitted from the lie told by his fellow agent Odette Sansom, who, when captured, claimed that they were married and that he was related to Winston Churchill.[11] Believing this, their captors deemed that both Churchill and Sansom could be valuable as bargaining chips, giving Churchill special status, and keeping Sansom in solitary confinement, rather than placing her in with the general prisoner population, when she was sent to Ravensbrück, the women's concentration camp in northern Germany. Sansom's treatment was hardly a privilege, but being kept in solitary, despite its extreme psychological and physical hardships, may nevertheless have improved her chances of survival.

Sansom was among those who gave evidence at the first in a series of seven British-run trials relating to crimes committed at Ravensbrück, including crimes against female agents, that took place in Hamburg between the end of 1946 and early 1948.[12] A few months prior to this, another British trial centred on what had happened to a group of female agents who were captured, sent to Natzweiler camp, and executed. As I will show, for a variety of reasons, the Natzweiler Trial was not widely reported in the British press,

---

[9] Under the Geneva Convention, captured servicemen were normally not obliged to undertake work and could receive Red Cross parcels and post from home (though the Nazis sometimes denied the latter as a punishment). Paul Brickhill describes one of the escapees from Sagan attempting to pass off his disguise as a customized uniform when recaptured. *The Great Escape* (London: Cassell, 2000 [1951]), p. 217. See also Victoria Stewart, 'Masculinity, Masquerade and the Second World War: Betty Miller's *On the Side of the Angels*', in *Conflict, Nationhood and Corporeality in Modern Literature: Bodies-at-War*, edited by Petra Rau (Basingstoke: Palgrave, 2010), pp. 124–42.

[10] Bruce Marshall explains that Yeo-Thomas gave a false name because he was concerned for the safety of his father, who lived in Paris: 'If [his captors] discovered his real identity and failed by normal methods to make him speak they would certainly arrest his father and torture the old man in his presence.' *The White Rabbit: A British Agent's Adventures in France* (London: Pan, 1954 [1952]), p. 109.

[11] At Buchenwald, Peter Churchill encountered another prisoner, Jack Churchill, who also benefitted from the accident of his surname: '[he was] no relation of mine or Winston's, but [was] always known as my cousin to our captors'. Churchill, *The Spirit in the Cage*, p. 150. Odette Sansom and Peter Churchill married in 1947.

[12] For an overview of these trials, see Michael J. Bazyler and Frank M. Tuerkheimer, *Forgotten Trials of the Holocaust* (New York: NYU Press, 2014), pp. 129–57.

but over the years that followed, a number of biographical accounts of the murdered agents, aimed at a popular readership, were published. Often these texts underlined that the women had been dealt with illegally by drawing a contrast between their treatment and the valid and proper legal proceedings against the perpetrators.

Incarcerated agents sometimes used the threat of future legal action as a way of attempting to gain influence over their captors. Indeed, in several cases to be examined here, including Peter Churchill's, captives essentially blackmailed Nazi officers, promising to give favourable testimony at any future trial in return for concessions during their imprisonment, making a proleptic appeal to a time when positions would be reversed, and their captor would be indicted. The very particular position of SOE agents as combatants, together with the relatively prominent status that their stories eventually attained in post–war British culture, therefore makes their biographies and autobiographies a striking case study in the consideration of how the crimes of the Nazis and attempts to bring them to justice were understood in the 1940s and 1950s, and, in particular, how the depiction of concentration camps in these works tended to overshadow the fates of the other, less 'privileged' inmates.

The Search for Justice in Biographies of Female SOE Agents

From late 1944, Vera Atkins, who oversaw the recruitment and training of female agents for SOE's French section (F-Section), attempted to establish where missing agents in the field believed to be in Nazi captivity were being held. As Sarah Helm has noted in her biography of Atkins, Atkins thought it more likely that the women would be found in concentration camps than in prisoner-of-war camps, and the information she received about the concentration camps came from a variety of sources. She 'monitored the press, spoke to exile groups', and examined information uncovered by postal censorship: 'Mail reaching, in particular, the Jewish Agency [in England] had consistently told a story of concerted horrific atrocity.'[13] Security concerns meant that Atkins was initially not allowed to circulate names of missing agents to other branches of the military. This concerned her because she

---

[13] Sarah Helm, *A Life in Secrets: The Story of Vera Atkins and the Lost Agents of SOE* (London: Abacus, 2006), p. 65.

believed that some agents might have attempted to maintain their cover identities after being captured and that they might therefore have difficulty establishing their bona fides and being repatriated if their actual names were not released to the Allied forces who were their potential liberators.[14]

Towards the end of the war, information eventually began to emerge as some agents, including Odette Sansom, made their way back to Britain, and a shift in political attitude, described by Helm as 'the new "market" for war crimes', was an additional factor in the publicizing of what had happened.[15] But Atkins was still sensitive about the potential repercussions of revealing what these women had been required to do in the field. When legal proceedings began to be planned in relation to four agents who were executed together at Natzweiler, she foregrounded the importance of countering any potential claim by defence counsel that the women were spies and that their executions were therefore not illegal.[16] This concern accounts for the paucity of the newspaper coverage of this trial, as the majority of British newspapers acceded to Atkins's request not to report on it while it was in progress. *The Daily Mail* complied by the letter though not the spirit of the request by noting it had been made on the grounds that 'details of [the women's] deaths would cause pain to the relatives', but while not naming the victims, its report nevertheless describes how the women were given lethal injections and then cremated, possibly while still alive.[17] However, at least partly because of representations made by relatives of deceased agents, including the father of Violette Szabo, an agent who was executed at Ravensbrück, their service was eventually given official recognition, and when a memorial to women of the SOE was unveiled in London in May 1948, *The Illustrated London News* was among the publications that gave the event prominent coverage, publishing photographs of agents who had died, where these were available, and providing brief accounts of the circumstances of the death of each where these were known.[18]

In 1949, William Hodge & Co published the proceedings of the Natzweiler Trial in their *War Crimes* series, and both the preliminary material and the account of the trial itself underline the importance to a successful

---

[14] Helm, *A Life in Secrets*, p. 80.
[15] Helm, *A Life in Secrets*, p. 190.
[16] Helm, *A Life in Secrets*, p. 241.
[17] Anon, '4 Women Whose Names Will Never Be Known', *Daily Mail* (30 May 1946), p. 1.
[18] Anon, 'The Women Who Died For Their Country: Courageous Secret Service Agents', *Illustrated London News* (22 May 1948), p. 573. Not all the information given in this article was accurate; the photograph labelled as 'Eliane Plewman' is actually of Violette Szabo.

prosecution of establishing that the women had not themselves received anything resembling a fair trial, which, even if they were deemed to be spies, would have been required under international law. In his preface to this volume, Hartley Shawcross emphasizes this intention when he remarks that the purpose of publishing accounts of such proceedings is:

> [n]ot to encourage a morbid interest: not to keep alive feelings of ill-will against our late enemies. But because the horror through which the world passed in those dark years was [...] something against which [...] asserting the law in international affairs as in municipal ones, must protect us.[19]

Similarly, in his closing remarks at the trial, the Judge Advocate, A. A. H. Marlowe, asserted: 'This Court is not concerned with whatever "strange Courts" there were in Germany in the last few years. [...] [T]he German idea of justice had completely departed from that which was ordinarily accepted to humanity, and it is no sort of answer to say: "Well, it was a sort of Court".'[20] He was responding here to the claim, outlined in his opening speech by Grobel, the German lawyer who acted as lead defence counsel, that the women were indeed spies and that 'the sentence by a full Court was not required in this case, but that the sentence by a single person might have sufficed.'[21] Grobel used the term *special Courts*, or in German *Sondergerichte*, to refer to the various types of proceedings, including 'S. S. Courts, and S. D. Courts' that took place in Nazi Germany, and Marlowe's term *strange courts* could be a loaded misremembering of this term.[22] But Marlowe's comments underline a sense that regardless of what might be argued about the peculiarities of wartime, part of the task of these post-war proceedings, in his view, was to re-establish internationally recognizable standards of the rule of law.

From this perspective, the Natzweiler Trial was a consequence of the failure of the rule of law in Nazi Germany as much as it was a result of the

---

[19] Hartley Shawcross, 'Foreword', in *Trial of Wolfgang Zeuss et al (The Natzweiler Trial)*, edited by Anthony M. Webb (London: William Hodge and Company, 1949), pp. 13–15.

[20] Webb, ed., *Trial of Wolfgang Zeuss*, p. 205.

[21] Webb, ed., *Trial of Wolfgang Zeuss*, p. 99. At this trial, defendants chose to have German defence counsel.

[22] Webb, ed., *Trial of Wolfgang Zeuss*, p. 98. Grobel appears to have been speaking English when he used the term *special courts*. Anita Lasker-Wallfisch, whose involvement in the Belsen trial was discussed in Chapter 1, recalls being tried, along with her sister Renate, by a 'Sondergericht, a special court. [...] We were given the option of legal representation, which [...] was a charade [...] it really was in our interest—absurd though it may sound—to get as long a sentence as possible. If by some chance the court were to find us "not guilty", and we were released from prison, we would never walk out free. We would be instantly rearrested by the Gestapo.' *Inherit the Truth 1939–1945* (London: Giles de la Mare, 1996), pp. 63–64.

specific brutality of the women's treatment, and this failure was now, in the form of the British-run trial itself, being reasserted. The full details of what had happened to the women who died at Natzweiler, insofar as they could be reconstructed, would not emerge until some years later, and indeed the identity of one of the women killed was not established until long after the trial. Atkins initially believed that 'Sonia Olschanesky', reported as having been taken into captivity along with Diana Rowden, Andrée Borrel, and Vera Leigh, was an alias for SOE agent Noor Inayat Khan. Further information emerged about what had happened to Khan, correcting this error, and, in the mid-1950s, Elizabeth Nicholas was able to establish that Olschanezky (as she was properly known) was a locally recruited member of an SOE circuit. When Nicholas came to undertake her own investigation into the case, in the context of wanting to find out more about what had happened to Rowden, with whom she had been at school, she expressed disquiet at existing discourse that had emerged relating to the women, including both the Hodge volume and the London memorial.[23] Her work, like Jean Overton Fuller's, reshapes biography as a quest, and foregrounds the role of the biographer as investigator, an extra-judicial seeker-after-justice.

Overton Fuller's biography of Noor Inayat Khan, *Madeleine* (which takes its title from Khan's codename) was published in 1952, with Nicholas's *Death Be Not Proud* appearing in 1958. These texts engage either implicitly or explicitly with books including Jerrard Tickell's *Odette: The Story of a British Agent* (1949) and R. J. Minney's *Carve her Name with Pride: The Story of Violette Szabo G. C.* (1956). Tickell's work, which benefitted from access to material that was not available to later authors, was facilitated by the fact that he was attached to the War Office's public relations department, and in this capacity, he attended the first trial of personnel from Ravensbrück, which opened in Hamburg in December 1946. Ravensbrück was in the Soviet Zone at the end of the war, and Michael J. Bazyler and Frank M. Tuerkheimer argue that the British took responsibility for organizing this and other trials related to the camp because 'they viewed the Soviet-backed Polish government with suspicion', and did not want to hand over the suspects in their custody to the Poles.[24] Another factor influencing this decision was that, as I have noted, several British women, including Sansom, had been imprisoned at Ravensbrück, and it was where Violette Szabo was executed.

---

[23] Elizabeth Nicholas, *Death Be Not Proud* (London: Cresset Press, 1958), pp. 27–29.
[24] Bazyler and Tuerkheimer, *Forgotten Trials*, p. 137.

Tickell opens *Odette* with a description of the Ravensbrück trial, his chapter culminating in Odette Sansom's confirmation of her identity when she goes into the witness box to give her evidence. The narrative which follows, beginning with Sansom's family background, is thus framed by the validatory force of courtroom witness testimony. Of course, Sansom's evidence did not consist of her recounting her whole history in the detail that Tickell does, but in using the courtroom as a frame, Tickell authenticates his account. The 1950 film adaptation of *Odette* replaces this framing device with a different kind of authentication. Maurice Buckmaster, the head of SOE's F-Section, speaks directly to camera in a prologue, explains who he is, and affirms: 'I know [...] that this story is a true one.'[25] The Ravensbrück trial is not mentioned in what follows, and the film culminates in Odette (Anna Neagle) being reunited with Peter Churchill (Trevor Howard) after they have both managed to make their way back to England. Churchill registers the physical harm that Odette has suffered but nevertheless embraces her, thus promising the audience that her femininity has remained essentially undamaged and providing the narrative with romantic closure. Tickell's book, meanwhile, closes with Sansom's citation for the George Cross, emphasizing recognition of a professional rather than personal kind.

The film's reunion scene, like Tickell's description of Sansom's physical presence in the courtroom, is important because it evidences Sansom's resilience under torture.[26] She embodies survival. As Tickell puts it: 'Her face, pale in the strong light, was small-featured, delicate and oddly childlike. Her eyes were bright. A mass of dark hair swept upwards from her forehead, almost concealing the slanting beret, and fell thick upon her shoulders.'[27] Despite what she has endured, Sansom's femininity and vulnerability, signified by her 'child-like' face and luxuriant hair, are unharmed.[28]

---

[25] Rather oddly, in the body of the film, Buckmaster appears as himself, opposite professional actors in the other roles.

[26] The back cover of the Pan paperback edition of *Odette* does not pull its punches in describing what, infamously, happened to Sansom in captivity: 'The Gestapo put certain questions to her; she had nothing to say, even after they had pulled out all her toenails.' Jerrard Tickell, *Odette: The Story of a British Agent (Odette Churchill G. C. M. B. E.)* (London: Pan, 1955[1949]), jacket blurb. For an analysis of how *Odette* and other biographies of female agents depict scenes of torture, see Victoria Stewart, 'Representing Nazi Crimes in Post-Second World War Life Writing', *Textual Practice* 29.7 (2015): pp. 1311–30.

[27] Tickell, *Odette*, p. 16.

[28] As Deirdre Osborne has observed, the facts that Odette was 'A French woman domiciled in England, legally separated from her English husband' and that she had three daughters, complicate this characterization of her and are accommodated by Tickell largely by elision.

Positioned at an early point in the narrative, this is a guarantee for the reader that Sansom will emerge from her ordeal, and, importantly, having kept silent under torture, will eventually, in the safe confines of the courtroom, be able to speak about what she, and others, have endured.

Odette and other popular biographies of SOE agents from the 1940s and 1950s, such as Minney's *Carve Her Name with Pride*, have been criticized by M. R. D. Foot, author of the 1968 official history of SOE's F-Section, as 'good thrillers but bad history', and historian Mark Seaman concurs, commenting of *Odette* that 'at times the book reads like a novel'.[29] These comparisons construct the fictive realm as unreliable and inauthentic: it has no place in an account of historical events. Foot's and Seaman's dismissals of fiction underestimate the extent to which the techniques associated with fiction, such as figurative language and emplotment, are frequently, even inevitably, employed in historical or biographical writing, but whether or not these texts may be judged 'good', that is, reliable, history, they can nevertheless be highly revealing of the temper of the period when they were produced. Their 'fictive' aspects are symptomatic of attempts to describe historical events that are only partially understood. Indeed, when these texts were published, only limited official sources were available even to a relatively privileged researcher like Tickell. The attribution of thoughts, feelings, even dialogue to their subjects by these authors may not strike historians as good practice, but for the biographers, this is a legitimate means of creating a coherent account of their subject's behaviour, forming a connection with the reader, and bridging the gaps in the historical record.

Not all authors of biographies aimed at a general audience made extensive use of these devices. In her preface to *Madeleine*, Overton Fuller emphasizes the challenges that confronted her in attempting to find out what happened to her friend Noor Inayat Khan. Her interviewees include those who knew Khan because of their work with the Resistance as well as others who collaborated with the Nazi regime. In either case Overton Fuller makes an

'"I do not know about politics or governments ... I am a housewife": The Female Secret Agent and the Male War Machine in Occupied France (1942–5)', *Women: A Cultural Review* 17.1 (2006): pp. 42–64 (p. 45).

[29] M. R. D. Foot, *SOE in France: An Account of the Work of the British Special Operations Executive in France 1940–1944* (London: Her Majesty's Stationery Office, 1968), p. 453; Mark Seaman, 'Good Thrillers, But Bad History: A Review of Published Works on the Special Operations Executive's Work in France during the Second World War', in *War, Resistance and Intelligence: Essays in Honour of M. R. D. Foot*, edited by K. G. Robertson (London: Leo Cooper, 1999), pp. 119–33 (p. 121).

effort to 'present the material impartially.'[30] This extends to minimizing her narratorial interventions in the sections of the text dealing with parts of Khan's life of which she does not have direct knowledge, including Khan's active service. This technique has particularly interesting effects when it comes to the testimony of those who kept Khan in captivity.

Overton Fuller describes how she was prompted to undertake her investigation of Khan's work in France by the paucity of available information about how she died. Her only 'official source' is the Hodge & Co volume on the Natzweiler Trial. This contains a 'meagre' account, indicating that 'Nora Baker', a name by which Khan was known, was taken from a civilian prison at Pforzheim to Dachau for execution in July 1944.[31] While at Pforzheim, Khan was kept 'in chains by day and by night, in solitary confinement', or so Overton Fuller learns from an interview with the former prison governor, Wilhelm Krauss. Krauss claims that, fearful of defying the Gestapo, he nevertheless eventually decided to make the conditions of Khan's captivity less harsh: 'In all the fifty years of his service he had never known a prisoner to be kept under such conditions.'[32] As Overton Fuller explains: 'It is impossible to tell how long [Khan] was kept completely chained [...] That the conditions of her detention were gradually eased emerged from the statements of all my informants, though they naturally do not tally in every detail.'[33] This brisk, almost business-like tone is typical of Overton Fuller, who works hard to maintain an emotional distance from the disturbing events she describes while simultaneously acknowledging the challenges of producing a coherent narrative.

Although Overton Fuller indicates to the reader moments when she feels her 'informants' are prevaricating, then, she continues to adopt a studiedly objective stance, despite, or perhaps because of, the fact that her subject was known to her. The only slight departure from this comes in Overton Fuller's use of foreshadowing, specifically in relation to the deaths of Khan and other agents, who at one point are described as 'doomed to die'.[34]

[30] Jean Overton Fuller, *Madeleine: The Story of Noor Inayat Khan* (London: Victor Gollancz, 1952), p. 9. In his 'Foreword', Selwyn Jepson, senior recruiting officer for SOE's F-section, praises the author's 'painstaking and successful efforts to avoid the taint of fiction.' 'Foreword', in Overton Fuller, *Madeleine*, pp. 7–8 (p. 7).

[31] Overton Fuller, *Madeleine*, p. 186.

[32] Overton Fuller, *Madeleine*, p. 180.

[33] Overton Fuller, *Madeleine*, p. 181.

[34] Overton Fuller, *Madeleine*, p. 70. The paperback reissue of Madeleine was retitled *Born to Sacrifice*, a phrase from a letter sent to Overton Fuller by Khan's brother Vilayat quoted in the narrative, which frames her death as preordained. Overton Fuller, *Madeleine*, p. 67.

For the most part, although her personal link to Khan is the underlying rationale for the investigation underpinning the book, for Overton Fuller to place too much emphasis on this would, it seems, undermine the trustworthiness of the account, and the reader's trust in Overton Fuller is, paradoxically, fostered further by her admission of the fact that some questions about Khan will remain unanswerable.

Shortly after describing the nature of Khan's imprisonment at Pforzheim, and in search of more information about Khan's final hours, Overton Fuller decides to contact 'a certain Wassmer', a Gestapo clerk, who transported Khan and Diana Rowden from prison to Dachau and Natzweiler, respectively. The account Overton Fuller receives from Wassmer forms the short final chapter of the biography. Overton Fuller initially hesitates to contact Wassmer, who, she reflects, with a trace of irony, 'must be weary of interrogations', and, when she finally writes to him, her 'hope of receiving a reply was not very great'.[35] However, he does soon respond, and she finds the 'obvious sincerity' of his letter 'touching: it was clear that he was anxious to help me as best he could to complete my picture of Noor, and to show that her wonderful bravery had not failed her at this time'.[36] Overton Fuller's kid-gloves attitude towards a former Gestapo official might seem peculiar, but throughout the text, Overton Fuller reserves judgement on individuals whom she believes can help her with her quest, focusing on gleaning as much information as she can from whatever source, and writing not 'against the Germans—or for them'.[37] Notably, in this case, her source is able to emphasis Khan's endurance.

Wassmer describes the final journey taken by Khan and her fellow prisoners and tells Overton Fuller that they 'talked together in a very lively and spirited fashion', but his narrative ends once he has delivered the women to Dachau: 'Later, official information was received in Karlsruhe that the women had been shot'.[38] This is the final sentence of the body of the text. It is followed by two appendices which transcribe Khan's posthumous citations for the George Cross and the Croix de Guerre. The use of the passive voice—'information was received'—is an indication that Overton Fuller can

---

[35] Overton Fuller, *Madeleine*, p. 187.
[36] Overton Fuller, *Madeleine*, p. 187. Karlsruhe was the city where the Gestapo officers who oversaw Khan's incarceration were based. Following the publication of *Madeleine*, Overton Fuller received letters via her publisher, one from a former Dachau inmate and the other from an officer of the Canadian Intelligence, that cast serious doubt on Wassmer's version. See Shrabani Basu, *Spy Princess: The Life of Noor Inayat Khan* (London: History Press, 2008).
[37] Overton Fuller, *Madeleine*, p. 9.
[38] Overton Fuller, *Madeleine*, p. 187.

go no further. She is not willing to project emotions onto Khan, to imagine how she might have felt, or, to put it another way, to fictionalize her, preferring to present her narrative as one that will inevitably have gaps. In the absence of witnesses to testify to the precise circumstances of her death, a veil is drawn.[39] What is left in no doubt is the positive effect that contact with Khan could have on those around her even when she is in extremis: Ernest, one of her interrogators at the Avenue Foch admits to being 'impressed by her steadfastness and her self-control.'[40] No one was ever convicted as having been responsible for Khan's death, and Overton Fuller's account thus stands instead of the juridical process of building a case, uncovering a network of individuals who each played a part in Khan's eventual end with the final judgement on questions of responsibility being left to the reader.

Overton Fuller's treatment of Khan can be contrasted to R. J. Minney's more hagiographic description of Violette Szabo's imprisonment and death. Minney compensates for a lack of testimony from his subject and an absence of eyewitness accounts of Szabo's incarceration by speculating about what he believes to be likely sentiments to her, drawing on his prior construction of her as single-minded in her desire to defy the Nazis. Describing how women were 'processed' on their arrival at Ravensbrück, Minney comments:

> Through all these unpleasant preliminaries [Szabo's] mind, trained to take in everything, was already seeking a possible mode of escape. Had anyone ever got out of Ravensbrück, she wondered? It did not seem at all possible, but a way might be found—would have to be found. On that she was resolved.[41]

Minney aligns Szabo with other wartime British captives of the Nazis with whom his readers might well be familiar, namely the determined British officers who made often highly organized escape attempts from prisoner-of-war camps. But it soon becomes clear that even if the largely unprovable determination attributed here to Szabo was actual, the nature of her captivity was very different from that of the men kept at Sagan or Colditz, or

---

[39] More recent research has provided disturbing details of Khan's final days. See Shompa Lahiri, 'Clandestine Mobilities and Shifting Embodiments: Noor-un-nisa Inayat Khan and the Special Operations Executive, 1940–44', *Gender & History* 19.2 (2007): pp. 305–23 (pp. 315–16)
[40] Overton Fuller, *Madeleine*, p. 152. Overton Fuller explains in her acknowledgements that she has deliberately kept back Ernest's surname and that when they met, he showed her documentation relating to his de-Nazification, including a paper 'certifying that he was not a War Criminal' (p. 192).
[41] R. J. Minney, *Carve Her Name with Pride: The Story of Violette Szabo G. C.* (London: Pan, 1956), p. 170.

even from Peter Churchill's. Not only is she required to undertake physical labour such as making roads, but over the course of the next few months she is moved from Ravensbrück firstly south to Torgau, near Leipzig, then back to Ravensbrück for a spell in the Bunker, the isolation cells where Sansom was also kept, then east to Königsberg (now Kaliningrad) before being returned finally to Ravensbrück. Szabo did attempt to escape, including on one occasion asking a fellow prisoner to make a skeleton key for her. This took planning rather than being opportunistic, but by foregrounding her desire to escape, mentioning, for instance, that Szabo was moved frequently because 'she had been set down as a difficult prisoner—intractable and quite ungovernable', Minney avoids having to dwell in detail on the nature of her experiences when in these various camps.[42]

After Szabo is sent back to Ravensbrück for the final time, Minney switches his focus to her parents' search for news about her at the end of the war. Like Overton Fuller, he describes his subject's death indirectly, weaving together the testimony of a fellow prisoner of Szabo's at Ravensbrück and the account gleaned from the camp's second-in-command, Johann Schwarzhuber, by Vera Atkins. (The commandant of Ravensbrück, Fritz Suhren, fled the camp by car ahead of the Russian advance taking Odette Sansom with him and attempted, unsuccessfully, to use her to bargain with the Americans for his freedom.[43]) Schwarzhuber's account of the deaths of Szabo and the women executed alongside her states: 'The shooting was done [...] with a small-calibre gun through the back of the neck. [...] All three were brave and I was deeply moved. Suhren was also impressed by the bearing of these women. He was annoyed that the Gestapo did not themselves carry out these shootings.'[44] This final buck-passing remark could be read as Suhren's attempt at self-exculpation, but of course his annoyance does not go so far as condemning the fact that the executions are carried out at all, only that he has to take responsibility for them. By this account, Suhren and Schwarzhuber, like Szabo, are caught in circumstances beyond their control.

Minney then supplements this account with his own imaginative reconstruction of the execution, from the perspective of other prisoner-witnesses, and of Szabo herself:

---

[42] Minney, *Carve Her Name*, p. 175.
[43] Suhren was taken into custody but escaped shortly before the start of the first Ravensbrück trial. After three years on the run, he was eventually recaptured and was tried and convicted of war crimes by the French. He was executed in 1950. Bayzler and Tuerkheimer, *Forgotten Trials*, p. 130.
[44] Minney, *Carve Her Name*, p. 185.

Violette, they say, was the last to be executed and had to suffer the agony of seeing her friends put to death, aware all the time that the same fate awaited her. She did not flinch. Her spirit was indomitable. Again and again in the past, when all seemed lost, she had fought her way out [...] Even in captivity she tried repeatedly to break away so that, returning she could fight on. But now there seemed to be no way out at all. [...] Lifting her head with haughty scorn, she walked the last few paces to her death.[45]

Given how Minney has characterized Szabo throughout the narrative ('again and again [...] she had fought her way out') her 'haughty' raising of her head is a necessary culmination. The whole framing of Szabo's life has been gravitating towards this end. Her death is not the result of particular historical circumstance, but something less contingent: it is her fate. The various documentary, eyewitness and other accounts that underpin *Carve Her Name* are subsumed to a character study, as is made plain by the juxtaposition of these two descriptions of Szabo's death. Schwarzhuber describes the women as 'brave' but could himself be telling Atkins what he believes she wishes to hear.

Where Minney's biography is situated towards what Seaman might characterize as the novelistic end of the spectrum, Elizabeth Nicholas's *Death Be Not Proud*, like *Madeleine*, situates the investigative narrator prominently. In *Madeleine*, Overton Fuller describes her own pre-war friendship with her subject at the start of the text, and, towards the end gives a first-person account of contacting and going to meet Wassmer. Nicholas traces the progress of her research in much more detail, noting in her introduction: 'I wrote this book as my researches progressed.'[46] Nicholas is far more explicit than Overton Fuller about the continuing problems and frustrations she experiences on her quest to find out what happened to her friend.

Noting the official assistance that Tickell received when writing his biography of Sansom, Nicholas states: 'Every obstacle is now placed in the way of those who wish to write of the unlucky ones—those who lost their lives when with F-Section, SOE; those whose story, if published, would be painted in more sombre colours.'[47] Nicholas acknowledges that she is presenting a fragmented text rather than, in words that can be read as a

[45] Minney, *Carve Her Name*, p. 186.
[46] Nicholas, *Death Be Not Proud*, p. 14.
[47] Nicholas, *Death Be Not Proud*, p. 19.

sideswipe at Tickell, reconstructing 'in [her] own imagination the missing elements'.[48] Despite her reservations about its approach, *Odette* is relevant to Nicholas's work because of its prominence as an account of an F-Section agent and as a counter-text to her own. It is from this book that Nicholas picks up the threads of her friend Diana Rowden's story, as Rowden and Sansom were transported to Germany together after being captured. Tickell's book, in Nicholas's view, was not only 'written in a style that suggested it was fiction' but 'reeked of the cops and robbers approach to subversive activity',[49] this latter simplification following from the former.

Like Overton Fuller, Nicholas consults the Hodge volume on the Natzweiler Trial. She characterizes the proceedings as 'repellent', largely because 'each one of the guilty sought to incriminate his fellows in order to save his own skin'.[50] Whereas the Nazi personnel from the camp are shown attempting to manipulate the Allies' legal process in order to escape being blamed for war crimes, the captured agents, with the exception of Sansom, were denied a trial when in Nazi hands, and, with grim irony, or what Tickell, cited by Nicholas, called a 'sardonic twist', Sansom, the only one of the women actually condemned to death, is the only one who survives.[51] This is another reason for Tickell to foreground Sansom's court appearance at the start of *Odette*. The opportunity to give evidence in an Allied court contrasts starkly with the 'hearing' Sansom herself received, which, as described by Tickell, is only just recognizable as a form of legal process and is conducted in German:

> There were several officers there [... .] They were [...] addressed by a hard-faced civilian [... .] As all the proceedings had been conducted in a language she did not understand, she had no idea what they were saying. That they were sitting in judgment on her was plain. But where was the counsel for defence? Where was the interpreter?[52]

Eventually 'a Colonel with the Iron Cross', being told by Sansom that she does not understand German, delivers the sentence to her in 'slow, guttural French'. According to Tickell's narration, Sansom reflects that the proceedings 'seemed to bear no relationship to reality. The words the

[48] Nicholas, *Death Be Not Proud*, p. 31.
[49] Nicholas, *Death Be Not Proud*, p. 31.
[50] Nicholas, *Death Be Not Proud*, p. 71.
[51] Tickell, qtd in Nicholas, *Death Be Not Proud*, p. 31.
[52] Tickell, *Odette*, p. 227.

Colonel had made were only sounds... and his French was execrable'.[53] Sansom's snobbery about the Colonel's poor French, situated here as a defence against acknowledging that the sentence delivered might actually have any force, underlines one of the minimal expectations for judicial proceedings in a democracy: that the defendant should understand what is being said.[54] (In the film, probably to facilitate the audience's under-standing, Odette interrupts the officer who is reading her sentence to her in German, telling him that she is unable to understand and he contin-ues in broken English; the hearing itself takes place without Odette being present.) The lack of propriety in the conduct of this 'strange Court' is fur-ther underlined by the fact that, fortunately for Sansom, the sentence is not carried out, whereas others who did not receive any form of trial at all were executed.

Tickell describes how, immediately following this incident, Sansom receives a visit from Hugo Bleicher, known as Colonel Henri, an officer of the Abwehr who claims to be attempting to work on Sansom's behalf, and apologizes to her for the treatment she has received at the hands of the Gestapo: 'Believe me when I say how sorry and utterly ashamed I am.'[55] Bleicher also features in Nicholas's account, and, interviewed by her, is

---

[53] Tickell, *Odette*, p. 228.

[54] A key case in the English/Welsh context is that of Lee Kun, a Chinese national who had been found guilty of murder. He had the services of a translator when interviewed by the police and at the preliminary hearings, but no translator was requested for his trial. As Celia Brown-Blake describes, notwithstanding the rejection of the appeal, the case established 'the general principle that testimony must be interpreted for an accused who does not understand the English language'. 'Fair Trial, Language and the Right to Interpretation', *International Jour-nal on Minority and Group Rights* 13 (2006): pp. 391–412 (p. 395). See also *Rex v Lee Kun* (1916) 11 Cr. App. R. 293. In Germany, Article 113 of the Weimar Constitution stated: 'Sections of the population of the Reich speaking a foreign language may not be restricted, whether by way of legislation or administration, in their free racial development; this applies specifically to the use of their mother tongue in education, as well as in question of internal administration and the administration of justice.' In Elmar H. Hucko, ed., *The Democratic Tradition: Four Ger-man Constitutions* (Leamington Spa: Berg, 1987), p. 175. Karl A. Schleunes notes, however, that 'the idea of civic or legal equality was rejected by the Nazis'. 'From Civil Rights to Civic Death: Dismantling Rights in Nazi Germany', in *Two Cultures of Rights: The Quest for Inclusion and Participation in Modern America and Germany*, edited by Manfred Berg et al (Cambridge: Cambridge University Press, 2002), pp. 77–93 (p. 78).

[55] Tickell, *Odette*, p. 230. Peter Churchill was also visited by Bleicher, whom he refers to as 'Henri', during his time in Fresnes, and he describes how he reacts with suspicion to Henri's claim that 'since the beginning of hostilities a small percentage of good Germans have been doing everything in their power to put out peace feelers to the Allies in the hopes of putting an end to this crazy war'. Churchill, *The Spirit in the Cage*, p. 42. Despite Churchill's reservations about Henri's motives, Henri arranges for Churchill to see Odette and to receive a visit and parcels of supplies from a friend.

able to give her information about investigations into F-Section with which he was involved. Nicholas finds Bleicher, 'against all probability, sympathetic' as a personality, even 'appealing'.[56] She puts his success in wartime down to the 'bizarre blending of a strong sexuality with a powerful paternalism' and points out that 'no atrocities were even pinned on Bleicher',[57] despite him having been interrogated by both the British and the French. But Nicholas nevertheless asserts that, even if there was no evidence that could form the basis of a charge against Bleicher, he still bore '[g]uilt by association' for having handed prisoners over to the Gestapo.[58] Nicholas characterizes Bleicher as one of many who, despite not being enthusiastic supporters of Nazism, 'did not see why they should not jump on the bandwagon'.[59] Bleicher's culpability may not be such as could be proved in a court but in Nicholas's analysis, he should take his share of the blame for not resisting the regime. This is a judgement that has moral rather than legal force.[60]

These examples illustrate a range of approaches with some authors being readier than others to share with the reader the difficulties they have encountered in reconstructing their subjects' stories. But each author nevertheless has a sense of their work contributing to the exposure of injustice. For Nicholas and Overton Fuller this extends from critiquing the Nazis treatment of the women in their captivity to questioning, even if only implicitly, the adequacy of post-war legal proceedings.

---

[56] Nicholas, *Death Be Not Proud*, p. 224.
[57] Nicholas, *Death Be Not Proud*, p. 225.
[58] Nicholas, *Death Be Not Proud*, p. 225.
[59] Nicholas, *Death Be Not Proud*, p. 228.
[60] Bleicher's moral ambiguity is underscored in the film adaptation of *Odette*, in which he is played by Marius Goring. Goring, although sometimes presumed to be of German heritage because of the similarity of his surname to that of Hermann Göring, was English and grew up on the Isle of Wight, where his father, Charles Goring, was a criminal psychiatrist based at Parkhurst prison. Marius Goring spent time in both France and Germany while a student before the war, becoming fluent in French and German. During the war, he broadcast anti-Nazi propaganda for the BBC German Service in the guise of a disaffected German army officer, and after the war his proficiency in German saw him frequently cast as German characters, often prototypical 'good', or at least ambivalent, Germans. See for instance *So Little Time* (1952) in which romance, facilitated by a shared love of classical music, blossoms between a German officer and the daughter of the Belgian household with whom he has been billeted. In the late 1940s Goring undertook a theatre tour of Germany with his wife, Lucie Mannheim, a German-Jewish actress who had fled Germany in 1933. For the role of Bleicher he affects a pair of sunglasses, a choice which could be intended to remind the audience of Göring, who, like a number of the defendants, wore sunglasses during the Nuremberg proceedings, supposedly to protect his eyes from the glare of the lights set up to enable the filming of proceedings. In *Odette*, this habit serves as shorthand for the character's evasiveness and duplicity.

Unorganized Justice among British Prisoners

The sense that underlying principles of justice can persist in defiance of a system that seeks to abolish the democratic rule of law, and that individuals may be held accountable, or threatened with being held accountable to such principles, is in evidence in other texts the deal in more detail and more directly with the experience of incarceration. A number of memoirs and biographies, particularly those by and about male SOE agents, show that the structures of self-regulation identified by Elie Cohen as having emerged among the general populations of concentration camps operated within subgroups such as those to which 'special' prisoners like Peter Churchill were assigned. For example, Churchill describes becoming suspicious that one of the other inmates, whom he calls 'Judd', is a 'stool pigeon', that is, that he is reporting on the activities of the British to the Germans. As the Senior British Officer, Churchill decides to carry out an impromptu court martial, demoting Judd from corporal to private after physically assaulting him when Judd refuses to stand to attention in his presence.[61] When Judd is discovered to have reported this treatment to the Germans, Churchill organizes for him to be 'sent to Coventry', not just by the British prisoners but by those of other nationalities.[62] This punishment, which involves not speaking to or even acknowledging the existence of an individual deemed to have gone against the interests of the group, is characteristic of practices of intragroup discipline among school pupils, especially in public schools. But if 'sending to Coventry' has infantilizing associations, it is merely one end of a troubling spectrum of punishments or potential punishments. Churchill reflects: 'In the Resistance a man like Judd would have been attended to a long time ago without bothering any court of law, and although this kind of thing is highly illegal it is curious at times how little one is exercised by such a consideration.'[63] The subtext of this comment is that Churchill understands why summary execution or other forms of summary justice—'being attended to'—might be resorted to in extremis and it is notable that

---

[61] Churchill, *The Spirit in the Cage*, p. 162.

[62] Churchill, *The Spirit in the Cage*, p. 162,

[63] Churchill, *The Spirit in the Cage*, p. 164. Marshall recounts how, prior to his capture, Yeo-Thomas became suspicious of a messenger sent to his resistance group and 'was going to kill the boy' but 'dismissed him with a warning' after another member of the group intervened. Marshall, *The White Rabbit*, p. 70.

he appears to empathize with situations where strict legality seems to be secondary to (supposedly) consensual moral codes.

Churchill's sentiments have an echo in Cohen's work: 'One of the few standards recognized by unorganized justice was that spies were not tolerated.'[64] In the camp, any betrayal of the solidarity between the inmates as a group, resulting in a blurring of the dichotomy between prisoners and guards, upsets the ad hoc hierarchy of the organization. This is different from the form of 'licensed' collaboration represented by the actions of concentration camp Kapos, not least because the kind of activity that exercises Churchill is carried out covertly. In the event, Churchill does not use the ultimate sanction against Judd, and instead he practises a form of blackmail that has a corollary in other memoirs by captives of the Nazis. Judd is unable to tolerate being sent to Coventry and agrees to comply with Churchill's demands. Churchill writes a confession in Judd's name, saying that if Judd can 'behave until the end of the war' the confession will be destroyed in front of him.[65] Judd, with some reluctance, signs the document. Here, then, we see Churchill improvising a form of unorganized justice with a reformatory or reparatory intent, by making reference to how Judd's actions might eventually be judged after the end of the war, basing this on the assumption, with which Judd concurs, that the Allies will be the winning side.[66] This reinforces a continuity between pre- and post-war standards of justice that, when Churchill writes the letter, is a hope rather than an actuality. Appearing in print in the post-war period, the description of his actions asserts that standards were and indeed are maintained, notwithstanding his acknowledgement of the lure of more peremptory treatment of those deemed to be traitors.

---

[64] Elie A. Cohen, *Human Behaviour in the Concentration Camp*, trans. M. H. Braaksma (London: Jonathan Cape, 1954), p. 150.

[65] Churchill, *The Spirit in the Cage*, p. 166.

[66] The individual called 'Judd' by Churchill was in fact called John Spence and was one of four British soldiers of Irish origin whom the Nazis attempted to recruit as part of their propaganda effort. See Tim Carroll, *The Dodger: The Extraordinary Story of Churchill's Cousin and the Great Escape* (London: Random House, 2012). Churchill mentions that Judd 'boasted of the fact that he had broadcast for the Germans in English' and had betrayed Jews to the Gestapo. Churchill, *The Spirit in the Cage*, p. 159. In the Appendix to his memoir, Churchill notes that, having decided at the time of the writing and signing of the confession that, despite his promise, he would report Judd to the authorities at the end of the war if others did, he indeed makes a report after his return to England, but, inexplicably to Churchill, no charges were pursued. Churchill, *The Spirit in the Cage*, p. 246. Glen O'Hara notes that after the war Spence was cleared of having worked for the Nazis. O'Hara, 'The Parliamentary Commissioner', p. 773.

Elsewhere in *The Spirit in the Cage*, Churchill underlines his own awareness, during his captivity, of his particular status in the camp. When Dodge and Day, two of the former Sagan prisoners, decide to escape via a tunnel, Churchill, questioned afterwards by the camp authorities, explains that he did not join them because: 'I am not a prisoner of war, captured in uniform, whose escape is recognised by the Geneva Convention.'[67] Churchill indicates to his captors that he, at least, is behaving in accordance with protocol. In contrast, SOE agent Yeo-Thomas, known by the nickname 'White Rabbit', gave a false name when he when was captured and was sent to Buchenwald without any of the 'privileges' afforded to Churchill. His biographer Bruce Marshall notes that Yeo-Thomas was condemned to death without having been told that this had happened, and was saved from being executed when a fellow member of his Resistance group found out and was able to bribe a Gestapo officer, resulting in Yeo-Thomas's file being 'lost'; the money for the bribe was provided by the British government.[68] Later, at Buchenwald, Yeo-Thomas, together with fellow captured agent Christopher Burney, became involved in a plan that relied on the relationship that had been established between Eugen Kogon, later to be the author of *Der SS-Staat* (1946), and Ding-Schuler, the German officer for whom Kogon worked in a clerical role.[69]

In Marshall's account, Kogon acted as an intermediary, persuading Ding-Schuler that 'in return for a promise from Yeo-Thomas to testify on his behalf at the war crimes trials he should agree to save the lives of [...] twenty-one prisoners [...] by substituting their identities for those of other prisoners who died of typhus' as a result of the medical experiments Ding-Schuler was overseeing.[70] Dietzsch, a Kapo who oversaw the so-called 'Guinea Pig' block where these experiments took place, demanded a similar undertaking, requesting that Yeo-Thomas write 'a detailed statement of all [he] had done to save his life.'[71] In return, following the death from typhus of three French

[67] Churchill, *The Spirit in the Cage*, p. 154.
[68] Marshall, *The White Rabbit*, p. 123.
[69] Burney describes how Kogon (whom he calls 'Emil Kalman') became close to Ding-Schuler, to the extent that the officer's children referred to him as 'Onkel Emil'. He recounts Kogon's later attempts to 'encourage [the] inclination' of another officer, Pister, to 'betray Berlin and to think for himself and his family' by concocting a letter implying that the Allies had sent an agent observe Pister's behaviour. *Solitary Confinement and The Dungeon Democracy* (London: Macmillan, 1984 [1945]), pp. 137–248(p. 218; p. 227).
[70] Marshall *The White Rabbit*, p. 209.
[71] Marshall, *The White Rabbit*, p. 220.

prisoners, Yeo-Thomas and two others were declared dead in their places and given the deceased's identities.

The notion that some Nazis, despite continuing to work for the regime, might have been willing to acknowledge that its days were numbered, is also expressed in Hugo Bleicher's memoir. Reflecting on the events of early 1943, when he was stationed in France, he recalls: 'I doubted no longer that the war was lost to Germany'. He nevertheless 'had no hesitation [...] in doing [his] duty as before', explaining this decision with reference to the 'men' who 'depended' on him: 'I could not leave them or abandon them to their enemies'.[72] This statement could, of course, be read as an attempt at partial retrospective self-exculpation by Bleicher, allying himself not with the regime but with his 'men'; the plot involving Ding-Schuler's compliance takes place rather later, in the autumn of 1944.

The extraction of statements attesting to assistance provided seems to be the reverse of the way in which Churchill uses his account of Judd's wrong doing. In Yeo-Thomas's case, individuals request testimony as a form of insurance, acknowledging that while they may have helped to save others, this will eventually be weighed in the balance against their behaviour during the whole course of the war. In fact, such testimony could not guarantee a favourable outcome at a later date. Marshall describes what happened between Yeo-Thomas and Dietzsch:

Because Dietzsch had risked his life to help [the prisoners], Yeo-Thomas now risked his life to help Dietzsch [...] he signed [his statement] with his real name, rank and number, and gave [it] to Dietzsch. [...] [T]his document, while it may have saved Dietzsch's life, did not prevent the Kapo from being sentenced to a long term of imprisonment by the same Allied Courts that pardoned Ilse Koch.[73]

---

[72] Hugo Bleicher, *Colonel Henri's Story: The Memoirs of Hugo Bleicher, Former German Secret Agent*, edited by Ian Colvin (London: William Kimber, 1954), p. 72–73.

[73] Marshall, *The White Rabbit*, p. 220. Peter Churchill recalls that the officer in charge of his group of prisoners was eventually given an order to execute them, but was not able to carry it out, and, having been convinced that the Allies were approaching, decided to flee, taking the order with him: 'With these hostages alive this piece of paper would have a certain protective value if shown to the Allies.' Churchill, *The Spirit in the Cage*, p. 221. In this case, then, no Allied intermediary is required: the officer realises that the unfulfilled order will give him leverage to plead on his own behalf.

The implication here is that Yeo-Thomas's statement ought to have had more force. In the context of how Ilse Koch was treated by the court, Dietzsch, Marshall suggests, should have received a more lenient sentence.[74] The rationale for this lies not so much in the quality of Dietzsch's actions but in the value of Yeo-Thomas's word and the extent to which he was willing to put himself at risk in order to give Dietzsch his support. Dietzsch's lengthy sentence is constructed as not honouring appropriately the risk taken by Yeo-Thomas on his behalf. Ding-Schuler was arrested in April 1945 and committed suicide while in custody in August the same year before he could be brought to trial.

Kogon, concerned that Yeo-Thomas might suffer reprisals from French Communist prisoners if his adoption of a French identity is discovered, later arranges for Yeo-Thomas to be moved on to Rehmsdorf. When Rehmsdorf is to be evacuated in the face of the Allied advance, Yeo-Thomas makes proactive use of the potential power of his testimony to persuade Otto Möller, one of the guards in charge of the evacuation, to facilitate an escape attempt. With a fellow prisoner acting as an interpreter, Yeo-Thomas reveals that he is 'a colonel in the British Intelligence Services', embellishing his story with the detail that he has been 'sent to Rehmsdorf specially in order to check up on the action of the SS' and that he has already sent a list of SS members to the Allies.[75] He manages to persuade Möller that unless he—Möller—has someone to speak up for him, he is 'liable to be shot when he's captured.'[76] Möller believes this story and misdirects the other guards when the escape takes place. It is notable that, as well as being based on the presumption that the Nazis will soon be on the receiving end of Allied justice, something which it has in common with Yeo-Thomas and Kogon's earlier use of blackmail at Buchenwald, this manipulation of Möller also rests on the

[74] Ilse Koch was the wife of Karl Koch, who served as Commandant of Buchenwald and later Majdanek, and who was removed from the latter after a prisoner escape. He was executed by the Nazis in April 1945, after facing charges of forgery and embezzlement, as well as in relation to the collection of human skin and skulls while at Majdanek. Ilse Koch was sentenced to life imprisonment for war crimes by the Americans, but was pardoned in 1949, then rearrested and resentenced to life-imprisonment in 1951. She took her own life in prison in 1967. See 'Ilse Koch', in Robert Rozett and Shmuel Spector, *Encyclopaedia of the Holocaust* (New York: Taylor & Francis, 2013), pp. 875–76, and, for public and press perceptions of Koch, Alexandra Przyrembel, 'Transfixed by an Image: Ilse Koch, the "Kommandeuse of Buchenwald"', trans. Pamela Selwyn, *German History* 19.3 (2001): pp. 369–99. Given that Marshall's book was first published in 1952, it is possible that his comments were written prior to Koch's rearrest.
[75] Marshall, *The White Rabbit*, p. 239.
[76] Marshall, *The White Rabbit*, p. 240.

suggestion that the Allies might resort to summary justice, shooting prisoners on capture. That Yeo-Thomas is lying to Möller when he levels these
threats against him is less important in the narrative than Möller's own
credulity. Whereas previously, with Dietzsch, Yeo-Thomas used his position
to guarantee the force of the account he gives of the other man's behaviour,
here his status is employed as a threat, as much as a potential form of
protection.[77]

The final irony for Yeo-Thomas is that it is only with difficulty that he
manages to establish his own bona fides when he eventually reaches Allied
lines. Having decided to retain the guise of a Frenchman, Yeo-Thomas, by
this stage suffering from dysentery, is recaptured by the Germans and rouses
the suspicions of some of the French officers who are being held with him,
and who do not believe him when he reveals that he is actually a British SOE
agent: '[W]hat proof have we that you are not working for the Germans?'
Marshall suggests that this was 'a natural enough suspicion in a war in which
the Queensbury rules had been thrown overboard, the kick in the testicles
called strategy and the greater lie used to outwit the lesser'.[78] Indeed, as his
narrative of Yeo-Thomas's story illustrates, such improvisatory, 'ungentle-
manly' tactics were used by both sides. Yeo-Thomas, having no papers to
guarantee his 'true' identity is eventually able to persuade the French by
showing them a chess set with a British manufacturer's stamp which had
belonged to a fellow prisoner at Buchenwald, and was kept as a memento
by Yeo-Thomas after the other man's death. But this incident momentarily
opens up for the reader the hall of mirrors in which the undercover agent
exists, switching between different identities according to the demands of
the situation, trusting that he will eventually be able to reclaim his original allegiance. In due course, having reached the Allied lines, Yeo-Thomas,
tells the French officer who has been tasked by the Americans with debrief-
ing him that he is 'Yeo-Thomas, better known to the Resistance as Shelley
[his SOE codename]', a revelation which, according to Marshall prompts
the French officer to comment: 'We've been moving heaven and earth to
find you.'[79] By the time that Yeo-Thomas has made this claim, of course, his
role as an SOE field agent has been made defunct by the wider progress of
the war.

---

[77] Möller's eventual fate is not described within Marshall's account, but the 'Author's Foreword' tells us that he 'is now working on a farm in Germany'. *The White Rabbit*, p. 7.

[78] Marshall, *The White Rabbit*, p. 260.

[79] Marshall, *The White Rabbit*, p. 265.

Glimpses of the Holocaust

While questions may have later been raised as to whether Peter Churchill and his fellow prisoners were actually in a concentration camp while held at the Sachsenhausen Sonderlager, no similar doubts were aired about Yeo-Thomas's captivity at Buchenwald. In both *The Spirit in the Cage* and *The White Rabbit*, however, the central subject of the narrative is shown to be aware of the difference between his own status and that of other prisoners. This awareness can be a way of acknowledging that other prisoners, specifically Jewish prisoners, experienced worse treatment than the British did, but it tends to underline a feeling that the other prisoners, and what happened to them, are largely unknowable. As I have noted, this can be understood as a sign of respect for those prisoners and their stories, but it can cement, for the reader, a sense of the Jewish prisoners having only a peripheral place in the larger narrative of the war to which texts like *The Spirit in the Cage* and *The White Rabbit*, as well as *Odette*, belong. It is understandable that a biography or autobiography should prioritize the story of a single individual, but I want to consider here the extent to which these texts contributed, albeit inadvertently, to the misunderstanding or downplaying of the specific fate of the Jews in post–war British culture.

Marshall describes how, arriving at Buchenwald with a group of other political prisoners, Yeo-Thomas observes the inmates: 'The compound was filled with emaciated, hairless wretches shuffling wearily round and round in heavy wooden clogs. The eyes of those listless sub-human creatures were mean with terror.' The new arrivals are described as sharing the same thought on contemplating this scene: 'how long is it going to be before we look like them?'[80] What seems to be a reflection on how incarceration has deindividualized and dehumanized the 'creatures' is reframed as being largely about appearance: when will we 'look like' them? Further, the fact that the thirty-seven new prisoners are described as having the same thought 'simultaneously' means that the erosion of subjectivity that they are contemplating and which is described for the reader, is countered by a more positive group identity: they have arrived at the same time, they are all political prisoners, and they are assigned to the same hut.[81] A large part of what follows describes Yeo-Thomas's efforts to maintain this positive sense of group identity even while concealing who he actually is from many of his

[80] Marshall, *The White Rabbit*, p. 192.
[81] Marshall, *The White Rabbit*, p. 193.

fellow prisoners. This is reinforced when, soon after his arrival, he encounters Burney, his fellow F-Section officer, who explains that the population of the camp is characterized by in-fighting, particularly between the 'common law offenders and the political prisoners',[82] a kind of internal dissent that, as I have shown, was fostered by the camp system, and is described in some detail in Burney's *The Dungeon Democracy* (1946). Burney's words, however, help Yeo-Thomas to orientate himself and become allied to the group of which Burney is a member.

When the Jewish prisoners are specifically mentioned, it is to highlight how bad their conditions were:

> [I]f conditions in the main camp were bad those in the lesser camp were worse. [...] [T]he tenants, who were mostly Jews, were systematically starved: every day, hundreds of lean, famished men yelped, squealed and grunted as they kicked and clawed each other in the struggle to get at a few pounds of potato peelings.[83]

This description of the small compound is followed by a visit from some other British prisoners that is said to have cheered up Yeo-Thomas's group. The conjunction of these two events—observing the condition of the Jews, who are described in terms that liken them to animals, and the reassuring encounter with men who provide the beginnings of a supportive network and a potential escape plan—serves to widen again the gulf between the Jews and the political prisoners. This emphasizes the effectiveness of the 'divide-and-rule' policy of the Nazis. Although this policy is to some extent subverted by the bonds that form between existing and new inmates, these are bonds based on shared nationality, and, in the cases of Yeo-Thomas, Burney, and other prisoners including brothers Alfred and Henry Newton, the common factor of having been SOE agents.[84] The very different circumstances that have led to the Jews being in the camp in the first place (or indeed, interpellated as Jews in the first place) are not considered.

Peter Churchill's first sight of other inmates on arriving at Buchenwald also conveys his sense of feeling separate from them. He sees a 'large squad' being marched over broken ground while wearing heavy rucksacks, and

---

[82] Marshall, *The White Rabbit*, p. 195.
[83] Marshall, *The White Rabbit*, p. 200.
[84] On the Newtons, see Jack Thomas, *No Banners: The Story of Alfred and Henry Newton* (London: W. H. Allen, 1955).

later learns that 'these starving wrecks of humanity' were testing 'the wearing power of some new boots'.[85] The 'starving wrecks' are said to have been
wearing 'striped jackets',[86] but we are not told what category of prisoner they
might be. Interestingly, when Churchill describes glimpsing a road sign for
'Oranienberg' on his journey to the camp from Gestapo Headquarters, he
realizes where he is being taken, but he is mistaken when, in this connection, he cites a literary reference point: 'Just before the war I had read Louis
Golding's *Dr Emanuel* which unfolded the doubtful pleasures in store for
anyone who entered the gates of Sachsenhausen Concentration Camp.'[87]
Golding was a prolific and popular British Jewish author active between
the 1920s and 1950s. The novel Churchill recalls was actually called *Mr
Emmanuel* (1939), and it describes how the eponymous mild-mannered,
widowed retiree travels from the Manchester suburbs on behalf of one of
his neighbours to try and find the mother of Bruno, a German-Jewish child
refugee who has been taken in by a local family. Emmanuel is arrested
but although he experiences solitary confinement at Berlin's Moabit prison,
contrary to Churchill's recollection, he is not sent to a concentration camp.[88]

Churchill's misapprehension both indicates the relative paucity of reference points in pre-war British culture where the concentration camps were
concerned and evidences the kind of confusion between different types
of incarceration that Rawlinson sees as characterizing post–war British
culture.[89] Perhaps the key aspect of this comparison, from Churchill's perspective, is that in both his own case, and that of Golding's protagonist,
a British subject is imprisoned by the Nazis. This of course elides a key

---

[85] Churchill, *The Spirit in the Cage*, p. 125.
[86] Churchill, *The Spirit in the Cage*, p. 125.
[87] Churchill, *The Spirit in the Cage*, p. 125. In April 1945, having been moved to Dachau en
route to Italy, Churchill meets two women who have been incarcerated at Ravensbrück and are
able to give him news of Odette. He comments that the name of the camp 'was new to [him].'
Churchill, *The Spirit in the Cage*, p. 210.
[88] Emmanuel is eventually released after Elsie Silver, the daughter of another of his neighbours, who is now resident in Berlin and who, despite being Jewish herself, is the mistress of a
member of the Reichstag, persuades her lover to intercede on Emmanuel's behalf. Emmanuel
gets home safely, though only after discovering that Bruno's mother has become the mistress
of a Nazi officer and appears to be beyond redemption. He tells the boy that she died resisting
the Nazis.
[89] See Mark Rawlinson, 'This Other War: British Culture and the Holocaust', *Cambridge
Quarterly* 25.1 (1996): pp. 1–25. British newspaper reports throughout the 1930s did discuss the
use of concentration camps in Germany and, for instance, the fact that prisoners were kept there
without trial, but there was little detail about the conditions in such camps. Sachsenhausen in
particular was mentioned in reports about the incarceration of Pastor Martin Niemöller, who
was sent there in March 1938, later being moved to Dachau.

difference between Churchill and Emmanuel, and Churchill and many of
the other prisoners at Sachsenhausen: Churchill was not Jewish.

Once he has been settled into the hut in 'a pine-tree studded enclosure'
that seems very much preferable to the conditions of his earlier experiences
in German captivity, the population of the main camp does not feature
prominently in his account, though Churchill does make some effort to
show that the wider context of the camp did not completely disappear from
the 'privileged' prisoners' view:

> We were always very conscious of the hardships and misery in the main
> camp from which we were merely separated by a common wall. An occa-
> sional burst of machine-gun fire in the night told us that some poor wretch
> had been caught in the search-lights outside his hut. When smoke rose
> from the crematorium [...] it was best to think that another soul was out
> of his misery [...] [T]o those who believe in the sanctity of human life,
> something is lost forever by the sound and smell of bestiality and sadness
> comes to eyes that see what the mind can never forget.[90]

The lack of specificity in this passage is striking. Where Marshall attributes
negative emotions and sentiments to a group being observed by Yeo-
Thomas, Churchill here moves from 'We' to a much more impersonal form
of expression. The 'noise of gunfire' prompts a realization that 'some poor
wretch' has been caught in the lights, rather than in the gunfire itself, and
so the actual object of these reflections (the execution of a prisoner) is not
directly perceived or described: attention is diverted from the body to the
'soul'. Violent death, followed by cremation, is reframed as, in the cliched
sentiment that in other contexts is applied to those who have suffered from
long-term illness, a form of release. Indeed, the idea of putting a living thing
'out of [its] misery' is one that is more readily applied to an injured animal than a human. Asserting that someone else is like an animal is a way
of asserting that you are still holding onto your humanity, and the logic
here is similar to that which underpins Churchill's bartering with promised
testimony.[91] In both cases the prisoner indirectly acknowledges that he is
currently powerless, but asserts that at some future point he will again have

[90] Churchill, *The Spirit in the Cage*, p. 144.
[91] See my discussion of such comparisons in Chapter 1. In the context of the use here of
the expression 'put out of its misery', I am reminded of Primo Levi's recollection of a Kapo
at Auschwitz using the word *fressen (to feed)*, usually applied to animals, rather than *essen (to
eat)*, usually applied to people, when referring to the prisoners, and that, further, the prisoners
themselves used the same term.: '[The Kapo] does not say it from derision or to sneer, but

agency, and positions himself as at least not being as degraded as the others, be they Jewish prisoners or traitorous stool-pigeons.

Churchill's final reflection here seems to reach towards how a belief in the 'sanctity' of human life has been eroded by the witnessing of 'bestiality', but the implication is that he is referring not to bestial behaviour on the part of the Nazis, but to the reduction of the prisoners to the condition of beasts. 'Sadness' seems an oddly watered-down word to use in the context, and Churchill's apparent reluctance to write in more detail about how he felt about the other prisoners in curious. He seems to want both to assert that anyone who sees terrible things is bound to be affected by the memory of them, while at the same time not wanting to actually describe in any detail what he did see, or indeed hear, or smell; the more senses he invokes, the less clear the image. But perhaps this is precisely the point. Churchill is struggling because he knows he ought to say something about what happened beyond his own compound, but he either did not actually see anything specific that he can offer to the reader as representative of what went on in the camp or is indeed too pained by the memory to depict it directly.

After being evacuated from Sachsenhausen with other 'privileged' prisoners, Churchill spends a short period of time at Flossenburg and has greater exposure to the conditions experienced by other prisoners, not least because: 'Here there was no wall as there had been at Sachsenhausen to prevent us seeing what our imagination had pictured. [...] Truly Sachsenhausen was a rest camp for its inmates compared to Flossenburg.' He notes his group were kept in a hospital ward and shared toilets with men from the next ward, who to Churchill's eye, 'weighed no more than five stone [...] and would look at us over the next stall with the eyes of those who have not long to live'. Notably, this description does not dwell on specific interaction between Churchill and any particular prisoner: the group of dying prisoners are not individuated from each other. Having recalled this scene, Churchill goes on to reflect:

> How many camps of this sort existed in Germany? How many hundreds of thousands of human beings—men and women—would see the

because this way of eating on our feet, furiously, burning our mouths and throats [...] really is *"fressen"*, the way of eating of animals, and certainly not *"essen"*, the human way of eating [...] *"Fressen"* is exactly the word, and is used currently among us.' *If This Is a Man/The Truce* trans. Stuart Woolf (Harmondsworth: Penguin, 1987), p. 82.

gates opened by healthy soldiers in khaki, only to look at them with uncomprehending eyes before death closed them for good?[92]

The rhetorical questions here, unanswerable by Churchill himself, ask the reader, in turn to contemplate death of an indeterminate scale and scope, and, at the point when this text was written and published, would have acted as a reminder that for many, the arrival of the Allies was always going to be belated. The sense, however, of Churchill being deeply affected by being confronted with the imminence of mass death at the camp is eroded when, at their next stopping point, Dachau, he meets other 'privileged' prisoners, a 'galaxy of historical figures', who have arrived from other camps and mentions many of them—including Martin Niemöller—by name.[93] Churchill is evidently much more at ease recalling his interactions with these individuals than remembering the nameless, dying men at Flossenburg.

In both these texts, the question of perspective, and the rightness or otherwise of attempting to depict the experiences of others, hover in the background. What I identify as awkwardness, inconsistency, or tentativeness is symptomatic not only of the inadequacy of these descriptions but of the very difficulty of encompassing linguistically what is being described. Tickell's *Odette* reaches for different, though no less problematic, imagery, when attempting to provide readers with an insight into conditions at Ravensbrück. During his account of the trial, the organization and running of Ravensbrück are explained, including the process of *Selektion*, the identification of those who would be gassed: 'Nearly forty thousand women were ordered to parade bareheaded and with naked feet before the huts. Fear travels fast and those who were forced to take part in this fiendish Folies Bergères were fully conscious of its dread purpose.'[94] This allusion to the 'Folies Bergères' is apparently justified by Tickell's description of the women's efforts to make themselves appear younger and healthier prior to the *Selektion* itself: 'they attempted to step out strongly with swollen ankles and feeble feet; they [...] knew that the old and the ill were to be killed and that the young and strong might live to work a little longer'.[95] Such tactics are depicted in other accounts, including the

---

[92] Churchill, *The Spirit in the Cage*, p. 200.
[93] Churchill, *The Spirit in the Cage*, p. 205.
[94] Tickell, *Odette*, p. 15.
[95] Although prisoners were earlier transported to other camps for gassing, gas chambers were only in operation at Ravensbrück itself from the opening months of 1945. Contrary to Tickell's account, Sarah Helm suggests that 'rumours and lies were circulated' to try to mask what

film *Schindler's List* (1994), where, before a *Selektion* women pinch their cheeks or rub blood onto them to mimic a 'healthy glow'. Tickell's analogy points to the fact that in each case, men are looking, and women being looked at, but the comparison is nevertheless shocking to a contemporary reader because it brings into conjunction two things—a Parisian nightclub that was associated with a particular kind of illicit entertainment and the choosing of individuals to undergo death by gassing—that seem utterly incomparable.

The ethical problems of comparing the concentration camps with anything and indeed of using figurative language to describe them at all are now familiar, and, as I suggested in the introduction, in many early representations, an emphasis on indescribability was characteristic.[96] Tickell's choice of image also sexualizes the process he describes, but it is not impossible that this is precisely the point. Tickell (perhaps) attempts to indicate that, for the Nazis, this process was indeed akin to ogling women in a nightclub. Considered this way, the choice of analogy seems (marginally) more explicable, but it underlines the difficulty that Tickell has in establishing a consistent narrative voice and perspective, a difficulty that refracts the nature of the events described. His use of the phrase 'fiendish Folies Bergères' is in fact embedded in a sentence that attempts to evoke the women prisoners' emotions. The women, we are told, are 'fully conscious of [the event's] dread purpose'.[97] In this context, the implication is that the women themselves might have conceived the selection in this light, but this is both improbable and unprovable. Tickell's choice of image, then, disjunctive as it is, stands as a symptom of the difficulties of representation that it is attempting to solve.[98]

In *Carve Her Name with Pride*, R. J. Minney largely resists using figurative language in his description of Ravensbrück. If Tickell's description of the camp veers towards the lurid, Minney's is studiedly detached and

was happening and avert panic. *If This Is a Woman: Inside Ravensbrück, Hitler's Concentration Camp for Women* (London: Abacus, 2015), pp. 544–45.

[96] Barbie Zelizer cites Ed Murrow's comment during a report from Belsen: 'I saw it, but will not describe it.' *Remembering to Forget: Holocaust Memory Through the Camera's Eye* (Chicago: University of Chicago Press, 1998), p. 85.

[97] Tickell, *Odette*, p. 15.

[98] In the light of Rawlinson's identification of prisoner of war camps as a comparator in writing about public schools in the late 1930s, it is notable that Tickell later describes Ravensbrück as a 'diabolic Roedean' (p. 52), referring to a famous English girls' school, with Kapos likened to school prefects. See Rawlinson, 'This Other War', pp. 16–17.

starkly unevocative. His initial description of the camp focuses on facts and figures:

It was the largest prison camp in Europe, indeed the largest prison for women the world had ever known [...] [I]t was designed to accommodate 7000 women prisoners [...] [B]y the time Violette arrived, there were 40, 000 women crowded together in large huts [...] In all nearly 120, 000 prisoners are known to have entered it. Of these fewer than 12, 000 were alive when the Russian advance overshot the camp and gave them their freedom. The Soviet soldiers, tough and hard-bitten, were appalled by the pitiful condition in which they found the survivors.[99]

Describing the camp as a prison may provide a point of reference for the general reader, but it implies that some of the 'inmates' might have deserved their incarceration. While the mismatch between there being capacity for 7000 in place where 40,000 were being kept is shocking, the impact this might have actually had, day-to-day is only touched on very indirectly, via the responses of the 'hard-bitten' Soviets. The reader is asked to imagine what conditions might have shocked these apparently hard-to-shock individuals and, as a result, is led further away from what Minney ostensibly wishes them to contemplate.

Minney does explain that the 'bulk' of the prisoners 'were there for no crimes that they were aware of committing', and he enumerates the nationalities of the captives: 'Russians and Poles [...] Czechs too and Danes, Norwegians, Belgians, Dutch, French and even Germans'.[100] Szabo first arrived at Ravensbrück in August 1944, by which point many of the Jewish prisoners who had been kept there had been moved elsewhere. Nevertheless, Minney gives no acknowledgement that being Jewish, or indeed a Jehovah's Witness or a gypsy, was one of the 'crimes' for which individuals might have been sent to the camp. The phrase 'even Germans' is the only slight acknowledgement that the war facilitated the Nazis' victimization of sections of the German population and that other identities folded into, or deemed more important than, nationality.

The 1958 film adaptation of Minney's biography, with Virginia McKenna in the role of Violette Szabo, is more cursory in its treatment of Szabo's incarceration. The action moves swiftly from Szabo's capture and her interrogation and torture at the Avenue Foch, via a brief reunion, with

---

[99] Minney, *Carve Her Name*, p. 169
[100] Minney, *Carve Her Name*, p. 171.

her fellow agent Tony and the never-to-be-fulfilled promise of a love affair between them, to a short sequence in a camp that is not named. Where *Odette* uses striped uniforms and a smoking chimney to signify Ravensbrück, prior to focusing in on Odette's cell, *Carve Her Name* presents an establishing shot of uniformed female prisoners seen through barbed wire. Violette and her two fellow agents Denise Bloch and Lilian Rolfe are taken to be executed seemingly immediately after arrival and are the only prisoners to be individuated in any meaningful way. Although Minney, as I indicated earlier, describes the women being shot at close quarters, in the film, they stand before a machine gun, and, as the sound of the shots rings out, the film cuts to show the sun breaking through the clouds above them. This reframing of the biography's account references the established film trope of the firing squad, displacing in the process the more intimate brutality of what actually happened to the three women.

Following this, in a brief epilogue, Szabo's daughter Tanya is shown being presented with her mother's posthumous George Cross before being taken home by her grandparents and going out to play in the street with other children. Where the film version of *Odette* provides romantic closure, *Carve Her Name* offers hope for the future via the next generation. Her grandparents stand in for the parents Tanya will never know, and Tanya herself is embedded in a supportive local community of neighbours, her compensation for the loss of her mother being the knowledge that by her mother's actions, that community has been freed from the threat of tyranny.

The focus on varieties of resistance in these biographies and autobiographies can have the effect of making other prisoners seem passive merely 'background' for agents' activities, and this has the effect of shoring up the perception of members of the Special Operations Executive as an exemplary type of service personnel. British prisoners, especially those who were accustomed to using cover identities, could exploit the complexity of the camp organization to bargain on their own behalf. Whether or not participating in such deals is enough to exculpate, or should have been enough to exculpate, the Nazi officers concerned is a question that for the most part remains in suspense in these texts. This is not to downplay the bravery with which women and men like Szabo and Churchill carried out their work, simply to note that their emphasis on activity rather than passivity may be one reason why these texts, despite their harrowing content, were so popular in the 1950s. Even where agents were executed, it is easier to contemplate the stories of these individuals than to try to grasp the mass suffering of their fellow concentration camp prisoners.

Writing about one's war experiences, allowing another to write about them and offer their account for publication, or taking on the task of writing on behalf of one or more of those who did not survive, can be a way of supplementing judicial proceedings or even an attempt to substitute for them. These texts are also, in various ways, compensatory: authors such as Overton Fuller and Nicholas in particular attempt to rescue their subjects from the misapprehensions that they believe have been promoted by more official kinds of memorialization. Telling one's own story, as Churchill does, is a means of attempting to reassert agency (so to speak) after a period when that agency has been denied or delimited, and this can be seen as another form of compensation, and not only because the story, once published, can bring a financial return. These writings from the 1940s and 1950s can thus be seen as an early manifestation of how, as Charles S. Maier puts it, 'historical narratives are increasingly conceived of as compensatory [...] in that they introduce new agents who have hitherto been left in obscurity'.[101] The omissions or deficiencies that I have identified in these texts are evidence of the problems faced by these authors in coming to terms not just with a traumatic period in their own or their subjects' lives, but with the wider trauma of which the story is itself only a fragment.

In the wake of Airey Neave's campaign, Peter Churchill did eventually receive some financial compensation. Yeo-Thomas died in February 1964, while the legal arguments were still being rehearsed, having struggled, as his most recent biographer Mark Seaman describes, with an eating disorder in the years following his release.[102] The Newton brothers returned to England after their release from Buchenwald to discover that the belongings that they had left for safe-keeping when sent on their mission had been 'lost in transit' and that their promotions in the field had not been honoured and were therefore not reflected in their accumulated back-pay.[103]

---

[101] Charles S. Maier, 'Overcoming the Past? Narrative and Negotiation, Remembering and Reparation: Issues at the Interface of History and the Law', in *Politics and the Past: On Repairing Historical Injustices*, edited by John Torpey (Langham MD: Rowman & Littlefield, 2003) pp. 295–304 (p. 303).
[102] Mark Seaman, *Bravest of the Brave: The True Story of Wing Commander 'Tommy' Yeo-Thomas SOE Secret Agent Codename 'White Rabbit'* (London: Michael O'Mara, 1999), p. 213.
[103] Thomas, *No Banners*, pp. 342–43. The extended Newton family had lived in France prior to the war, and the brothers' parents, both their wives, and Alfred's young children, were all killed when the *SS Avoceta*, on which they were making their way as refugees from Lisbon to Liverpool, was torpedoed in September 1941.

In April 1964, *Guardian* journalist Terence Prittie wrote an article in which he described Yeo-Thomas's recent death as 'a forcible reminder that [...] nearly 20 years after the war, British citizens who were illegally imprisoned in Hitler's concentration camps have still not received compensation for their suffering', and placing the blame for this on the British government.[104] Prittie was also the author of the two articles published in the *Guardian* in November 1965 and January 1967 that described Gertrude Sington's struggle to have her compensation claim against the German government recognized. As I indicated in Chapter 2, these articles include harrowing details, which Gertrude Sington evidently consented to being made public, of what she went through during her captivity. They allow us a glimpse of another story, a different kind of bravery. The issue they bring to light is not who was more or less deserving of compensation, but how difficult it could be for other victims of the Nazis, to ensure that their stories were, at the very least, told.[105]

[104] Terence Prittie, 'Compensation Held Up', *Manchester Guardian* (27 April 1964), p. 16.
[105] Terence Prittie, 'A Victim of Nazism Still Awaits Her Compensation', *Guardian* (2 November 1965), p. 12; 'Nazi Concentration Camp Victim Is Still Denied Justice', *Guardian* (23 January 1967), p. 3.

4

Holocaust Survivors and Refugees in 1940s Detective Fiction

What detective fiction shares with the other kinds of writing that I have been considering here is a concern with the issues of identity and belonging that criminality and victimhood bring in their train.[1] Broadly speaking, interwar British detective fiction centres on how the disruption caused to a society by a crime can be repaired through the identification and bringing to justice of the criminal. But in this context, 'a society' often means a circumscribed locale with interrelated protagonists within which, either explicitly or implicitly, broader social concerns and values are explored, and 'bringing to justice' may get no further, within the narrative, than guilt being asserted or admitted, rather than involving courtroom proceedings. In an often-cited essay from 1948, W. H. Auden describes the 'closed society' of the detective story. As he explains, this has a structural function, in that it gives the narrative a spatial focus and promotes reader engagement, but it also has symbolic ramifications.[2] The examples of closed societies offered by Auden include 'the country house [...] the old world village [and] the theatrical company',[3] and the prisoner-of-war camp can be added to this list, as Michael Gilbert's *Death in Captivity* (1952) illustrates. The action of Gilbert's novel opens in a camp in Italy in June 1943, just as news of the invasion of Sicily has reached the prisoners, and the German advance adds urgency to the investigation into the murder of a prisoner who has been suspected by his fellows of working for the Italians.

Although the concept of the closed society may seem to reduce setting to an aspect of structure, with the precise nature of the different locations unimportant in and of themselves, Gilbert's novel is just one example of how

---

[1] The classic form of detective fiction emerged in Britain in the interwar years, and there was lively debate among authors and reviewers about how it should be defined. For an overview, see Victoria Stewart, *Crime Writing in Interwar Britain: Fact and Fiction in the Golden Age* (Cambridge: Cambridge University Press, 2017), pp. 7–14.

[2] W. H. Auden, 'The Guilty Vicarage', in *The Dyer's Hand and Other Essays* (London: Faber & Faber, 1962 [1948]), pp. 146–58.

[3] Auden, 'The Guilty Vicarage', p. 150.

Literature and Justice in Mid-Twentieth-Century Britain. Victoria Stewart, Oxford University Press.

detective fiction adapted to and actively engaged with the changing political context of mid-century Britain. In some cases, the threat to the closed society was reconfigured to incorporate an explicitly politicized aspect, thus disturbing the dichotomy between the closed society of detective fiction and the 'open society' that, in Auden's account, is more usually associated with the thriller.[4] Lacking the spatial boundaries of the closed society, the open society is one in which any individual encountered by the protagonist is relatively decontextualized and therefore has to be weighed up as a potential threat.

Considering the 'wartime adaptability of the detective formula', Gill Plain argues that the 'ideological compatibility between espionage and detection is obvious: the detective must identify the "enemy within", and it matters little whether this enemy takes the form of a murderer or a traitor'.[5] Plain's comments come in the context of a discussion of Agatha Christie's *N or M?* (1941), a novel that centres on the identification of the German spy among the residents at a boarding house. Characterizing Christie's works more generally, Plain contends that they 'famously depend on the premise that every character is guilty in thought if not in deed'.[6] Part of what allows the detective narrative to expand to novel-length (the predominant though not sole form of post–First World War detective fiction) is the fact that characters not only have guilty thoughts, but may have committed (noncriminal) acts that they wish to keep concealed. Their attempts at concealment complicate the investigation and therefore the plot. For instance, the mysterious stranger who enters a community and later proves not to be the criminal but to have a hidden connection with one or other of the inhabitants is a common feature of the work of Christie and many of her contemporaries.

These characteristics of detective fiction are relevant to the consideration of how particular types of closed society or community and particular types of outsiders are depicted in the form in the 1940s. The refugee and the former concentration camp inmate can be caught sight of in detective fiction of this period, and in many cases, the secrets these individuals conceal relate not to their own shameful actions in the past, but to the shame associated with victimhood and survival. The crimes of which they are victims are not domestic, and not, as a rule, central to the action. Attempting to incorporate

[4] Auden, 'The Guilty Vicarage', p. 149.
[5] Gill Plain, *Twentieth-Century Crime Fiction: Gender, Sexuality and the Body* (Edinburgh: Edinburgh University Press, 2001), p. 44.
[6] Plain, *Twentieth-Century Crime Fiction*, p. 53.

war crimes into detective fiction can therefore lead to their marginalization in favour of more familiar or, in narrative terms, manageable types of crime. But even when situated at the periphery, this material destabilizes the detective narrative precisely because it cannot be fully encompassed by the tropes and strategies usually associated with that genre.

Discussing how minor characters function in nineteenth-century fiction, Alex Woloch argues that, 'simply through their subordinate multiplicity', such characters 'hover vulnerably on the borderline between name and number'.[7] Not all characters can take centre stage, but the stories of minor characters and their interactions with the central protagonists can raise the question of why some stories are indeed central and some marginal. This 'borderline' echoes the characterization of refugees in mid–twentieth century fiction as, in Katherine Cooper's analysis, 'authentic [...] truth-tellers', who trouble the status and nature of home by their position as 'threshold figures'.[8] The stories they bring may be as threatening and as inassimilable as they themselves seem to be. In the novels to be examined here, the scope that refugees are given to tell their stories tends to be limited, but it is notable that they are often, if only temporarily, positioned as the focalizer of the narrative, a function that more usually in detective fiction is reserved for the investigator or for a 'Watson'-type assistant who helps the reader make sense of the investigation. Marginalization may be taken to imply that stories about war crimes are being addressed only in a token or even opportunistic fashion to give a veneer of contemporary relevance to an otherwise formulaic narrative. But these stories cannot be viewed apart from the often-considerable impact, in relation to both form and theme, that they have on the narrative as a whole despite this marginality.

The presence of these figures therefore provides the opportunity for an assessment of how new understandings of Britishness and Britain's relation to Europe were being broached in popular writing in the post–Second World War years. Indeed, although the Holocaust survivor is a very specific type of incomer to Britain, this figure can be contextualized in relation to pre-war refugees who make an appearance in detective fiction throughout the 1930s and into the war years, some of whom are explicitly described as having been concentration camp inmates. These depictions are not necessarily

---

[7] Alex Woloch, *The One vs. The Many: Minor Characters and the Space of the Protagonist in the Novel* (Princeton: Princeton University Press, 2004), p. 17.
[8] Katherine Cooper, 'Figures on the Threshold: Refugees and the Politics of Hospitality, 1930–51', *Literature and History* 27.2 (2018): pp. 189–204 (p. 197).

nuanced, and the reasons why individuals have left their homelands are not always specified, so that an Austrian refugee, who could have fled anti-communist measures in the early 1930s, may not be distinguished from a German-Jewish escapee from Nazi persecution, and the different experiences of pre- and post-war refugees are not always elaborated upon. The economy with which characterization and setting are typically evoked in detective fiction can lead to a reliance on stereotypes of either a positive or negative kind. But some authors do successfully use the detective form, for all its supposed limitations, to raise questions about justice, guilt, and responsibility that echo the debates I have identified in other kinds of writing about crime and the law from this period.

As I have indicated, although there are exceptions, detective fiction tends to focus its attention on the investigation of crime rather than the judicial processes that might follow. The detective's identification of the guilty party is sufficient to provide closure, and justice is felt to have been done on behalf of the victim (the crime at the centre of these novels is almost always murder). This is complicated if the murder has been carried out in order to compensate for perceived deficiencies in the legal system; the murder of a blackmailer, for instance, might be condoned.[9] Including a survivor of persecution in a narrative can prompt a scenario in which a victim of crime feels that they may never gain recompense through the legal system, and here too a desire to seek retribution by enacting rough justice may be constructed as a motive, and at times a justifiable one. This is the situation that arises in Harriet Rutland's *Blue Murder* (1942) and Ellis Peters's *Fallen into the Pit* (1951). But though such rough justice may not be wholeheartedly condemned in the narrative, the desire for the maintenance of social order means that it has to be contained. This containment can be linked to the issue of belonging and assimilation, which is not only played out in relation to refugees' attempts to 'fit in', but in another aspect of these novels which mirrors those attempts: the construction of residual or resurgent fascism as a threat to the post-war social order in Britain. The defeat, or, in some instances, elimination of figures with extremist views at home acts as a proxy for a global threat, constructing it as controllable.

---

[9] In 'Raffles and Miss Blandish', George Orwell comments that it is a 'fairly well-established convention in crime stories that murdering a blackmailer "doesn't count"', in *Collected Essays, Journalism and Letters of George Orwell Volume III: As I Please 1943–45*, edited by Sonia Orwell and Ian Angus (London: Secker & Warburg, 1968 [1944]), pp. 212–24 (p. 215, n. 1).

Fifth Columnists and Others

Continuities, then, can be identified between wartime and post-war depictions of Jews and other refugees in detective fiction, with identity, national identity, and allegiance become increasingly complicated, especially when the detective form intersects with the thriller. As Plain points out in her discussion of *N or M?*, the impact of the 'Fifth Column' scare, when fears that undercover Nazi agents might be active in Britain were at a height, can be discerned in fiction from the early 1940s. Neil Stammers notes that although the press and public in Britain were largely sympathetic towards refugees in the pre-war period, 'by March [1940] enemy aliens, as a collective group, were beginning to be portrayed in a new light—as a potential fifth column and a threat to national security'.[10] This is echoed by Tony Kushner's observation that memories of the November 1938 pogrom (sometimes referred to as *Kristallnacht*) soon 'dimmed in the democratic world'.[11] Where internment was concerned, Rachel Pistol argues that there 'was no great public agitation' for this 'until the fall in 1940 of France, Belgium and the Netherlands'.[12] At this point internment, which had been reserved for those who were categorized as a threat to national security, was expanded by a series of Emergency Regulations. Wholescale internment of Italians began following Italy's entry into the war in early June 1940, and the policy extended to Germans and Austrians at the end of June. Those affected were 'men aged 16-70 with less than 20 years residence in Britain' as well as men and women who were on 'MI5's suspect list'.[13] Noting that the impact of internment on individual internees varied according to factors including age and previous history, Pistol reinforces the importance of public opinion in the extension of the practice of internment: 'Internment can only be considered a success in that it helped allay the fears of the public, who were afraid there was a Fifth Column presence in the country, quite possibly disguised as refugees'.[14] Such fears were rapidly incorporated into popular fiction.

---

[10] Neil Stammers, *Civil Liberties in Britain during the Second World War: A Political Study* (Beckenham: Croom Helm, 1983), p. 37.

[11] Tony Kushner, *The Holocaust and the Liberal Imagination: A Social and Cultural History* (Oxford: Basil Blackwell, 1994), p. 55.

[12] Rachel Pistol, "'I Can't Remember a More Depressing Time but I Don't Blame Anyone for That": Remembering and Commemorating the Wartime Internment of Enemy Aliens in Britain', *Patterns of Prejudice* 53.1 (2019): pp. 37–48 (p. 38).

[13] Stammers, *Civil Liberties*, p. 39.

[14] Pistol, "'I Can't Remember'", p. 40.

Set shortly before but written and published after June 1940, *N or M?* centres on the hunt for a spy that unfolds at a boarding house, an archetypal 'closed society'. The guests are assessed by the investigators, Christie's recurring protagonists Tommy and Tuppence, who themselves adopt false identities to facilitate their search. One figure who comes under scrutiny is Carl von Deinim, a German research chemist, who tells Tuppence: 'I came to this country to escape Nazi persecution. [...] My brothers are in concentration camp. My father died in one. My mother died of sorrow and fear'.[15] Carl is not Jewish, however: Tuppence learns that '[h]is father got into trouble for criticising the Nazi regime'.[16] His Germanness is important, in plot terms, because it complicates the issues of political loyalty that are key to the sifting of potential suspects. When, shortly after telling Tuppence his story, Carl hears someone talking about him in the street and is insulted, Tuppence reproves him: 'You're a refugee. You have to take the rough with the smooth [...] You can't expect the mere man in the street [...] to distinguish between bad Germans and good Germans'.[17] In terms of the trajectory of the plot, Christie wants to exploit the difficulty of distinguishing between these two types of individuals, the good and the bad German, who appear at first glance to be the same. Carl is presented as 'typically' German in appearance, 'very stiff, fair-haired and blue-eyed'.[18] Making Jewishness the reason for Carl's persecution would have complicated this either/or, good/bad German dichotomy for Christie, not least because Jewishness cannot easily be mapped onto either national identity or political belief.

Carl, the suspect so obvious that he cannot really be the culprit, turns out not to be all that he appears. He is in fact a British agent who adopted the identity of the real Carl after Carl himself, faced with being blackmailed into working for the Nazis, took his own life. (Similarly, in Gilbert's *Death in Captivity* a presumed stoolpigeon turns out to be a British agent, tasked with gathering evidence for future war crimes trials.) The false Carl explains that he was suited for this role because '[the real] Carl and I had a certain superficial likeness (my grandmother was a German), hence my suitability for work in Germany. Carl was not a Nazi'.[19] While the ringleader of the Fifth Column in this novel, Major Bletchley, turns out to be a German, or, more

---

[15] Agatha Christie, *N or M?* (London: HarperCollins, 2015 [1941]), pp. 29–30.
[16] Christie, *N or M?*, p. 20.
[17] Christie, *N or M?*, p. 30.
[18] Christie, *N or M?*, p. 17.
[19] Christie, *N or M?*, p. 239.

specifically a Prussian, passing himself off as 'a "hearty Englishman"', his co-conspirators are British people with Nazi sympathies who have 'pledged to assist an invasion' and who include 'two Chief Constables, an Air Vice-Marshall [...] a Cabinet Minister [...] and various military and naval lesser fry, as well as members of our own Intelligence Force'.[20] The situating of Nazism, or, more broadly fascism, as a domestic problem is one that recurs, as I will show, in post-war detective fiction.[21]

When she still believes him actually to be a refugee, Tuppence pragmatically advises Carl that he should be grateful to be alive rather than complaining about a lack of understanding of his situation on the part of the British with whom he comes into contact. Negative opinion of refugees is voiced in the novel by Bletchley before his real identity is discovered. After a foreign woman has been seen in the neighbourhood, Bletchley says that he noticed her because: '[W]e are all on the look-out nowadays for Fifth Columnists, aren't we? [...] I noticed this woman. A nurse, I thought, or a maid—a lot of spies came over here in that capacity.'[22] Referring to Carl, he opines: '[T]his refugee business is dangerous. If I had my way, I'd intern the lot of them [...] the Government is a great deal too easy with these enemy aliens. Anyone who cared could come over here and pull a long face and talk about their brothers in concentration camps.' He goes on to accuse Carl of 'arrogance'.[23] Christie partially defuses such prejudices by having Tuppence express a marginally more measured view, and by the later revelation that Bletchley is in fact a German agent. But these beliefs are not confronted directly. Vanda Polonska, the woman who rouses Bletchley's suspicions, is eventually revealed to be a 'penniless refugee', but only after she and her family members are described as being 'looked upon with suspicion' by the authorities. That Polonska has 'been through scenes of great horror in Poland' is revealed at the inquest that takes place after she is summarily shot by a member of the spy ring before she is able to tell her own story and assert her innocence.[24] Meanwhile, 'Carl' turns out not really to be a refugee at all; he is an impostor, though not in the way Bletchley suggests. The question of how refugees would or should be dealt with or in what circumstances

---

[20] Christie, *N or M?*, p. 161, p. 235.
[21] Nazi Germany is the regime most commonly mentioned in this connection, although Nap Lombard's *Murder's a Swine* (1943) features a British fascist group who style themselves the 'Free British Mussolites'. ('Nap Lombard' was a penname adopted by Pamela Hansford Johnson and her then-husband Gordon Neil Stewart.)
[22] Christie, *N or M?*, p. 130.
[23] Christie, *N or M?*, p. 41.
[24] Christie, *N or M?*, p. 233, p. 137, p. 136.

they might be able to tell their own stories, is therefore deferred, though for Christie's first readers, the intemperate Bletchley's comment 'intern the lot' would have echoed current government policy.

The vagueness or imprecision that characterizes Carl's story, with the phrase *concentration camp* standing metonymically for the apparatus of Nazi repression, is typical of refugee stories in detective fiction of the 1940s and 1950s. This can be explained partly by a desire to give only information about characters that is essential to the working of the plot. The relevant point in Carl's case is that he has a story to tell about his family being victimized; the detail is not pertinent, and the same goes for the 'scenes of great horror' that Vanda Polonska has witnessed. Christie and other authors who use references to concentration camps or other aspects of the Nazi regime in this way might be presuming that their readership will be able to fill in some of the gaps, that they will have a general sense of what the term *concentration camp* refers to, even if, in 1941, their knowledge is as vague as, by his own account, Peter Churchill's was a year or two later.[25] This becomes problematic when the term seems to drift away from its referent and is used in a nonspecific way, and when, especially at the end of the war, it comes to be applied to quite different types of camp. What Christie and her contemporaries bring to the surface, however awkwardly, is a sense that storytelling and the credibility (or not) of stories, together with the desire, or lack of desire, on the part of refugees to tell their stories, is a central part of how refugee experience is engaged with at this period.

Part of what raises suspicion about the 'false Carl' is that his story, as Tuppence reflects, is told as though 'he had learned it by heart'.[26] Flatness of delivery could be the consequence of trauma, the necessity of having to repeatedly tell a painful tale, or, indeed, it could signal detachment born of the fact this is not the teller's story at all, as transpires in *N or M?* This uncertainty about whether aspects of an individual's demeanour signify pretence also finds its way into other representations of refugees. The action of G. D. H and Margaret Cole's *Toper's End* (1942) unfolds at Excalibur House, the home of scientist Dr Sambourne, who has made it a sanctuary for refugee academics. During the murder investigation Superintendent Wilson 'hesitates' when he encounters Wauters, a Dutch professor of Fine Art, who is one of Sambourne's guests: 'The one thing Wilson could feel certain of was that the Dutchman's exquisite polish was carefully studied; but that fact need have no sinister meaning. Wilson had met before professors of the fine arts

---

[25] See Chapter 3.
[26] Christie, *N or M?*, p. 30.

whose manners appeared to have been designed as practical illustration in aesthetics.'[27] Whereas Tuppence wavers between believing Carl to be pretending and believing him to be showing evidence of trauma, Wilson is unsure whether Wauters is pretending or just pretentious.[28]

Willi Hilfe, the Austrian refugee who initially seems to be supportive and helpful to Arthur Rowe in Graham Greene's *The Ministry of Fear* (1943), is a more complicated example, not least because Rowe, to whom Willi explains his origins, has himself been presented to the reader as a damaged individual. This novel engages in a self-conscious fashion with the tropes and conventions of detective and spy fiction. At his first meeting with Rowe, Willi explains that his sister Anna 'got [him] out of Austria', adding, merely: 'That's another story.'[29] While this might initially seem to be a tactful statement on the part of Willi, who does not want his own and Anna's story to distract from Rowe's predicament, his passing reference to his escape from his homeland helps to construct him as a worldly-wise and interestingly enigmatic figure in Rowe's eyes.

When Anna doubts that the charitable organizers of the fête which led to Rowe's unwitting entanglement in what is at this point an ill-defined conspiracy could have any responsibility for his problems, Willi corrects her perception. His comments echo how detective fiction was shifting, or being obliged to shift, at this period.

There's no longer a thing called a criminal class. We can tell you that. There were lots of people in Austria you'd have said couldn't ... well, do the things we saw them do. Cultured people, pleasant people, people you had sat next to at dinner. [...] Your old-fashioned murderer killed from fear, from hate—or even from love. [...] But to murder for position—that's different, because when you've gained the position, nobody has a right to criticize the means.[30]

---

[27] G. D. H. and Margaret Cole, *Toper's End* (London: Collins, 1942), p. 200.

[28] Kushner points out that refugees were advised to perform a version of Englishness which led to some, by their own accounts, feeling that they had to try to become 'more English than the English' or 'almost hyper-English.' Kushner, *The Holocaust and the Liberal Imagination*, p. 57. In Michael Innes's novel *Operation Pax* (Harmondworth: Penguin, 1964 [1951]), Professor Kolmak, a Viennese art historian who has been living in Oxford for some years, is nervous about how women in a bus queue respond to him politely removing his hat: 'Perhaps taking off his hat had been a mistake. And he still hated all the mistakes, worrying over them far more than was reasonable in a man endowed with philosophic views, dedicated to liberal purposes...' (p. 90).

[29] Graham Greene, *The Ministry of Fear*, (Harmondsworth: Penguin, 1973 [1943]), p. 46.

[30] Greene, *Ministry of Fear*, p. 47.

The very fact that Willi does not tell his story in detail indicates to Rowe that Willi does indeed *have* a story, and his reticence about what exactly he 'saw people do' reinforces Rowe's construction of him as 'a young man of great experience': Willi's experience is too 'great' to share.[31] Willi suggests that the people who would usually be regarded as civilized have adopted the behaviour of the 'criminal class'. Members of the 'criminal class', understood as habitual criminals, are not generally the perpetrators in detective narratives. Rather, to follow Willi's typology, it is the 'old-fashioned murderer', driven by intense passion, and therefore cloaked in the remnants of respectability, who tends to feature in such texts. Murdering for political position is a different matter, and, as Willi indicates, can cause a blurring of the boundaries of acceptability: 'Nobody will refuse to meet you if the position's high enough. Think of how many of your statesmen have shaken hands with Hitler.'[32] 'Shaking hands with Hitler' means conniving at the way in which he has gone about achieving and maintaining his position. But these comments of Willi's, which here read as an indictment of both political terror and attitudes of appeasement, are cast in quite a different light when it emerges that Willi is in fact a player in the espionage conspiracy from which he claims to be helping Rowe to extricate himself. Rowe's sympathy, invoked by Willi's hints at his troubled past, proves to be misplaced.

In a startling moment towards the end of the novel, Rowe, having had his suspicions about Willi confirmed by Anna, goes with her to confront her him, and they find Willi sleeping. The scene is described a way that communicates the deep ambivalence that the ostensibly charming but actually fascist Willi has provoked in Rowe, and, perhaps, the reader.

Hilfe lay on the bed on his back without his jacket, his shirt open at the neck. He was deeply and completely at peace, and so defenceless that he seemed to be innocent. [...] He looked very young; he didn't, lying there, belong to the same world as Cost [his co-conspirator] bleeding by the mirror [... .] One was half-impelled to believe, 'It's propaganda, just propaganda: he isn't capable...' [.] Watching the sleeping man [Rowe] could realize a little of the force and the grace and the attraction of nihilism—of

---

[31] Greene, *Ministry of Fear*, pp. 47–48. There is no mention of the Hilfes having been interned, though during his first conversation with Rowe, Willi, indicating that he would like to be making more of a contribution to the war effort than he is currently allowed, admits: 'it's something not to be interned'. Later, after his treachery has been revealed, he speculates that Anna may be sent to 'an internment camp' as punishment for letting him escape. Greene, *Ministry of Fear*, p. 48, p. 213.

[32] Greene, *Ministry of Fear*, p. 47.

not caring for anything, of having no rules and feeling no love. [...] It was as if [Hilfe] were the only violence in the world and while he slept there was peace everywhere.[33]

Rowe's attraction towards Willi is the logical conclusion of the triangular relationship between Rowe and Willi and Anna Hilfe that was established at the outset: Anna, who reminds Rowe of his dead wife, serves temporarily as a substitute focus for these complicated feelings. Willi, who in repose resembles a figure on 'the tomb of a young student',[34] has been reading Rilke and therefore seems to hark back to pre-Nazi Germanic culture, but any nostalgia is undercut by the identification of nihilism as part of what makes Willi an attractive figure. On the most superficial level, this moment tells the reader that appearances can be deceptive, and that charming people can have obnoxious political views. But Greene goes further, implying the seductive force of a world-view that demands the abrogation of responsibility, 'not caring for anything [...] having no rules'. Willi, however, does not remain asleep. Indeed, like what would later be termed a 'sleeper', an agent placed undercover in an organization or society and 'woken' sometime later when his mission really begins, he is still causing damage even when in repose.

Writing in 1940, F. Lafitte suggested that the presumption that refugees could be spies in disguise was an emotional response that ignored the practicalities of working undercover: '[T]he refugee disguise is the last one which an enemy agent would adopt, because it would be a hindrance to any spy worth his salt to have [...] so much information about himself lodged with official bodies.'[35] In the context of Lafitte's attempt to point out how unlikely it would be for a spy to disguise himself as a refugee, Willi Hilfe might be considered the exception who proves the rule. Certainly, other novels from the early 1940s give a contrasting view of the refugee predicament. In *Toper's End*, Dr Franck, a new arrival at Dr Sambourne's house who has recently been released from internment on the Isle of Man, is apprehended by the Home Guard while walking from the train station, after he is heard singing 'an Irish rebel song', which the Home Guard take to indicate that he 'may be a parachutist, signalling to his confederates'.[36] This moment is framed as a wry comment on the over-zealousness of the Home Guard, but notably, when attempts are made to verify Franck's identity, the assurances of his

[33] Greene, *Ministry of Fear*, p. 203.
[34] Greene, *Ministry of Fear*, p. 203.
[35] F. Lafitte, *The Internment of Aliens* (Harmondsworth: Penguin, 1940), p. 41.
[36] Cole and Cole, *Toper's End*, p. 52.

fellow refugees, some of whom have known him since before the war, are not considered sufficient. Franck is only walking to Excalibur House in the first place because he has given up his lift from the station to Dr Sambourne's racist sister.

If Excalibur House is the 'closed society' in the Coles' novel, it is striking that Franck gets into difficulties while he is en route there. Being in transit, even if this does not involve crossing national borders, disturbs the integrity of the closed society. From this perspective, the setting of Raymond Postgate's *Somebody at the Door* (1943) takes on special significance. Postgate was the brother of Margaret Cole and, like the Coles, politically left leaning, and his novel uses the close official scrutiny to which refugees were subject to provide an alibi for a refugee protagonist. The action centres on the investigation of a group of suspects who travelled in the same train compartment as the murdered man. One of these passengers, Albrecht Mannheim, is German: 'The German refugee was the least difficult to investigate. For Inspector Atkins had already a great deal of information about him, for the end of 1939, when he had settled in Croxburn; and the Home Office had a little earlier information.'[37] But Mannheim was brought out of Germany in an amateur rescue operation rather than as part of an official scheme and he later acknowledges to Atkins how difficult it is to prove his story:

> I could copy all that from the British Museum. I tell you where I lived, and whom I knew [in Germany]: that too, I might have been told by the Nazis, if I am a spy. I did not take part in politics very much: I do not know those who are refugees here, In Germany I was not the sort of person who was photographed in picture papers. I can think of nothing else.[38]

Paradoxically then, although his movements are closely monitored because of his refugee status—he has been warned by the police for having a radio without a permit—the more fundamental question of whether he himself has a right to that status and to the identity he claims is very difficult to prove.

---

[37] Raymond Postgate, *Somebody at the Door* (London: British Library, 2017 [1943]), p. 110. A related point is made in Kathleen Hewitt's crime novel, when, describing the body of a murdered man, David comments: 'The chap looked like a southern European, Italian maybe,' to which his friend Bob responds: 'Italians are listed pretty thoroughly these days.' *Plenty under the Counter* (London: Imperial War Museum, 2019 [1943]), p. 19.

[38] Postgate, *Somebody at the Door*, p. 240.

The reader, however, is in a different position to the police because Postgate describes the circumstances of Mannheim's escape in some detail in the novel. For the reader, then, there is no doubt that Mannheim really has had to flee Nazi persecution, whereas in *N or M?* and *The Ministry of Fear*, the refugees' reports of their escapes have to be taken on trust (or not). Mannheim's predicament is designed to prompt sympathy on the part of the reader, and readers' potential suspicions about refugees are not exploited either as an element of the plot or to cast doubt on the veracity of refugee stories more generally.

Mannheim's escape is told from the perspective of David, the young Labour Party activist who undertakes to help him, and who loses his life in the process and is thus unable to speak on Mannheim's behalf during the later investigation. Postgate's novel is unusual for the genre, not only because the action expands from its original focal point of the railway compartment to include an escape across Europe, but for its use of multiple narrative perspectives. More commonly in detective fiction, the action is focalized solely via the investigator or his or her assistant, and the reader is invited to engage and concur with the judgements that the investigator makes about the suspects and the evidence. Sharing the perspective of a character other than the investigator will often mean ruling out the possibility of that character being a suspect. It is therefore notable that in a number of examples under examination here, authors, as I will show, do try to explore what it might feel like to be a refugee (that is, to be, either potentially or actually the victim of a war crime), and to be suspected of committing a criminal offence. The formal shifts that are discernible in novels by Postgate and others are thus intrinsically connected to the attempt to incorporate different voices into the narrative. But especially where such refugees are explicitly marked as Jewish, the balance between exposing and critiquing stereotypes and simply perpetuating them can be a difficult one to maintain.

The Refugee at Work

Mannheim, a research scientist before he is forced to flee Germany, eventually finds a job 'in the chemical research side of a large munitions factory', with a break in employment when he is 'arrested with others in the panicky round-up of 1940'.[39] The nature of his work is another reason, aside from his

---

[39] Postgate, *Somebody at the Door*, p. 163.

refugee status, for him coming under suspicion, because the murdered man is found to have been killed by poison gas, though in a twist that complicates the idea of volunteering for Home Front defence as a purely positive contribution to the war effort, it transpires that knowledge gained during ARP duties has enabled the actual culprit to commit the murder. In a slightly later example, Patricia Wentworth's *The Key* (1946), the death of Michael Harsch, a German-Jewish refugee scientist, whose past experiences are encoded in a reference to his 'leg which had been crippled in a concentration camp', is initially presumed to be suicide, but this suggestion is dismissed by his friend Janice: 'The Nazis had stripped him of everything. He hadn't got anything left except his mind, and they couldn't touch that.'[40] Harsch has just made a discovery that will help win the war and therefore give him some recompense for the loss of his family in the camps, and his death indeed proves to have been a murder.

Mannheim, Harsch, and indeed Carl von Deinim in *N or M?* are all able to continue to work as scientists, supporting the British war effort, but more common in fiction of this period are refugees who find that their professional expertise is undervalued or misunderstood in their new homeland. In *Toper's End*, writing to a friend about her new job as Dr Sambourne's secretary, Mary Philip observes that 'the foreigners come one after the other and tell me how really important they were in their own countries and how nobody loves them here—poor things'.[41] Later, the senior police officers involved in the investigation note that although many of Sambourne's visitors use the title 'Dr', this is 'Nothing to do with medicine. [...] Just means they've got university degrees, and like going round being labelled.'[42] Similarly, in Michael Innes's *Operation Pax* (1951), unable to recall Kurt Kolmak's name, one of the other fellows at his college calls him 'Doctor': 'It is always in order to address a learned Teuton as Doctor'.[43] This cynicism about the supposed self-importance of the refugees, which emerges from a lack of familiarity with the European university system, is to some extent mitigated in the Coles' novel when Franck's fellow refugee Glück uses her psychoanalytical training to help Franck recover a memory that provides key to identifying the murderer.

[40] Patricia Wentworth, *The Key* (London: Hodder and Stoughton, 2005 [1946]), p. 7 (p. 38).
[41] Cole and Cole, *Toper's End*, p. 11.
[42] Cole and Cole, *Toper's End*, p. 97.
[43] Innes, *Operation Pax*, p. 115.

More common in detective fiction are representations of refugees taking on work as domestic servants. As Rose Holmes explains: 'Women domestic servants were the largest single professional category of refugees from fascism to enter Britain, totalling between a third and a quarter of all refugees in the country before the Second World War.'[44] Intersecting tensions can be discerned here. There is a presumption that domestic service is unskilled work that anyone should be able to do, and that refugees should be grateful for any work that is offered them, even if they have undertaken specialized training for a profession. Certainly, according to Kushner, 'It is clear that for some German and Austrian Jews, coming to Britain on a domestic permit was a last resort.'[45] In Britain in the interwar years, domestic service had become a less popular choice for young women and, as Holmes puts it, 'middle-class British women were desperately seeking servants.'[46] This is echoed in what Nicola Humble describes as 'the intense preoccupation with servants and their treatment' in literature of this period, which she characterizes as amounting to an 'obsessive concern',[47] and which reflects wider insecurities among the middle and upper-middle classes. In detective fiction, domestic servants are anomalous figures. They are of low social status but nevertheless have a degree of access to their employers' private lives; where the 'closed society' is concerned, they are ideally placed to be 'enemies within'.

Offering an alternative to a negative stereotype can sometimes result in authors resorting to equally stereotyped, albeit ostensibly more positive, figurations. As Bryan Cheyette has argued in relation to literary representations of Jews, thinking in terms of an opposition between antisemitism and philosemitism downplays the extent to which, 'the protean instability of "the Jew" as a signifier' characterizes modern literature.[48] Similarly, Zygmunt Bauman notes the usefulness of the term *allosemitism*, coined by Arthur Sandauer, which 'refers to the practice of setting the Jews apart as people radically different from all the others'. Allosemitism 'does not unambiguously determine ether hatred or love of Jews, but contains the seeds of both,

[44] Rose Holmes, 'Love, Labour, Loss: Women, Refugees and the Servant Crisis in Britain, 1933–1939', *Women's History Review* 27.2 (2018): pp. 288–309 (p. 288).

[45] Kushner, *The Holocaust and the Liberal Imagination*, p. 101.

[46] Holmes, 'Love, Labour, Loss', p. 288.

[47] Nicola Humble, *The Feminine Middlebrow Novel, 1920s to 1950s: Class, Domesticity, and Bohemianism* (Oxford: Oxford University Press, 2001), p. 118.

[48] Bryan Cheyette, *Constructions of 'the Jew' in English Literature and Society: Racial Representations, 1875–1945* (Cambridge: Cambridge University Press, 1993), p. 8.

and assures that whichever of the two appears, is intense and extreme.'[49] This ambivalence can result in the expression of either positive or negative stereotypes, both of which are problematic because of their reduction of individuals to a set of simplified gestures and tics and because they do not allow the complexity of lived experience to be conveyed. From an author's perspective, however, such simplification can be an economical way of connecting the action of a novel to wider cultural debates and, in some cases, can facilitate critique, rather than reinforcing presumptions. In relation to wartime and post-war texts, stereotypical depictions of refugees can help to provide a sense of how these wider cultural debates about displacement, justice, and the aftermath of the war were constituted.

In Harriet Rutland's *Blue Murder*, Arnold Smith, a novelist who has been excused from active service, leaves the disruption of London and goes to lodge with the Hardstaffe family in the countryside. The family employ a maid called Frieda: 'Swarthy skin, black hair and eyes, and curved nose pronounced her to be of Jewish descent.'[50] Unlike Willi Hilfe, who is described as having 'excellent English' with 'only a certain caution and precision [marking] him as a foreigner',[51] Frieda's grasp of English is poor, and she is said to speak 'gutturally', an adjective intended to indicate German intonation.[52] After Mrs Hardstaffe is murdered, the members of the household are questioned, and the detective, Cheam, canvasses their views on whether Frieda could be responsible. Leda, the Hardstaffes' grown-up daughter, who has already been characterized as bullying and prejudiced in her behaviour towards Frieda, does not hesitate to say that she believes the maid to be capable of murder, claiming to have seen morphine among Frieda's belongings and adding: 'She has the most violent temper and flies into hysterics over nothing.'[53] The cook, however, takes a different view:

Frieda? Oh no, she never did it. A bit queer she is, right enough, but so'd we be if we'd been through half of what she has. I never did hold with Jews, me being a good Church of England Christian, but I don't hold with torturing

[49] Zygmunt Bauman, 'Allosemitism: Premodern, Modern, Postmodern', in *Modernity, Culture and 'the Jew'*, edited by Bryan Cheyette and Laura Marcus (Cambridge: Polity Press, 1998), pp. 143–56 (p. 143).

[50] Harriet Rutland, *Blue Murder* (London: Dean Street Press, 2015 [1943]), p. 15.

[51] Rutland, *Blue Murder*, p. 43.

[52] Rutland, *Blue Murder*, p. 16. Later in the novel, Frieda is described as 'a refugee from Germany, born in Austria' (p. 126), and she reminisces about her apparently middle-class upbringing in 'Nürnberg' (Nuremberg) (p. 106).

[53] Rutland, *Blue Murder*, p. 68.

an animal, let alone a decent-living human-being, and the bits of tales that girl manages to tell you would fair make your hair curl [...] you may as well have a down on a sausage-dog for being a German. They can't neither of them help it.[54]

The cook's apparent sympathy is here overlaid with comparisons between Jews and animals, and with an exceptionalism that often characterizes expressions of prejudice, the 'some of my best friends are...' defence.[55] The implicit equivalence of the cook's claim that we would be 'queer' had we gone through what Frieda has gone through, shifts the focus from Frieda's actual suffering, the 'bits of tales', while seeming to promote empathy with her plight. But, like Frieda, the cook, a character who has a low status in the household, is a working-class woman, constructed through the use of stereotypes. Many readers of this novel might well congratulate themselves for holding more sophisticated views.

From this perspective, Cheam's questioning of Frieda is notable. Aware of her limited grasp of English, and in the absence of an interpreter, he reflects that he will need to 'frame his questions within the three-hundred-word vocabulary of a two-year-old child.'[56] The relative simplicity of Frieda's response to his questions evidences the lack of detail and reliance on the metonymic force of terminology that is characteristic of other examples of fictionalized refugee testimony:

You do not understand? No. Because you are no German Jew. You say 'Itler is bad man, must be kill. But if you are not Jew, you do not know how bad. You understand bombs and Luftwaffe, but you do not understand Gestapo and torture if you are not a Jew like me. I am told to get up from my bed one night. I must go to the frontier. If I do not go, I am sent to Poland in a cattle-truck or to a concentration camp.[57]

[54] Rutland, *Blue Murder*, p. 78.
[55] In his essay 'The Meaning of Working Through the Past' (1960), Theodor Adorno recalls hearing about a woman who, 'upset after seeing a dramatization of *The Diary of Anne Frank*, said, "Yes, but that girl at least should have been allowed to live." [...] The individual case, which should stand for, and raise awareness about, the terrifying totality, by its very individuation became an alibi for the totality the woman forgot.' *Critical Models: Interventions and Catchwords* trans. Henry W. Pickford (New York: Columbia University Press, 1998), pp. 89–103 (p. 101).
[56] Rutland, *Blue Murder*, p. 80.
[57] Rutland, *Blue Murder*, p. 81.

She explains why morphia was found in her possession: '[P]erhaps I do not get to the frontier [...] It is better then to die, being a Jew.'[58] Frieda here echoes the view expressed by Smith earlier in the narrative, that while conditions for civilians in Britain are difficult, 'it's a great deal worse to have to [...] flee for your life across Europe.'[59] Indeed, it is important that similar views have already been expressed by a sympathetic British character because this undercuts any sense that Frieda might somehow be exaggerating for effect, and she, unlike Smith, has actually experienced both wartime Germany and wartime Britain.

Frieda evidently does not need a sophisticated vocabulary in order to characterize the nature of her suffering. Her language here contrasts with later moments that are narrated from her own perspective, in which the deficiencies of her English are corrected, perhaps over-corrected, by more lyrical reflective passages, supposedly representing her interior monologue in her native tongue. (Similarly, the Coles attempt to evoke a German accent in their approximation of Glück's broken English, and this contrasts with her eloquence when she and Franck are supposed to be speaking German.) In the wake of Mrs Hardstaffe's death, Mr Hardstaffe, the tyrannical head of the household, is murdered, and it is Frieda who discovers the body:

> For a second, she stood rocking on her feet as if she had just received a blow between the eyes. And in that fraction of time, a kaleidoscope of shifting horrors came to her mind. Rubber truncheons, screams of pain horrible to hear, the sickening crunch of a crushed skull, sticky jags of broken bone, coagulated clots of blood ... But this man wasn't a Jew.[60]

Detective fiction does not tend to dwell on the condition of the corpse, although as Plain has observed, in Christie's work, while some bodies are presented as whole, undamaged, and 'made safe', the second corpse in these narratives often comes under closer scrutiny than the first and bears the 'uncomfortable trace of authentically shocking violence'. A dynamic is therefore established between 'corporeal repulsion and fascination'.[61] In the case of Rutland's novel, it is difficult to unpick which elements of this description relate to what Frieda can see in front of her, and which are elements of a form of traumatic flashback. Momentarily, Gestapo violence seems to play out in

[58] Rutland, *Blue Murder*, p. 81.
[59] Rutland, *Blue Murder*, p. 18.
[60] Rutland, *Blue Murder*, p. 109.
[61] Plain, *Twentieth-Century Crime Fiction*, p. 33, p. 38, p. 41.

an English domestic interior. Though the evocation of a victim's interiority could itself be deemed an act of appropriation on the part of the author, there is an attempt here to convey the difficulty Frieda might have in telling her story, and to communicate an awareness that it may be in any case be challenging for the reader to grasp that story's implications, especially when transmission occurs between different languages.

On the one hand, then, this passage illustrates how impossible it is for Frieda to leave her story behind when she leaves mainland Europe; on the other it suggests that the violence she witnessed before could happen here and now, that fascism could find a foothold in Britain. This overlaying of past and present is echoed in *The Key*, when, as Harsch goes into a room in a pub, we are told that he thinks he has 'seen a ghost'. Only at the end of the novel is it deduced that the person he glimpsed, and who left him feeling disturbed, was known to him from the war:

[H]e would have seen [...] a silhouette, light striking at an angle on the side of the head, the cheek, the jaw, the shoulder [...] enough to give you a horrid shock if it was what you had seen before, perhaps many times, when you were in your cell in the dark in a concentration camp and the door opened from the lighted corridor to let one of your tormentors in.[62]

The scene in the pub is disjunctively combined with a scene from Harsch's past, and notably, because it was the spur for his murder, the full significance of this not-quite encounter is explained not by Harsch himself but by Sergeant Abbot, who has been investigating the crime. The use of 'you' in the passage quoted above invites the reader, as well as Abbot's interlocutors in this scene, to occupy the position of the camp survivor, but its coupling with the conditional 'would' has the effect of distancing what is described: the encounter remains hypothetical, unamenable to being described any more directly. The man who kills Harsch is Mr Everton, an apparently harmless local, who, as Maud Silver, Wentworth's Marple-esque investigator, explains, is in fact the son of Germans who 'became a fanatical Nazi' during pre-war visits to his parental homeland. Everton is apprehended but his enemy contact, the man recognized by Harsch, vanishes from the narrative, and the question of how the threat he represents might be contained is left in suspense.

[62] Wentworth, *The Key*, pp. 293–94.

In *Blue Murder*, the threat of fascism is represented in more purely domestic but no less threatening terms by the racism and authoritarianism of Leda Hardstaffe, who is eventually identified as the culprit but who, in an ending that is shocking not only in its disruption of the conventions of classic detective fiction but also in its political pessimism, is not apprehended. The novel's climax is narrated from the perspective of Smith as he realizes that he is in the process of becoming Leda's next victim and he has not been saved when the novel ends. Thus, the sufferings of the Jewish refugee as a consequence of Nazi crimes are again over-written by a domestic crime, but the boundaries between the violence of war and violence motivated by other causes are shown to be fragile.

This ending, which implies that justice may not ever be done, and which, in making a novelist the next victim, questions the efficacy of the literary representation as a means of engaging with violent acts, is chillingly apt given that the war was still ongoing when *Blue Murder* was published. It might be presumed that post-war authors writing in the wake of the publicization of the fate of the Jews and others under Nazi rule, and in some cases, in the wake of war crimes trials, might be more inclined to fall back on stereotypes of Jews as either long-suffering victims or self-righteously vengeful, reflecting Cheyette's view that 'writers do not passively draw on eternal myths of "the Jew" but actively construct them in relation to their own literary and political concerns'.[63] In fact, novels from the post-war period continue to display a range of attitudes, especially when the Jewish character is placed in a principally domestic context, or, as in Agatha Christie's *A Murder Is Announced* (1950), shown to be undertaking domestic work, and therefore troubling the boundaries of the home.

Tackling the question of antisemitism in Christie's novels, Laura Thompson, Christie's most recent biographer, separates attitudes conveyed by the narrator or by characters within the novels from attitudes that Christie herself might have held, while suggesting that Christie's shock when she encountered extreme expressions of antisemitism in real life underscores how 'meaningless' references to antisemitic stereotypes in her books really are. Thompson gives the example of a character in *The Hollow* (1946) who is described as 'a Whitechapel Jewess with dyed hair and a voice like a corncrake'.[64] By Thompson's logic, this description should be read as a throwaway aside that reflects contemporary prejudices fostered over

---

[63] Cheyette, *Constructions of 'the Jew'*, p. 268.

[64] Laura Thompson, *Agatha Christie: An English Mystery* (London: Headline, 2007), p. 387.

the years in literary representations, rather than as an evocation of an attitude that might affect real-world relationships, though this is difficult to square with Thompson's contention that Christie, far from being an ahistorical puzzle-setter, was in fact deeply 'engaged' with 'contemporary thinking'.[65] What makes *A Murder Is Announced* notable for the present discussion is its inclusion of Mitzi whose behaviour reflects many antisemitic stereotypes.[66] Not labelling Mitzi as Jewish is a way for Christie, in Thompson's terms, to 'engage' with a contemporary issue without having to actually 'engage' with historical detail, and it shows how deeply embedded antisemitic stereotypes were for Christie and her contemporaries. They are legible even when not explicitly named, and as Jane Arnold notes, Mitzi is not the only example in Christie's work of a character who is constructed with reference to antisemitic tropes without ever being described as Jewish.[67]

In *A Murder Is Announced*, Jane Marple investigates a murder that takes place after a number of village residents are summoned to Miss Blacklock's house on a particular day at a particular time by a newspaper small ad. The plot that then unfolds involves disguised identities and the claiming of an inheritance. Miss Blacklock herself eventually proves to be the guilty party and is caught with the help of her housekeeper Mitzi. Mitzi—her surname is never given, but we are told it is 'unpronounceable'—is a pre-war refugee from Europe and is evidently Jewish, though she is not explicitly described as such. She has gone to work for Miss Blacklock despite the fact that, as she asserts early on in the novel, she over-qualified for the role:

'Has something upset you?'
    'Yes, I am upset', said Mitzi dramatically. 'I do not wish to die! Already in Europe I escape. My family they all die—they are all killed—my mother, my little brother, my so sweet little niece—all, all they are killed. But me I run away—I hide. I get to England. I work. I do work that never—never would I do in my own country—I-'

[65] Thompson, *Agatha Christie*, p. 388.
[66] As Jane Arnold suggests: 'It seems fair to assume that [Mitzi] is intended to be Jewish.' 'Jews in the Works of Agatha Christie', *Social History* 49.3–4 (1987): pp. 275–82 (p. 279). In Christianna Brand's novel *Heads You Lose* (Harmondsworth: Penguin, 1954 [1941]). Henry Gold is described as 'without having the characteristic features, unmistakably Jewish', implying that, as with criminality, Jewishness can be deduced from appearance even in the absence of its (supposedly) accepted markers.
[67] Arnold provides a list of Jewish characters in Christie's works in an appendix to her article (pp. 280–81) and notes other examples of strongly implied Jewishness, such as Herman Isaacstein in *The Secret of Chimneys* (1925).

'I know all that', said Miss Blacklock crisply. It was, indeed, a constant refrain on Mitzi's lips.[68]

Christie avoids having to specify where exactly Mitzi escaped from, or indeed exactly how her family were killed or by whom. She does not need to: Mitzi's story is only important in this novel inasmuch as it allows Christie to draw her, swiftly and economically, as a character motivated by (self)-righteous indignation. Further, when the police begin investigating the murder that has taken place at Miss Blacklock's house, Miss Blacklock tells the officers:

Please don't be too prejudiced against the poor thing because she's a liar. I do really believe that, like so many liars, there is a real substratum of truth behind her lies. I mean that though [...] her atrocity stories have grown and grown until every kind of unpleasant story that has ever appeared in print has happened to her or her relations personally, she did have a bad shock initially and she did see one at least of her relations killed. I think a lot of these displaced persons feel, perhaps justly, that their claim to our notice and sympathy lies in their atrocity value and so they exaggerate and invent.[69]

Miss Blacklock's comments could be read as an indictment of the British public's attitude to 'atrocity stories': it is the public's lack of understanding or acceptance that causes Mitzi and other 'displaced persons' to exaggerate. But what is underscored more strongly is Mitzi's status as a fabulist, and her apparent appeal to the ill-defined 'atrocity stories' mentioned by Miss Blacklock overshadows the more-or-less passing references to her having seen 'one [...] of her relations' (it evidently makes little difference to Miss Blacklock which) killed. 'Atrocity', as used here, is a word that gestures towards all manner of recent historical events and experiences, but the reader is not invited to confront what it might actually mean, least of all for Mitzi.

Mitzi eventually plays a key role in entrapping the murderer but the fact that the culprit turns out to be her employer does little to undermine the reliability of Miss Blacklock's earlier account of Mitzi's exaggerations. Miss Marple persuades Mitzi to put herself in the position of being Miss Blacklock's next victim, with the assurance that a rescue will be effected before Mitzi comes to any harm. The attack on Mitzi happens in the kitchen, the part of the house where she spends much of her time: 'Mitzi turned off the

[68] Agatha Christie, *A Murder Is Announced* (London: HarperCollins 2005 [1950]), p. 25.
[69] Christie, *A Murder Is Announced*, p. 58.

taps and as she did so two hands came up behind her head and with one swift movement forced it down into the water-filled sink. [...] Mitzi thrashed and struggled but Miss Blacklock was strong.'[70] Marple, hidden in the kitchen broom-cupboard, distracts Blacklock who releases Mitzi, and once Blacklock has been arrested, Mitzi congratulates herself on her own performance: 'I do that good, do I not? I am clever! And I am brave! Oh, I am brave! Very very nearly was *I* murdered too. But I am so brave I risk *everything*.'[71]

But although Mitzi asserts that she has risked 'everything', she was never in any real danger and her claim to have been brave is marked as further evidence of her propensity to exaggerate. Marple explains: 'I flattered [Mitzi] up, of course, and said I was sure if she'd been in her own country she'd have been in the Resistance movement [...] I told her stories of deeds done by girls in the Resistance movements, some of them true, and some of them, I'm afraid, invented.'[72] Suffering under the Nazis, the keynote according to Mitzi, of her European family's war experience, is displaced by the derring-do of Resistance heroines, eliding the fact that a number of these, including, as I have shown, British female agents of the Special Operations Executive, ended their days in Ravensbrück or Dachau. Marple's admitted fabrication in the service of solving the case is distinguished from the ingrained tendency to exaggerate by which Mitzi is characterized, even though both are attempts by socially marginalized figures—Mitzi the refugee, Marple the older female—to woo the listener into sympathy with their world-view. Where Wentworth and Rutland attempt to create for the reader some sense of what it might feel like for a refugee to be confronted, in their new home, with a stark reminder of the brutality they have escaped, Mitzi's past, the moment when she really did risk '*everything*', remains opaque.

Uncovering the Remains: Ellis Peters's *Fallen into the Pit* (1951)

A Murder Is Announced was Christie's forty-third novel, and although she was certainly willing, especially during and in the wake of the Second World War, to incorporate social commentary into her fiction, by the 1950s, she was competing with a new wave of detective authors who adopted a largely different approach. Many works from the later 1940s and 1950s do not presume that the threat of fascism has ended with the ending of the war. The 'thriller'

---

[70] Christie, *A Murder Is Announced*, p. 229.
[71] Christie, *A Murder Is Announced*, p. 230.
[72] Christie, *A Murder Is Announced*, p. 249.

elements that had proved apt during wartime were not simply be deaccessioned, and the place of professional, as opposed to amateur, investigator, increased in prominence. A comparison can be made between *A Murder Is Announced* and Ellis Peters's *Fallen into the Pit* (1951), the first in what would become a series with a professional policeman, George Felse at its centre. The action of *Fallen into the Pit*, which also unfolds in a village, centres initially on the murder of Helmut Schauffler, a German former prisoner of war, and the plot opens out to encompass issues of pre-war marital discord and post-war land ownership. Peters's novel, like Christie's, situates the refugee character in a domestic setting, though Gerd is the wife of a farmer rather than an employee. She has a number of highly fraught encounters with Schauffler and is a suspect in his murder before Felse's attention shifts elsewhere.

Like many of her contemporaries, Peters centres on an investigation run by the police rather than by a private investigator. The structure of the novel is largely recognizable from earlier examples of the form: a closed world of suspects, in Peters's case in an invented village in the English-Welsh borders; a second murder that complicates the investigation of the first; a resolution that removes the guilty party without recourse to legal remedy, following the convention whereby the identification of the culprit by the investigator provides a guarantee of the culprit's guilt, regardless of standards of legal proof. Peters, however, is much more concerted than Christie in her attempt to locate the action at a specific historical moment, and, for part of the action at least, to focus on concerns that extend beyond the boundaries of Comerford, its fictional setting.

Unlike Christie, Peters is specific about her refugee character's national origins: Gerd Hollins is a pre-war refugee from Germany. While Peters to some extent shares Christie's tendency to gloss over the detail of what may or may not have happened to the family that the refugee has left behind, her depiction of Gerd is different from Christie's portrayal of Mitzi in at least two key respects. Especially near the start of the novel, Peters's third-person narration is sometimes focalized via Gerd, and, partly as a consequence of this, Gerd, like Frieda in *Blue Murder*, is a much more immediately sympathetic character than Mitzi. This is not to say that Peters avoids stereotyping in her depiction of Gerd: by including a German former prisoner of war, Helmut Schauffler, among the other inhabitants of the village, Peters provides herself with the opportunity to go out of the way to stress Gerd's attempts at forgiveness, attempts that are sorely tested by Schauffler's unrepentant antisemitism.

The depiction of Schauffler itself draws on particular wartime and post-war stereotypes. He is not only 'blond' but 'blond as a chorus-girl', a comparison indicating that he is of Aryan stock while pointing towards degenerate effeminacy. He is a figure who provokes ambivalence on the part of George Felse, the sergeant on the case; his sentiments about Schauffler echo Arthur Rowe' reaction to Willi Hilfe: '[Schauffler] should, thought George, be a pretty impressive specimen when on his feet, broad-shouldered and narrow-flanked [...] His English was interestingly broken.'[73] Felse's opportunity to scrutinize Schauffler comes about when the young man gets into a fight with one of the locals, after being seen giving a Nazi salute, a gesture he claims has no meaning for him other than to signify the effects of his early life and upbringing: 'Never have I been a Nazi, only one must conform [...] I am young, I do as I am taught.'[74] Peters's introduction into the novel of contemporary debates about whether Nazis can be re-educated, and if so, how, is undermined by the fact that Schauffler is evidently being disingenuous when he makes this comment. After his involvement in the fight, he has to be moved to work on a different farm, and Gerd persuades her husband to offer him employment, framing this as a way for her to 'get used to the idea that Germans are much the same as other flesh and blood.'[75] But this experiment ends disastrously when Schauffler unleashes antisemitic invective at Gerd, and after Schauffler is murdered, there are initially suspicions that this might be an act of revenge on the part of either Gerd or her husband.

The reader is told that Gerd fled Germany in 1937 and hoped that her family would follow:

but nobody ever came. [...] Long after she had married Christopher Hollins she had gone on hoping and believing that the others would turn up, after the war; and after the war she had traced at least her youngest brother, but to a cardboard box of ashes on a shelf in a room of the crematorium of Osviecim [sic]. And that was all.[76]

Not even a body, then, but only a box of ashes, albeit an apparently individuated one, attributable to her brother. It is striking that Peters conjures this curious, sparse, almost antiseptic image rather than, for instance, alluding to the images of corpses that Gerd (and Peters's original readers) might

---

[73] Ellis Peters, *Fallen into the Pit* (1951; London: Futura 1991), p. 28.
[74] Peters, *Fallen*, p. 28.
[75] Peters, *Fallen*, p. 33.
[76] Peters, *Fallen*, p. 31.

have been expected to see in magazines and newsreels at the war's end.[77] Her attempt at transcribing 'Oświęcim', the Polish name of Auschwitz, while prompted by an urge to authenticity, serves to distance this place further from the anglophone reader. One explanation for this indirect treatment of the death of Gerd's family members, to which I will return later, is that in this kind of novel, there is only room for certain kinds of body.

Schauffler's threats to Gerd, when he approaches her in the farm kitchen, are based on the notion that England is not the safe haven it might seem to be:

> 'Do you think even the English do not tire at last? There are some who are tired already of harbouring you [...] You hear already, but a Jew crawls away only when he must. Even when you kick him out at the door he creeps in by the window again. [...] Even in this nice country', he whispered, with a stupid little giggling breath of excitement and pleasure in her ear, 'you will wear here, some day, a yellow star'.[78]

Peters's insertion of explicit antisemitic sentiments into the narrative contrasts with Christie's 'playful' use of stereotypes in the depiction of Mitzi. It is notable, however, that it is another outsider, indeed a Nazi, who voices these sentiments. Peters avoids the more extreme shock that is found at the end of *Blue Murder*, when an 'insider' is revealed to be not only a murderer but a racist one who appears to have completely evaded justice.

Gerd's passivity in the face of Schauffler's words—she does not speak, and does not further withdraw herself from Schauffler's presence when he approaches close to her—is underscored by her reflections once he has left her:

> She seemed to be contemplating some domestic complication such as the next week's grocery order. What she was actually seeing was a long, dark earth corridor, and six people walking down it, father, mother, Walter, Hans, Frieda, Josef; and at the end of it as crematorium trolley into which, one by one, they quietly climbed and vanished.[79]

---

[77] Similarly, in *Operation Pax*, on meeting his elderly landlady, Kolmak reflects: 'Because she was feeble and useless old woman, she conjured up in his mind the image of a gas chamber. It hung behind her now, a frame to the scant wisps of her silver hair' (p. 93). His heartless characterization of the woman as 'feeble' and the fact that at this point in the narrative his own political allegiance is not clear, adds to the shock of a 'gas chamber' materializing in a North Oxford hallway.

[78] Peters, *Fallen*, p. 37.

[79] Peters, *Fallen*, p. 38.

The conjunction of Gerd's domestic concerns with her imagining of her family's fate invites a parallel between her passivity in the face of Schauffler's bullying and the (presumed) passivity of her family, and by extension other Jews, in the hands of the Nazis: 'they quietly [...] vanished'. Gerd has chosen not to rise to Schauffler's taunts but pictures the most extreme outcome of this attitude. Although Gerd's family, unlike Mitzi's, do at least have names, the precise nature of what became of them, the fate that Schauffler implies could await Gerd too, is only hinted at, perhaps to signal Gerd's own inability or unwillingness to confront directly what her family might have gone through, perhaps because any more precise evocation would rupture the narrative irreparably. If detective fiction is about containing and controlling death, how can it control and contain those particular deaths?[80] In fact, the most explicit depiction of a dead body in this novel and the one most evocative of the Holocaust is the one that is ostensibly furthest removed from those events.

The murder of Schauffler and the subsequent killing of Charles Blunden turn out to be the responsibility of Selwyn Blunden, Charles's father and a local landowner and magistrate, and are part of a plan on his part to keep concealed his earlier murder of his wife, committed in 1941. She was believed locally to have left her husband for another man. This murder, the first in the chronological sequence, is not revealed until the very final pages of the novel, after Blunden has died while in prison awaiting trial. His wife's corpse, dug up in a field that Blunden had protected from excavation, is described in terms which are graphic, especially when compared with those used to depict Schauffler's and Charles's remains. Schauffler's body is discovered semisubmerged in an underground pool, by Felse's teenaged son Dominic, who has been undertaking some amateur sleuthing, and, like his father, Dominic seems to find Schauffler, even in death, strangely attractive:

Pale things at this hour had a lambent light of their own, and the back of the blond head, breaking the surface with a wave of thick fair hair, was the

---

[80] Notably, in the final volume of her trilogy about a serving soldier, published in 1947 under her real name, Edith Pargeter, the author gives a detailed account of her protagonist's involvement in the relief effort at an unnamed camp in Germany, though the prisoners are not specified as Jewish. See *Warfare Accomplished* (1947; London: Headline 1990), pp. 287–311. Pargeter visited Czechoslovakia with the WEA during 1947, travelling across Europe by train, and for the rest of her life maintained a strong interest in Czech culture and affairs. Her translation from Czech of Josef Bor's account of a performance of Verdi's requiem at Theresienstadt was published as *The Terezín Requiem* (1963).

first alien thing he had seen, and fascinated him still [...] He lay there half-obscured by the cloudy, ochreous quality of the water, which reddened him all over, all but the patch of fair hair.[81]

Schauffler's body matches Plain's definition of the 'sacrificial' corpse, 'the body made safe'.[82] Not only is the narration sparing in the description of Schauffler's head wound, focusing instead on his iconic fair hair, but he is framed as easily dispensed with. There is a surfeit of potential culprits, and the possibility that he, too, might have a grieving family is not entered into.

Charles's death is more disruptive from the perspective of the coherence of the village community, not least because he is initially thought to have committed suicide. As Felse reports laconically to Dominic, Charles is found 'in the woods there, with his own shot-gun lying by him, and both barrels in him'.[83] This indirect account serves its purpose. Charles's death, like many second deaths in detective novels, is a means of ruling out certain narrative possibilities and eventually sets the course for the identification of Selwyn Blunden as the person responsible for both his son's and Schauffler's deaths. Blunden's position as a landowner and a Justice of the Peace makes his act of filicide all the more troubling, and his removal from the village community can be read as symbolic of the cementing of a new, more egalitarian, post-war social order. The discovery of the final body, however, goes some way towards complicating this conclusion.

The description of the remains of Blunden's late wife, which have been buried for about ten years, is graphic even by the standards of what Plain calls the semiotic body, the body that bears the 'uncomfortable trace of authentically shocking violence'.[84] The fact that the reader is presented with this corpse so late on in the narrative is also unusual, limiting as it does the space available for explaining or 'making safe' this discovery:

There she lay, a short, tumbled skeleton, falling apart here and there in the dirty folds of cloth which had now only slight variations from the universal dirt-colour of buried things, among the soil and gravel and brick [... .] A few fragments of skin still adhering to the skull, and masses of matted hair.

[81] Peters, *Fallen*, p. 75.
[82] Plain, *Twentieth-Century Crime Fiction*, p. 33.
[83] Peters, *Fallen*, p. 207.
[84] Plain, *Twentieth-Century Crime Fiction*, p. 38.

Front teeth touched with distinctive goldwork standing forward in the jaw;
and two things round her neck, a necklet of carved imitation stones and a
twisted wire. Loose enough now, but once it must have been tight round a
plump, soft throat.[85]

The disrupted syntax gives the impression of the viewer, Felse, glancing from
one detail to another, and evokes a bureaucratic listing of 'distinguishing features'. As such it invites the reader to both 'see' and not see what is described.
The effect here is quite different from the earlier focus on Schauffler's blond
hair, a detail which links the discovered body with the individual as he was in
life, and which underlines his reduction to a stereotype. Blunden's nameless
wife only appears in the narrative in either mediated form—earlier, Felse has
seen a photograph of her wearing the necklace that he recognizes here—or
in fragments.

Interpreting this description as an occluded reference to the bodies of
Holocaust victims could, of course, be seen as a case of confirmation bias
on my part. It is exceedingly difficult to know whether a reader in 1951
would have made a link between the 'goldwork' on the victim's teeth and
the removal of dental gold by the Nazis as present-day reader might. I think
this is a plausible reading precisely because of the veering away from the
description of Nazi crimes that occurs elsewhere in the novel. This description supplements both Gerd's impressionistic reflections on the possible fate
of her family and Schauffler's racist rants. The Holocaust did not happen
here, Peters acknowledges, but we must nevertheless make some reckoning with it. By placing this discovery so close to the end of the novel and
indeed identifying the victim only in the final line of the text, Peters fore-
closes the possibility of reparation that Plain sees as characteristic even of
the most graphic depictions of the body in detective fiction. Although the
discovery of this final body provides an explanation for the earlier murders, it is itself simply presented for the reader to contemplate, implying
that it, and what it represents, exceeds the scope of the narrative. This discovery, ostensibly unconnected with the Holocaust, can be contrasted with
how Christie presents the attempt on Mitzi's life in A Murder is Announced.
Christie diverts her reader away from considering the actual danger that
Mitzi or her family might have confronted in a way that throws into relief

[85] Peters, Fallen, p. 277.

Peters's more nuanced treatment of the legacy of the Holocaust in post-war Britain. Peters's depiction of Gerd is certainly not without its problems, but *Fallen into the Pit* is a bold attempt to incorporate the troubling legacies of the war in Europe into a popular narrative form.[86]

Still Fighting Fascism

Peters uses the unrepentant former prisoner of war as a figure for the difficulties of reinstating democracy in war's aftermath, but domestic fascism or individual British subjects' collaboration with the Nazis feature far more frequently in post-war detective fiction than individuals of Helmut Schauffler's type, partly at least because these novels tend to choose English settings. In some examples, it is possible to identify references to figures or kinds of figure who would have been familiar to a contemporary readership. For instance, in Christianna Brand's *Green for Danger* (1945), which centres on a murder that takes place at a hospital late in the war, the suspicious behaviour of Nurse Woods leads to her becoming a murder suspect, until it transpires that she is in fact simply trying to keep hidden the fact that her brother has been making propaganda broadcasts from the continent on behalf of the Nazis. A patient has noticed the similarity between the nurse's voice and that of her brother, whose broadcast he was listening to when the house he was in was bombed. This plot point is a reference to individuals including most notably William Joyce who did indeed make radio broadcasts from Germany. Joyce is referred to in the text by Nurse Woods, who uses the nickname that would have been familiar to the novel's first readers: 'I mean, a bit off to have to lie pinned down by debris, heroically waiting to be rescued, while Lord Haw-Haw tells you how effete you are.'[87] Nurse Woods's mention of Joyce, who, as I discussed in Chapter 2, was later tried, found guilty, and executed for treason, turns out to be a piece of misdirection on

---

[86] Peters's decision to allow the reader access to Gerd's perspective can be compared to a later example, John Le Carré's *Call for the Dead* (1961; London: Penguin, 2012), in which George Smiley, investigating the murder of Samuel Fennon, a civil servant suspected of spying, meets his widow, Elsa, a Jewish survivor of the camps: '[Her's] was a worn face, racked and ravaged long ago, the face of a child grown old on starving and exhaustion, the eternal refugee face, the prison-camp face, thought Smiley' (p. 19). Smiley eventually realizes that his initial construction of Elsa as a figure to be pitied has blinded him to her own duplicity: 'He had been the fool of his own sentiment' (p. 116). Although Elsa seems here to be elevated from being a type to being an individual, her duplicity and single-mindedness in support of an ideology are not constructed as admirable, and she is killed by her handler before she can be uncovered.

[87] Christianna Brand, *Green for Danger* (1945; London: Pan, 1999), p. 165.

her part, and is intended to help conceal her own brother's treachery.[88] But Nurse Woods's shame about her family connection to a traitor, or what she describes as her 'ugly secret', is a blind for the real murder motive, which centres on the supposed inadequacies of those involved in rescuing and treating people trapped after bombing raids.[89] Brand introduces a critique of the supposedly united and irreproachable Home Front war effort, suggesting that propaganda broadcasts were only the most explicit means by which civilian morale could be undermined, although the culprit, Esther, who evades justice by taking her own life, is described as having been 'knock[ed] right over the edge, into real insanity' by her mother's death after an air-raid, a loss for which she blames the ARP.[90]

Many detective novels from the late 1940s are more explicit in reflecting concerns about the resurgence of British fascism in the wake of the war than there are in exploring the fate of Holocaust survivors. In this regard, they echo the preoccupations of earlier texts, such as Nicholas Blake's *The Smiler with the Knife* (1939), in which the plot is constructed around the potential for British fascists to work in collaboration with the Nazis. Whether or not this was ever an intention of Oswald Mosley's British Union of Fascists, who, as Daniel Sonabend points out, 'considered themselves to be patriots who would never take the side of another country against their own', Mosley and other BUF members were subject to internment after Defence Regulation 18B, the same legislation that allowed for the internment of enemy aliens, was extended.[91] This allowed the detention of:

> [...] anyone who [the Home Secretary] had reasonable cause to believe was, or had been, a member of, or active in the furtherance of the objects of, any organisation which was either subject to foreign influence or control, or whose leadership had associations with persons in the government of, or had sympathy with, the system of government of, any power with which Britain was at war.[92]

By August 1940, 1450 individuals were being held under these powers. Some of these were short-term detentions, and the figure had fallen to 529 by

---

[88] Brand's novel is set while the war is still in progress and was published in April 1945, prior to William Joyce's arrest (in May 1945) and execution (in January 1946).

[89] Brand, *Green for Danger*, p. 205.

[90] Brand, *Green for Danger*, p. 249.

[91] Daniel Sonabend, *We Fight Fascists: The 43 Group and Their Forgotten Battle for Post-War Britain* (London: Verso, 2019), p. 17.

[92] Stammers, *Civil Liberties*, p. 64.

July 1942.[93] Amid political protests, Mosley was released from internment in November 1943, on the grounds of ill-health; his movements and political activities remained restricted.[94] After the end of the war, Mosley attempted to revive his political career through a variety of fora: 'Four separate movements, the 18b detainees' aid fund, the League of ex-Servicemen, The Union of British Freemen and the Mosley Book Clubs [...] coalesced in the [United Movement] in February 1948', when Mosley finally re-emerged into the spotlight.[95] This development was met with violent opposition from the 43 Group, comprised largely of former servicemen.[96]

Regulation 18B was well-enough known for Gladys Mitchell to presume that readers of *Tom Brown's Body* (1949) would understand the implications of Conway, a school master, having been 'held under 18B for a bit at the beginning of the war'.[97] Evidently this has not ruled out the continuance of Conway's teaching career, though one of his colleagues later asserts that he only worked with Conway on sufferance: 'I was against [Conway's appointment] from the first, and I told the governors so. An 18B man has no place, in my opinion, in a school of any type.'[98] Certainly Conway's experience of internment has not tempered his antisemitism. But the reason his attitudes come under scrutiny is because a murder investigation is launched after his death. Conway is described as having 'baited' Issacher, a Jewish pupil at the school, and Issacher therefore comes under suspicion. Indeed, Mitchell does not depict Issacher as a paragon either. Another of the teachers tells Mitchell's investigator, Mrs Bradley: 'I'm afraid [Isaacher]'s had an unsatisfactory life, and then, even the best of Jews are upset by the trouble in Palestine, I believe. I don't like the boy as a boy; I'm sorry for him, though.'[99] What is meant here by 'the best of Jews' is unclear; from the context it could imply 'assimilated'. Equally 'upset' could refer not to the emotions of the Jews

---

[93] Stammers, *Civil Liberties*, p. 67.

[94] Richard Thurlow, *Fascism in Britain: From Oswald Mosley's Blackshirts to the National Front* (London: IB Tauris, 1998), p. 200–01.

[95] Thurlow, *Fascism in Britain*, p. 213.

[96] See Sonabend, *We Fight Fascists*, or for an account of their activities by one of their founder-members, Morris Beckman, *The 43 Group: Battling with Mosley's Blackshirts* (1992; London: The History Press, 2013).

[97] Gladys Mitchell, *Tom Brown's Body* (1949; London: Vintage, 2009), p. 116.

[98] Mitchell, *Tom Brown's Body*, p. 200. Discussing the career of Jeffrey Hamm, a former schoolteacher who was detained under 18B, Sonabend comments: 'with his ex-18B status, getting a position as a teacher was always going to be out of the question for Hamm', though this refers to the situation in 1944. Sonabend, *We Fight Fascists*, p. 24. By introducing a dissenting voice, Mitchell certainly indicates that having been held under 18B will have had some impact on Conway's employment prospects.

[99] Gladys Mitchell, *Tom Brown's Body*, p. 116.

themselves but to how others behave towards them. By this reading, all Jews have to take some responsibility for the violence against British servicemen in Palestine during the period prior to the withdrawal of Britain from the territory in May 1948.[100] Issacher is a reminder that not all Jews who appear in detective fiction at this period are identified as refugees (just as not all refugees are, either explicitly or implicitly, identified as Jews). It is notable that he is here linked not to Jewish victims but to Jewish aggressors, an alignment that fits with his identification as a potential suspect but over-simplifies British Jewish subjectivity.

Mitchell's novel shows that a focus on the re-emergence of fascism in postwar Britain tends to shift attention away from the Nazis' treatment of the Jews, as do allusions to Jewish violence in Palestine. Refiguring the Jews as aggressors, or even, as in Isaacher's case, ordinarily flawed individuals, is one way of evading stereotypes of Jewish victimhood, but only at the cost of perpetuating the idea that antisemitism could in some way be justified by the violent actions of the Jews themselves. A more complex example is Cyril Hare's *An English Murder* (1951), in which a Holocaust survivor and a fascist are brought face to face in an archetypal 'closed society', the isolated country house at Christmastime. Wenceslaus Bottwink, a professor of History, is undertaking research in the unheated muniment room at Warbeck Hall: 'He was accustomed to cold. It had been cold in his student's lodgings in Heidelberg, colder yet in Prague in the winter of 1918, coldest of all in the concentration camps of the Third Reich.'[101] This sentence condenses Bottwink's European life-story; it ventures as far as the concentration camp only to withdraw immediately to the safety of the muniment room. The grammar of the sentence in fact serves to place a distance between Bottwink and each of these places: the reader is told that 'it had been cold', not that 'he had been cold', and the phrase 'the concentration camps of the Third Reich' is much more generalized in its effect than if individual camps had been named.

But Bottwink's experiences in the camps are less important for the plot than the reason for him having been sent there, his Jewishness, which

---

[100] The abduction and murder of Clifford Martin and Mervyn Paice, whose bodies were discovered hanging in an orange grove in July 1947, is often considered to have prompted anti-Jewish riots in Britain. Tony Kushner argues that pre-existing attitudes towards Jews in Britain and particularly 'the image of the Jew at home as the economic "other"' were the 'root basis of so much of the riots themselves', and he also notes that, much later, it emerged that Clifford Martin 'was actually Jewish'. 'Anti-Semitism and Austerity: The August 1947 Riots', in *Racial Violence in Britain, 1840–1950*, edited by Panikos Panayi (Leicester: University of Leicester Press, 1993), pp. 149–68 (p. 164).

[101] Cyril Hare, *An English Murder* (London: Hogarth, 1987 [1951]), p. 7.

emerges when he encounters Robert Warbeck, heir to the estate and leader of the 'League of Liberty and Justice'. Before Robert even meets Bottwink, he deduces from the man's name that he is 'a Jew boy'.[102] When Bottwink mentions that coldness of the muniment room as a way of making conversation, Robert's response presses Bottwink to give an account of his origins:

> 'No doubt you found it colder in your own country', [Robert] said slowly. 'What is your country, may I ask?'
>   In the face of his studied rudeness Dr Bottwink became perfectly calm again.
>   'That would be a little difficult to say exactly', he replied. 'By nationality, I have been Austrian and Czech and German—in that order. But I am a bit Russian also, and it so happens that I was born in Hungary. So there are a good many ingredients in my make-up.'
>   'Including Jewish ingredients, I suppose?'
>   'Of course', said Dr Bottwink, with a polite smile.[103]

As in Peters's novel, it behoves the Jew to exercise forbearance even in the face of explicit prejudice. Once Robert leaves the room his father apologizes for his behaviour, which has compounded Bottwink's uncertainty about his position in the house over the holiday; he has already expressed doubts about whether it is appropriate for him to dine with the family. Certainly, Bottwink is much more highly attuned than even the more sympathetic members of the household to 'complex power dynamic' that Cooper sees as characterizing relations between refugee guests and hosts.[104] Later, taunting his cousin Camilla, Robert refers to Bottwink as her 'new friend': 'Has he asked you to go back to Palestine with him yet?'[105] Internal evidence points to the action of the novel taking place after the ending of the British Mandate, and Robert here appears to support a Jewish homeland as a convenient means of excluding Jews, especially post-war arrivals like Bottwink, from Britain.

The house in which the action unfolds encodes Robert's own origins. Although he is not permanently resident there, his main home being in London, he evinces a sentimental allegiance to the concepts of heritage and family that the house appears to represent. His second cousin Julius, also

---

[102]   Hare, *An English Murder*, p. 30.
[103]   Hare, *An English Murder*, p. 38.
[104]   Cooper, 'Figures on the Threshold', p. 193.
[105]   Hare, *An English Murder*, p. 48.

at Warbeck for Christmas, is Chancellor of the Exchequer in the Labour government and is a focus of Robert's resentment because of his party's modernizing aims: 'The last Christmas in the old home—thanks to Cousin Julius and his pack of robbers!'[106] By the time he proposes this toast, Robert is drunk, reminding Bottwink of the times he has seen 'other men who had professed principles not so very different from those of the League of Liberty and Justice, who had been noisy and genial in their cups, and had thereafter committed crimes beyond all reckoning'.[107] In its conjunction of the quotidian and the threatening, the phrase 'genial in their cups' echoes Willi Hilfe's observation that 'people you had sat next to at dinner' could turn out to be murderers, but before Robert can become any more of a threat, he is poisoned.

In the wake of Robert's death, Bottwink reflects, 'In less-favoured countries anything of this nature might be expected to have a political flavour—political repercussions, even.'[108] Any political rationale that might be discerned for Robert's death is immediately compounded by his unpleasantness in his personal relations: it is discovered, for instance, that he has secretly married Susan, the daughter of Warbeck Hall's butler, and has a son by her, but that he refuses to acknowledge or support the child. This personal failing provides another motive, just as Robert's antisemitism means that Bottwink comes under suspicion. Ultimately, after two further deaths, Bottwink identifies both the culprit and the actual motive. Another of the house guests, Mrs Carstairs, is the wife of one of Julius's colleagues, and, knowing that if Julius inherits his uncle's title, he will have to give up the post of Chancellor, she kills both Lord Warbeck and Robert so that this will indeed happen, and her husband will himself be able to become Chancellor. However, Mrs Carstairs does not bargain for the fact that Robert and Susan have a son, and she takes her own life once she realizes that this child will in fact inherit the title and so her plan will not succeed unless he too is killed; infanticide remains beyond the pale. The solution to the puzzle therefore twines together the personal and the political. Although Robert's death was not politically motivated and, according to Julius at least, his movement has no chance of having an impact in Britain, in another way, the death was indeed a political act, because his removal could have helped in the achievement of Carstairs's political ambitions.

[106] Hare, *An English Murder*, p. 69.
[107] Hare, *An English Murder*, p. 64.
[108] Hare, *An English Murder*, p. 89.

It is Bottwink, the outsider, who deploys his knowledge of the peculiarities of English constitutional conventions, to deduce the motive.[109] In the process, he proves himself to be a valuable contributor to the both the 'closed society' of the country house where the murders take place and to British society as a whole. He earns the right to belong. Underpinning Hare's largely sympathetic and positive depiction of the immigrant survivor is the sense, identifiable in other novels I have discussed here, that such individuals must be in some way exceptional in order to earn the right to remain. Bottwink is at times baffled by the unwritten rules of behaviour, customs, and idioms of the household, but he nevertheless wants to respect and understand them. The details of the events that have led to him being in England are never specified. But as I have suggested, this indicates the extent to which life-stories involving concentration camps and displacement between European countries were taken as read at this period. To say that a character has been in a 'concentration camp' seems almost akin to saying that they have been 'up at Oxford': even readers who have no direct experience of these places will deploy a variety of pre-existing cultural knowledge, including their prior reading of works of fiction, to decode such metonymies. The character of these two experiences is of course utterly divergent, but at this period, these two formulations could have similar narrative functions. In each case, the relationship between the metonymy and the experience it condenses is a reductive one. What happens in these novels is similar to the 'swerve' away from the depiction of evil that Robert Eaglestone identifies in much more recent fictional treatments of Holocaust perpetrators. A number of the texts that he discusses substitute other kinds of evil for the evil of genocide even while seeming to thematize the Holocaust itself.[110] In this context, the inclusion of individuals who have fled persecution, rather than being identified specifically as Holocaust survivors, is itself a form of engagement that is an avoidance of engagement. The question of genre is a factor here. To suggest that detective fiction as a form is simply inadequate as a means of representing the Holocaust would be to impose unhelpful

---

[109] D. W. Hayton identifies the historian Lewis Namier as a model for Bottwink, identifying the 'recherché nature' of Bottwink's research, as well as his European origin, as 'points of contact', though he omits to mention that Bottwink, unlike Namier, is a survivor of the camps. For Hayton, the echo of Namier in the depiction of Bottwink is a sign of Namier's status as a public figure at this period. D. W. Hayton, *Conservative Revolutionary: The Lives of Lewis Namier* (Manchester: Manchester University Press, 2019), p. 339.

[110] Robert Eaglestone, 'Avoiding Evil in Perpetrator Fiction', in *Representing Perpetrators in Holocaust Literature and Film*, edited by Jenni Adams and Sue Vice (London: Vallentine Mitchell 2013), pp. 13–24.

limitations on what constitutes 'proper' representation. What might now seem like unhelpful or ill-informed attempts at engaging with the Holocaust nevertheless warrant consideration as part of the early effort, uneven and inadequate as it often now appears, to reckon with the legacy of Nazism. Further, the disturbance of the usual forms of detective fiction that is effected by attempts to incorporate this legacy indicates the extent to which these 'usual forms' were themselves in flux at this period. While the reconstruction of the stories of the victims are at the heart of detective fiction, such texts, as these novels show, are also about community, and how communities may be regulated and made safe. The authors considered here engage in a wide variety of ways with the dead, and present very different images of what survival might mean in post-war Britain, and indeed, post-war Europe.

Conclusion
Debating Capital Punishment

Crime, especially the types of crimes I have been discussing here, can have consequences even for those who do not consider themselves to be either perpetrators or victims, not least because of the radical instability of these categories. Even when criminal activity is only known about via newspapers reports, memoirs, or novels, it can still be powerfully affective. Crime happens within communities and reactions to crime are one of the ways in which communities define themselves. This is in part what underlies Alan Moorehead's comment, after his April 1945 visit to Belsen: 'This touches me and I am responsible.'[1] Though focusing on himself as a singular individual, Moorehead identifies as part of the community from which these crimes emerged and which will have to reckon with their consequences. But as I will show, many commentators in the decades following the war, while acknowledging that the Nazis' crimes were without parallel, were concerned that the kinds of representations I have been discussing brought those crimes too close for comfort.

To conclude this book, I consider how, in the aftermath of the Second World War, war crimes were made a point of reference in protracted debates about the abolition of capital punishment in Britain. A key example here will be Victor Gollancz's writing on this topic. Gollancz's visits to Germany in the months following the end of the war included a trip to Belsen, but, like Derrick Sington, he critiqued how the Belsen Trial was reported in the British press and warned against the dangers of continuing to dwell on Nazi crimes, especially when, in his view, this led to the demonization of the German civilian population. In common with others who opposed capital punishment, including, for instance, Viscount Templewood whose pro-abolition essay he published, Gollancz made a connection between brutality in war and capital punishment at home. Writing in 1951, Templewood suggested that 'the very extent of the crimes against humanity begins to blunt the reaction against them. [...] With every new exposure to some devilish

---

[1] Alan Moorehead, 'Glimpses of Germany II—Belsen', *Horizon* 12.67 (July 1945): pp. 26–35 (p. 31).

Literature and Justice in Mid-Twentieth-Century Britain. Victoria Stewart, Oxford University Press.
© Victoria Stewart (2023). DOI: 10.1093/oso/9780192858238.003.0006

form of savagery, the public mind becomes less sensitive.'[2] Gollancz noted in particular that representations of war crimes trials in the press could prompt prurient interest. In Gollancz's view, war crimes trials were purely retributive, and, according to Aimee Bunting, he felt that they 'shifted [...] Allied thinking away from the suffering of the Jews to the criminality of the Nazis themselves.'[3] Like Templewood, then, Gollancz believed that modes of representation were a crucial factor in shaping public attitudes. During the early 1960s, Gollancz again picked up some of these themes in an essay that argued against Adolf Eichmann being put on trial and incorporated a restatement of his objections to the death penalty. Here, as in post-war parliamentary debates, the perpetrators of Nazi crimes are seen as the ultimate test-case for capital punishment as a practice.

Other commentators shared Gollancz's concerns with how the Nazis' crimes and the trials that dealt with them had been depicted in the press and elsewhere. These concerns could emerge even when war crimes trials were not the main focus of attention. For example, the idea that there might be a 'proper' way of representing the Nazis and their crimes emerges in the mid-1960s writings of novelist and journalist Pamela Hansford Johnson, especially her 1967 account of the trial of Ian Brady and Myra Hindley, which took place during the period when capital punishment was suspended in Britain prior to its abolition.[4] Brady was found guilty of three murders, and Hindley of two, with Hindley convicted of the additional charge of harbouring Brady in the knowledge that he was a murderer. Both during the trial and in the wake of the verdict, it emerged that one of the bonds between the pair was an interest in the Nazis.[5] This was seen by Hansford Johnson as evidence that individuals could be brutalized by exposure to inappropriate representations of Nazi crimes, an idea that, as Templewood's comments indicate, had emerged in earlier debates about capital punishment. Given

[2] Viscount Templewood, *The Shadow of the Gallows* (London: Victor Gollancz, 1951), p. 11. Viscount Templewood (Samuel Hoare) was Conservative Home Secretary when the 1938 Criminal Justice Bill was drawn up and entered the House of Lords in 1945.

[3] Aimee Bunting, 'Britain and the Holocaust: Then and Now', unpublished PhD thesis (Southampton: University of Southampton, 2006), p. 41

[4] Capital punishment for murder was suspended in 1965 and finally abolished in 1969. Brady and Hindley were tried in 1966 for crimes that had taken place between 1963 and 1965.

[5] During the trial, more emphasis was placed on Brady's reading of the Marquis de Sade than on his interest in Nazism. According to journalist Maurice Richardson, who attended the trial, the prosecution decided to 'play down' Brady's 'passion for the Nazis' in order not to 'appear to be overloading their case with politics'. 'What is one to make of the Moors Murderers?' *Observer*, 8 May 1966, p. 21. The term *Moors Murderers* was used to refer to Brady and Hindley because they buried the bodies of their victims on Saddleworth Moor, near Manchester where they both lived.

that the books that Brady owned were widely available, this raised for Hansford Johnson the issue of whether such material should be subject to censorship. The question, then, for both Gollancz and Hansford Johnson is: what purpose might a knowledge of Nazi crimes serve? The sense that these crimes, and the ways they were often represented, were so distasteful that nothing could be learned from them was cemented, in the British context, by coverage of Brady and Hindley's trial which framed an interest in the Nazis, and by extension the Holocaust, as disreputable.

As I have argued elsewhere, it is a characteristic of court cases concerning crimes committed in a domestic setting that they bring to light actions and events that have occurred in private or secretly, some of which may provide context for the crime without being criminal themselves. Such revelations are one way in which observers at trials or readers of trial reports, reinforce their sense of what constitutes acceptable behaviour in their community.[6] The crimes of the Nazis prompt the question of how the establishment and calibration of social norms might operate internationally, at the level of 'civilization' (to use a term that crops up frequently in both Gollancz's and Hansford Johnson's work). There is little scope here for what James E. Young terms 'antiredemptive' representations, those that, as Matthew Boswell puts it, 'refuse affirmative explanations for art's purpose after atrocity', nor is there space for the idea that different forms of representation may not only compete with but rather supplement and complement each other.[7]

Debating Abolition in Post-War Britain

Discussing why capital punishment was not abolished by the Labour government in the years immediately following the Second World War, Victor Bailey suggests that this was partly because voting was left as matter of conscience for MPs, rather than there being a party line, but he also cites the influence of war crimes trials, especially the IMT: 'Nuremberg lent justification to a retributive approach to indigenous murder'.[8] In the 1947–1948 parliamentary debates on the Criminal Justice Bill, direct reference was

---

[6] Victoria Stewart, *Crime Writing in Interwar Britain: Fact and Fiction in the Golden Age* (Cambridge: Cambridge University Press, 2017), pp. 3–4.

[7] Matthew Boswell, *Holocaust Impiety in Literature, Popular Music and Film* (Basingstoke: Palgrave, 2012), p. 5.

[8] Victor Bailey, 'The Shadow of the Gallows: The Death Penalty and the British Labour Government, 1945–51', *Law and History Review* 18.2 (2000): pp. 305–49 (p. 310).

made to war crimes trials not least because a number of members of both Houses had been involved in either British-run trials or the IMT. In Bailey's view, a 'more influential' factor 'was the rise in officially recorded crime [in Britain] and the "moral panic" the figures generated'.[9] Given that the war itself was deemed to be a cause of this rise, however, these two issues were not entirely separate from each other.

A Criminal Justice Bill had been debated in 1938 but was dropped because of the war, and the Bill introduced in 1947, while intended to continue with the programme of the earlier Bill, did so in a new context. The new Bill focused on reforming the treatment of young and persistent offenders, with measures including the abolition of corporal punishment (though it could still be used in prisons), the removal of 'the anachronistic nomenclature of "hard labour" and "penal servitude"', and changes to the operation of the probation service. As Bailey puts it, the Bill 'aimed to eclipse the idea of retribution by further extending the principle that punishment should fit the criminal, not the crime'.[10] It contained no provision for the abolition of capital punishment.

Presenting the Bill in November 1947, Home Secretary James Chuter Ede explained why the government had made the decision not to pursue abolition, despite a five-year suspension of capital punishment having been part of the 1938 Bill. Citing statistics that indicated a rise in violent crime in the intervening years, he commented:

> Hitherto, it has been unusual for criminals engaged in [violent crimes] to carry lethal weapons, particularly fire-arms. There has, however, in the post-war period, been unwelcome evidence that a regrettable change has taken place in this respect. At the time when they have to deal with a phenomenal increase in the cases of violent crime and with the emergence of the armed criminal, the police forces are below establishment.[11]

Retaining capital punishment was presented by Chuter Ede as one way of attempting to reduce the tendency of criminals to go armed, and even a

[9] Bailey, 'The Shadow of the Gallows', p. 310.
[10] Bailey, 'The Shadow of the Gallows', p. 308.
[11] Hansard, HC debate, vol 444 col 2150, 27 November 1947. https://hansard.parliament. uk/commons. Accessed 27 August 2020. A case that was often cited in this connection was the murder of Alec de Antiquis, a passer-by who was shot when he attempted to intervene and stop three men who were fleeing after robbing a London jeweller's shop in April 1947. Christopher Geraghty, who fired the fatal shot, and Charles Jenkins, who was unarmed, were both hanged for de Antiquis's murder in September 1947.

temporary suspension was deemed by him to be too risky in the context he outlined. The subsequent debate, in both the Commons and the Lords, included discussion about whether capital punishment did indeed act as a deterrent to potential criminals in the way that Chuter Ede maintained, and comparisons were drawn with how other countries dealt with this issue. The alignment of capital punishment with antidemocratic attitudes was one theme that emerged. The day following Chuter Ede's comments, his fellow Labour MP Reginald Paget, claiming to be citing the views of the 'Fascist Minister of Justice', stated: 'Judicial execution is the ultimate subjugation of the individual to the State'. He continued: 'Let the dictators have their gallows and their axes, their firing squads and their lethal chambers. We, the citizens of a free democracy, do not have to shelter ourselves under the shadow of the gallows tree.'[12] He noted, as did other speakers, that fascist Italy was one of the few countries to have reintroduced the death penalty. In December 1947, a cross-party group led by veteran abolitionist Labour MP Sydney Silverman tabled a clause proposing the suspension of capital punishment for five years.[13]

Paget's suggestion that capital punishment could be considered unworthy of a democratic nation was given a different inflection by Silverman when the debate resumed in spring 1948 following the Bill's committee stages. In the context of recent events, Silverman reflected, the scale of the loss of life involved in incidences of capital punishment might seem negligible:

> [A]fter we have had two world wars with infinite loss of human life, after we have had the bombardment of cities and the wiping out of whole populations, after we have had new crimes committed against whole peoples for which we have had to invent new names, after such incidents as those of Hiroshima and Nagasaki—I suppose it may seem a very small matter whether half a dozen worthless human beings, who have themselves taken human life, should die or live.[14]

---

[12] Hansard, HC debate, vol 444, col 2304, 28 November 1947. https://hansard.parliamnet.uk/commons. Accessed 27 August 2020. In 1949, Paget would act as Defence Counsel for Field Marshal Erich von Manstein, a case that centred on the actions of the Einsatzgruppen (execution squads). Paget wrote about the case in *Manstein: His Campaigns and His Trial* (1951). See also Donald Bloxham, 'Punishing German Soldiers during the Cold War: The Case of Erich von Manstein', *Patterns of Prejudice* 33.4 (1999), 24–45.

[13] The proposal was for the abolition of capital punishment for murder. Sington and Playfair note that although Silverman supported absolute abolition, he 'disclosed that only twelve members [of Parliament] believed that the taking of human life by the State was unjustifiable in any circumstances'. Giles Playfair and Derrick Sington, *The Offenders: Society and the Atrocious Crime* (London: Secker & Warburg, 1957), p. 238.

[14] Hansard HC debate, vol 449, col 987, 14 April 1948. https://hansard.parliament.uk/commons. Accessed 27 August 2020.

Notably, Silverman brackets together actions that were carried out by the Allies and by the Axis powers (aerial bombardment), actions for which the Nazis were responsible (the new name in question presumably being 'genocide'), and actions undertaken by the Allies (the use of atomic weapons). Implicitly, these are moral equivalents, and the guilt is far from being all on one side. But equally important for Silverman is the other equivalence that is drawn here, between the mass deaths of war and the individual deaths that are a consequence of the continued existence of capital punishment. Simply because those latter deaths are fewer, they should not be seen as somehow less significant. If anything, for Silverman, they are more like the thin end of the wedge. As he continues: 'But, surely, it is the duty of all of us who value our civilisation not to depress still further those moral and spiritual values, but to seek to raise them, and to seek to raise them at precisely this moment when they are most in danger.'[15] Having entered the moral and spiritual abyss of wartime, it behoves those who 'value [...] civilisation' to hold, if anything, to a higher standard.

What problematized this type of parallel for some members of both Houses was the proximity of the 1947–1948 debates to the British-run war crimes trials and the IMT (which was then still hearing cases). One counterview was expressed by Conservative MP Quintin Hogg, who, rather than seeing the post-war moment as a chance for the recalibration of the country's moral compass, suggested that 'consistency' was important:

> We have just concluded a great world war, in which we took millions of human lives quite deliberately in order to protect things which we thought more valuable. [...] We have just been hanging our defeated enemies after the trials at Nuremberg. The Attorney-General [David Maxwell Fyfe], prosecuted them, not as an act of war but as an act of what was claimed to be justice. If we were going to say [...] that it was at all times and in all circumstances wrong to take human life, whatever evil doing the malefactor may have committed, then the time to say so was before Nuremberg and not immediately after.[16]

Hogg suggests that there is something cynical or at least opportunistic about arguments such as Silverman's being put forward at this point in time, implying that the Nazis executed at Nuremberg and elsewhere were

---

[15] Hansard HC debate, vol 449, col 987, 14 April 1948. https://hansard.parliament. uk/commons . Accessed 27 August 2020.

[16] Hansard HC debate, vol 449, col 1017, 14 April 1948. https://hansard.parliament.uk/ commons. Accessed 27 August 2020.

the exceptions who would otherwise have been a stumbling block to the abolitionists. War crimes trials are constructed not as an extension of the conduct of the war but instead an opportunity to lay down an appropriate judicial standard for post-war Europe. The question then, is whether war crimes trials can offer a viable point of reference for domestic judicial practice.

Two members of parliament who presented different views on the day Hogg spoke had been part of the British prosecuting team at Nuremberg. Elwyn Jones, a Labour MP who in 1949 would be a member of the prosecution team at the trial of Field Marshall Erich von Manstein and later, as attorney general, led the case against Brady and Hindley, described his time at Nuremberg as 'a particular duty which was imposed upon [him] and which [he] had the honour to accept', a form of words which echoes Winwood's description of the circumstances in which he came to defend Josef Kramer. Jones notes that then he was 'enforcing the law that was applicable' but that he speaks 'as a humble legislator, thinking that the law applicable to this country now should be altered', and that these 'two activities' are separate.[17] He refers to the scope of the Nazis' crimes and, echoing Paget, points out that, like fascist Italy, Nazi Germany reintroduced the death penalty: 'They relied on terror. Our democracy is a democracy that does not need the terror of the death penalty.'[18] What Jones does not directly address is the fact that the death penalty was imposed by the IMT itself; instead, he makes a connection between the crimes the IMT exposed (referring, for instance, to Höss's evidence about the treatment of prisoners at Auschwitz) and the Nazis' own use of the death penalty.

Where Jones saw the death penalty as of a part with antidemocratic 'terror', his fellow IMT-prosecutor David Maxwell Fyfe drew a different parallel, suggesting that the 'right to take life judicially in appropriate cases is the self-defence of the community' and is as 'logically and morally' justified as 'that right of self-defence by which members of the community are ordered to kill foreign enemies'.[19] Maxwell Fyfe thus turns inside out the argument made by abolitionists such as Silverman, who presented the deaths caused by both

[17] Hansard HC debate, vol 449, col 1066, 14 April 1948. https://hansard.parliament. uk/commons. Accessed 27 August 2020.
[18] Hansard HC debate, vol 449, col 1067, 14 April 1948. https://hansard/parliament.uk/ commons Accessed 27 August 2020. The Basic Law of the Federal Republic of Germany, which came into force in May 1949, abolished capital punishment.
[19] Hansard HC debate, vol 449, col 1076, 14 April 1948. https://hansard.parliament.uk/ commons. Accessed 27 August 2020.

sides in the recent war as an indication that the values of the 'community' needed realigning. For Maxwell Fyfe, both war and the death penalty are justifiable forms of self-protection, and the question of scale or proportionality is an irrelevance.

While their experiences as prosecutors at Nuremberg gave Jones and Maxwell Fyfe particular perspectives on Nazi war crimes, other speakers in these debates had different types of experience that coloured their views. In the Lords, Lord Douglas explained that as Military Governor in charge of the Allied Control Commission courts in occupied Germany, he had been responsible for overseeing 'several hundred death sentences, not only [...] on war criminals, but also [...] on Allied nationals'. The 'magnitude of the legal slaughter involved' was a factor leading to his resignation from the role, though he nevertheless did not move to an abolitionist position, saying that he was unconvinced by the arguments on that side of the debate.[20] Personal experience of this kind could result in quite a different response. Lord Raglan, recalling his time as an Inspector in South Sudan, noted that having direct contact with prisoners in custody awaiting execution and indeed having to organise the execution itself had led him to conclude that the hanging was a 'preposterous anachronism.'[21]

Comments such as these, as well as reflections on whether retention might damage Britain's image in the eyes of the international community, indicate that, notwithstanding the influence of the war crimes trials, there was always going to be an international or intercultural aspect to debates about abolition. As in Playfair and Sington's work in the 1950s, other European countries and America were looked to as points of reference, and the Royal Commission into capital punishment that was established under the chairmanship of Sir Ernest Gowers in the wake of the 1948 Act, as a means of giving closer scrutiny to the issues relating to how murder was defined and dealt with, considered international practice during its deliberations. The nature of the engagement with war crimes trials in these parliamentary debates shows the extent to which war crimes were already solidifying as a point of reference, even when these references were coded or oblique. Silverman alludes to crimes for a which a new name has had to be devised

[20] Hansard HL debate, vol 156, col 140, 2 June 1948. https://hansard.parliament.uk/lords. Accessed 27 August 2020. As is indicated by John Pine, who served as a prosecutor in British military courts in Germany, the method of execution in Germany was the guillotine. Qtd in Hilary Gaskin, *Eyewitnesses at Nuremberg* (London: Arms and Armour, 1990), pp. 49–50.
[21] Hansard HL debate, vol 156, col 74, 1 June 1948. https://hansard.parliament.uk/lords. Accessed 27 August 2020.

without actually using that name; in the Lords, Lord Merthyr referred to the 'crime of Nuremberg', a metonymy which switches attention from the crimes themselves to the trial venue.[22]

The views that emerged during these debates tend to support Lizzie Seal's argument, based on her analysis of correspondence received from members of the public by the Home Office, that there is a strong connection 'between responses to crime and punishment and individual's constructions of community'.[23] Examining letters that either supported or argued against the imposition of capital punishment in specific cases, she notes that during the war, many letters arguing for reprieves emphasized the respectability and good character of the condemned with reference to their local community'.[24] In the post-war period, more letters came from those not directly acquainted or connected with the condemned prisoner, and therefore 'invoked the national, rather than local, community'.[25] As in the parliamentary debates, notions of what constituted a 'civilised' society were brought to bear: 'British justice stood for fairness, reliable authority and the moral character of the nation. It should not be outraged for petty revenge.'[26] But as the continuing reconsiderations of this issue within and without parliament showed, each of these concepts—fairness, authority, moral character—was historically shifty. For some individuals, accepting abolition meant accepting that what might have seemed to be absolutes were in fact ideals that it was essential to reinstate in the wake of historical catastrophe.

Subsequent debates about the death penalty in the context of international human rights legislation and judicial practice show that the concept of community, both national and international, have had continuing resonance. As William A. Schabas explains, 'Whereas in the late 1940s and early 1950s the death penalty had been taken for granted, by the late 1980s and early 1990s, international jurists were not only favorable to its exclusion in the realm of international justice, they were also eager to use the international fora to promote abolition within domestic criminal law systems.'[27] Debates in Britain in the late 1940s gave some consideration to

---

[22] Hansard HL debate, vol 156, col 70, 1 June 1948. https://hansard.parliament.uk/lords. Accessed 27 August 2020.
[23] Lizzie Seal, 'Imagined Communities and the Death Penalty in Britain, 1930–1965', *British Journal of Criminology* 54 (2014): pp. 908–27 (p. 910).
[24] Seal, 'Imagined Communities', p. 915
[25] Seal, 'Imagined Communities', p. 916.
[26] Seal, 'Imagined Communities', p. 917.
[27] William A. Schabas, 'War Crimes, Crimes against Humanity and the Death Penalty', *Albany Law Review* 60.3 (1997): pp. 733–70 (p. 744).

how national practice might reflect or engage with international tendencies; the later development of international human rights legislation would act as a means of attempting to bring national legislatures into line with what was by then the more widely accepted abolitionist position. The debate in the late 1980s and early 1990s itself sprang from the question of how war criminals should be treated. Notably, as Schabas points out, some countries, in a stance that might have found favour with Giles Playfair and Derrick Sington, objected to life-sentences, a common alternative to capital punishment in many legislatures, on humanitarian grounds.[28] Reaching a consensus on what constituted a war crime, not straightforward in itself, was no less complicated than reaching an international agreement on what might be an appropriate penalty for committing such crimes.

Victor Gollancz, The Death Penalty, and Eichmann

Shortly before the debates on the Criminal Justice Bill began, publisher and campaigner Victor Gollancz visited Germany and wrote in impassioned terms about what he saw there. The Nazis' treatment of the Jews does not figure prominently in *In Darkest Germany* (1947), not least because Gollancz makes a separation between the perpetrators of those crimes and German civilians, whose living conditions under Allied occupation are his focus. This separation echoes the oppositional stance that Gollancz adopted in response to Lord Vansittart's *Black Record: Germans Past and Present* (1941), a book that saw Nazism as arising from German national character and did not allow for a distinction between Germans and Nazis. In *Shall our Children Live or Die?* (1942), written as a direct riposte to Vansittart, Gollancz argued, on the contrary, that 'the war was being fought as much for the benefit of the ordinary German—oppressed by a ghastly tyranny—as

---

[28] Schabas observes that Yugoslavia was one of a small number of countries that retained capital punishment for murder but maintained that life imprisonment was inhumane. Schabas, 'War Crimes', p. 759. Joseph Redenbaugh, one of the case-studies discussed in Playfair and Sington's *The Offenders*, was serving what they term a 'natural life' sentence (in the UK, this would now be called a *whole life tariff*). This is viewed as a 'purely retributive' measure, one which undermines any pretence that prison might provide a route to reform. Giles Playfair and Derrick Sington, *The Offenders: Society and the Atrocious Crime* (London: Secker & Warburg, 1967), p. 92. *The Offenders* expresses wariness about campaigns that focus on abolition 'as an end in itself rather than as a part of an assault on the whole expiatory theory of punishment' (p. 125).

for the persecuted Jews or conquered peoples of Europe'.[29] This is not to say that he neglected the plight of the Jews in his campaigning. As Tony Kushner explains, Gollancz's meeting with Polish resistance worker and courier Jan Karski in December 1942 prompted Gollancz to write *Let My People Go* (1943), a pamphlet urging the government 'to allow increased Jewish immigration to Palestine and to provide the necessary visas for refugees reaching neutral countries'.[30] Gollancz was a member of the National Committee for Rescue from Nazi Terror, founded in spring 1943 with the intention of exerting further pressure on the government in relation to this issue.[31] Viewed in the context of his involvement in this campaign during the war, Gollancz's focus on the living conditions of German civilians at the conflict's end can be seen as evidence of his lack of partisanship where humanitarian issues were concerned. In each case, it is characteristic that he asks the reader to focus on the plight of a specific group, but, like many of those who intervened in the parliamentary debates, he underlines that, where both the Jews and the German civilians are concerned, broader issues relating to what he terms 'the typical values of western civilization' are also at stake.[32]

A reference point for Gollancz when he considers this issue in *Our Threatened Values* (1946) are the attitudes that he believes were manifested in Britain in relation to war crimes trials. For Gollancz, the trials marked 'a collapse into the intolerance, the savagery, the revenge, the extra-legal exercise of power, and the dismissal of a man's motives as irrelevant which are among the worst characteristics of fascism itself'.[33] Being confronted with individuals who have committed terrible crimes is no reason, in Gollancz's view, for the loss of what he calls 'respect for personality'. Rejoicing 'when [William] Joyce and [John] Amery are sentenced to a shameful end' and thinking 'with pleasurable triumph of those wretched men in the dock at Nuremberg' are symptomatic, for Gollancz, of this loss of respect, a tendency that is compounded by the manner in which such trials were represented in the press.[34] He admits that he even felt sorry for 'the man Kramer of Belsen whose face

[29] Ruth Dudley Edwards, *Victor Gollancz: A Biography* (London: Victor Gollancz, 1987). Kindle edition.

[30] Tony Kushner, *The Holocaust and the Liberal Imagination: A Social and Cultural History* (Oxford: Blackwell, 1994), p. 177.

[31] Kushner, *The Holocaust*, pp. 177–181.

[32] Victor Gollancz, *Our Threatened Values* (London: Victor Gollancz, 1946), p. 7.

[33] Gollancz, *Our Threatened Values*, p. 46.

[34] Gollancz, *Our Threatened Values*, p. 11. John Amery, executed for treason in December 1945 after a trial at the Old Bailey, had been involved in attempts to recruit British prisoners of war to a battalion that would fight alongside the Germans, and, like William Joyce, delivered propaganda broadcasts from Germany.

was pilloried in almost every newspaper for the baser public to make a mock of', and cites the publication of images of Irma Grese being sentenced, and photographs of Mussolini's corpse, as expressing 'certain traits that are in the human nature of us all', but that should not be indulged.[35] In this context, it is hypocritical of the Allies to see themselves as being in a position to 're-educate' or 'de-Nazify' the German people.

There are echoes here of the two strands that emerged during the parliamentary debates and that would recur in Gollancz's later writing about the Eichmann trial: the idea that Nazism could prompt an inappropriate type of interest from 'the baser public'; and the idea that there was a contradiction between the Allies' behaviour towards their former enemies in the post-war period and their supposed upholding of civilized values. Indeed, these two strands are entangled with each other because, for Gollancz, putting Kramer and Grese on trial and allowing them to be the focus of press attention itself fed the prurience that he is concerned to critique. Gollancz's use of this example points to the prominence of the Belsen Trial, as well as the IMT, as a means of communicating an account of the Nazis' crimes to the public, but Gollancz recognizes that any such account cannot be ideologically neutral and can easily oversimplify what was at stake in the proceedings.

One way that Gollancz attempts to overcome some of these problems of mediation in his book *In Darkest Germany* is by foregrounding his own representational choices. The book is constructed from a series of articles and letters that were either written by Gollancz to his wife Livia or published in the press during the course of his visit to Germany, and they therefore have an immediacy that might have been lacking in a retrospective account. Gollancz illustrates his text liberally with photographs that provide evidence of the living conditions he has seen, and of the poor physical condition of the people, particularly the children, whom he encounters. As Jessica Medhurst points out, Gollancz himself appears in some of the photographs: in one instance, he informs the reader that it is his hand that can be seen holding the leg of an emaciated child as it is framed by the photographer.[36] At the start of the book he apologizes for what might be seen as his intrusion

---

[35] Gollancz, *Our Threatened Values*, p. 23. Mussolini and his partner Claretta Petacci were shot by partisans in April 1945, and their bodies left on display in a square in Milan. As an example of the coverage Gollancz cites, a photograph of the bodies after they were taken down was reproduced in *The Daily Mail*, 1 May 1945, p. 4, under the headline 'Retribution for Tyrants'.

[36] Jessica Medhurst, 'Representing and Repetition: Victor Gollancz's *In Darkest Germany* and the Metonymy of Shoes', *German Life and Letters* 69.4 (2016): pp. 468–84 (p. 478).

into these images, explaining: 'I thought that my visible presence would add verisimilitude, and obviate the charge, for instance, that these were really agency photographs taken in China in the year 1932.'[37] Medhurst argues that the 'anxiety that these photographs might be taken to be fraudulent' leads Gollancz to add 'something that the photographs are not apparently "of"', in the form of his own body, or part of it, though notably Gollancz suggests not that the pictures might be thought of as completely constructed, but that they might be inferred to have emerged from an earlier historical moment and a non-European context.[38]

Taking these images alongside the epistolary form of the text, I perceive an echo in *In Darkest Germany* of the attempts by commentators including Patrick Gordon Walker and Alan Moorehead to verify their reports from the camps by asserting that they were indeed there and are recounting what they saw. This rhetorical manoeuvre simultaneously expresses and counters a presumption that the public will be incredulous, a presumption that springs from the extremity of what the reporter is seeing. Gollancz's own shock is communicated by his belief that the reader in turn will be, or should be, shocked by his revelations and may even find them so shocking as to doubt their truth.

It is significant that Gollancz's aim is ultimately a political one. He offers the reader images of starving German civilians and their appalling living conditions as part of a campaign to persuade the British government to improve those conditions. Again, as in the case of the war crimes trials, the question of how a government might set itself up as a moral arbiter when, by Gollancz's account, it has left innocent people on starvation rations, is what underpins his argument. This would presumably be Gollancz's defence against an accusation that he is indulging the kind of prurience that he critiques elsewhere: this is not exposure for the sake of exposure but for a clearly delineated purpose.

During the early 1950s, in the wake of the failure to bring about either long-term suspension or abolition of capital punishment via the 1949 Criminal Justice Act, and spurred on by a number of high-profile criminal cases that culminated in the death sentence, Gollancz was involved in the

---

[37] Victor Gollancz, *In Darkest Germany* (London: Victor Gollancz, 1947), p. 15.

[38] The title of *In Darkest Germany* has an historical echo, alluding to William Booth's *In Darkest England and the Way Out* (1890), an exposé of working-class poverty by the founder of the Salvation Army. Booth's title in turn references the trope of the 'dark continent' or 'darkest Africa': H. M. Stanley's *In Darkest Africa* was also published in 1890.

founding of the National Campaign for the Abolition of Capital Punishment.[39] By the time that Adolf Eichmann was captured in Buenos Aires by the Israeli secret services and taken to Israel to stand trial, the laws relating to murder in England and Wales had been revised again, in line with some though not all of the recommendations of Royal Commission, which had reported in 1953. Among other measures, the 1957 Homicide Act introduced the concept of diminished responsibility as a potential mitigating factor; the Commission had not been asked to focus on abolition though it had considered whether the method of execution should be changed. In *The Case of Adolf Eichmann*, Gollancz argues against both the trial of Eichmann and what he saw to be as its highly likely end result: the execution of the defendant. He was thus able to revisit the question of how the crimes of the Nazis should be dealt with while remobilizing his arguments against capital punishment, which in his view were equally as applicable to this high-profile international case as to domestic cases that had made the headlines in Britain.

Early in his pamphlet, Gollancz notes that, inevitably, Eichmann's trial will include the recounting of some of the Nazis' crimes, and indeed he provides some examples for the reader of the Nazis 'unspeakable bestiality [...] These things happened, and now they will be happening all over again: they will be happening, this time, in the human imagination [...] There is only so much room in our consciousness: the more we live in the presence of evil, the less we live in the presence of good.'[40] The question here is whether anything can be learned by contemplating these crimes, or, as Gollancz puts it, allowing them to happen again in our 'imagination'. Gollancz goes so far as to suggest that being reminded of evil may 'by a process of morbid fascination, reinforce our own evil [...] [Y]esterday's cruelty should be forgotten as soon as is humanly possible for nothing can be done about it.'[41] Other commentators expressed similar sentiments, with Hugh Moran of the *Daily Mail*

[39] Often-cited cases at this period include the trial of Reginald Christie in 1953, which cast doubt on the earlier murder conviction and execution of Timothy Evans, the execution of Derek Bentley in 1953 for the shooting of a policeman that was actually carried out by his juvenile associate Christopher Craig, and the 1955 hanging of Ruth Ellis for the murder of her lover David Blakely. I discuss these cases in Stewart, *Crime Writing in Interwar Britain,* pp. 173–86. Gollancz published Ludovic Kennedy's *Ten Rillington Place* (1961), on the Christie and Evans case.

[40] Victor Gollancz, *The Case of Adolf Eichmann* (London: Victor Gollancz, 1961), p. 15. The text is dated 20 May 1961, roughly six weeks into the trial.

[41] Gollancz, *The Case of Adolf Eichmann,* p. 16.

commenting: 'This is a horror trial, and one wonders how much bestiality one can absorb day after day without it becoming commonplace.'[42]

Gollancz has some more specific objections about the trial, regardless of it potentially offering an opportunity for victims to tell their stories. 'If Eichmann was to be tried at all', he argues, 'he should have been tried either by an international court or by Western Germany, preferably the former.'[43] This is because, in Gollancz's view, all Israeli jurists, in common with their fellow Israeli citizens are 'emotionally involved' in the case, having family ties to victims of the Nazis. Gollancz sees this as akin to a judge in an English court presiding over a murder case in which he is 'the father of the alleged murderer's victim', or in which the 'jurymen [are] the victim's mother and brothers and sisters'.[44] The problem with this parallel is that, from another point of view, judges and juries, even if they do not have actual family ties to victims or perpetrators of crimes, may nevertheless have affective or symbolic bonds, by dint of shared gender, racial or cultural identity, and the assumption is that these will always be put to one side when it comes to considering the particular case.

Gollancz's doubts as to whether Eichmann could get a fair trial were echoed by Eichmann's own defence counsel, Robert Servatius, who, as Lawrence Douglas points out, 'did not challenge the objectivity of any one member of the panel; rather he claimed that because "the entire Jewish people were drawn into the holocaust of extermination", the specter of judicial prejudice would arise "from the very material of the proceedings"'.[45] Where Gollancz is concerned, it is interesting that he falls back on what he sees to be the default objectivity of English domestic courts, despite his engagement, especially via his involvement in the NCACP, in bringing to light miscarriages of justice that seemed to bring this objectivity into question.

Objecting to the trial on the grounds that Eichmann has already been presumed guilty, Gollancz again turns to English law as a point of reference, noting that 'to anticipate the result of judicial proceedings' in news reports would lead to a charge of 'contempt of court'. Admitting that he has read very little of the Israeli press coverage, he nevertheless suggests that 'the whole climate of public opinion everywhere has assumed Eichmann's guilt from the

[42] Hugh Moran, 'How Much of This Horror can one Stand?', *Daily Mail*, 29 April 1961, p. 4.

[43] Gollancz, *The Case of Adolf Eichmann*, p. 22.

[44] Gollancz, *The Case of Adolf Eichmann*, p, 21.

[45] Lawrence Douglas, *The Memory of Judgment: Making Law and History in the Trials of the Holocaust* (New Haven: Yale University Press, 2001), p. 116.

outset.'[46] The specific issues Gollancz raises about how the trial is being run are therefore underpinned by a more fundamental objection to Eichmann being put on trial at all.

Like Derrick Sington, Gollancz is inclined to stress the importance of environment in normalizing or legitimizing certain kinds of behaviour that in other contexts would be taboo: 'If we live amidst violence, if violence is more or less taken for granted by our neighbours and is generally "the thing" (as in Hitler's Germany), we may become in some measure *predisposed* to it.'[47] But, more broadly, placing blame on particular individuals diverts attention from the extent to which the international community should share responsibility for the rise of Nazism, a phenomenon that Gollancz connects to the unsatisfactory post–First World War settlement. Having failed at that point, the international community should, in Gollancz's view, have done more to help the Jews when their plight became increasingly evident during the war. No one, in this analysis, has clean hands.

The closing pages of the pamphlet argue against the capital sentence that Gollancz rightly foresaw as the likely outcome of the trial: 'It is precisely the ultimate evil in Hitler's "final solution" that calls, by way of reply to it, for an act of ultimate good [... .] If six million have been slaughtered, what can it profit to make the number six million and one?'[48] Gollancz is not principally concerned here with the particular sentencing powers of the Israeli court, though as Douglas notes, Servatius also questioned whether it was legitimate to try Eichmann under the Nazi and Nazi Collaborators (Punishment) Law of 1950, arguing that he should have been tried instead under current German law.[49] Where sentencing was concerned, the death sentence was not mandatory under the 1950 law and was not a penalty for any other offence under Israeli law.[50] Though the eventual sentence was described as having the dual purpose of punishing Eichmann and deterring others from committing similar crimes, Gollancz argues that taking the life of one

---

[46] Gollancz, *The Case of Adolf Eichmann*, p. 22.

[47] Gollancz, *The Case of Adolf Eichmann*, p. 28.

[48] Gollancz, *The Case of Adolf Eichmann*, p. 60.

[49] Douglas, *The Memory of Judgment*, p. 117. The 1950 law was framed as retrospective in scope and was drawn up principally with the intention of enabling trials of Jews who had been Kapos in the camps. In response to Servatius's argument that the court did not have jurisdiction to try Eichmann, the Israeli judges' position was that 'because the crimes were of the sort universally considered to be crimes, any nation would have the jurisdiction to try a perpetrator of those crimes'. Michael J. Bazyler and Julia Y. Scheppach, 'The Strange and Curious History of the Law used to Prosecute Adolf Eichmann', *Loyola of Los Angeles International and Comparative Law Review* 34.3 (2012): pp. 417–60 (p. 442).

[50] Schabas, 'War Crimes, Crimes Against Humanity and the Death Penalty', p. 765.

person as a form of compensation for the death of six million serves only to 'trivialize [...] the crucifixion of a whole people'.[51] But in enumerating Eichmann's death as number six million and one, Gollancz seems awkwardly to conflate that death with those of the Nazis' victims, while compounding the anonymity of those six million.

Gollancz's essay was a polemic: it was not intended to be even-handed, and, in it, as I have indicated, he uses the Eichmann trial as a means of refracting his views on a variety of issues. Others, including David Astor, the editor of the *Observer* and a friend of Gollancz's, also used consideration of the trial to reflect more widely on current attitudes towards the events that the trial dealt with. In response to the question of whether 'we should inform ourselves about these horrors', whether they are 'our business', Astor suggests that a 'scientific' approach might best overcome the 'emotional numbness' that he sees as being engendered by 'the most terrible crime in history'.[52] Gollancz's intervention illustrates how by this point in the early 1960s, even as the Eichmann trial promised to give voice to the victims of Nazism in a way that had not been the case at previous trials, there could still be calls for restraint, not only in the treatment of a perpetrator but in the depiction of the crimes of which that perpetrator was accused.

Pamela Hansford Johnson and the Trial of Brady and Hindley

By coincidence, *Judgment at Nuremberg* was released in Britain in December 1961 just a few days after the verdict and sentencing in the Eichmann case.[53] The film dramatized the 1947 Justices' Trial, one of the American-led trials that had formed part of the IMT, during which judges who had presided over trials during the Nazi period had their actions in upholding Nazi laws scrutinized. (Schabas notes that some of the defendants at the trial that was the inspiration for the film were found guilty of abuse of the death penalty, but, 'prudently', were not themselves condemned to death.[54]) The film incorporates some of the documentary footage that was

---

[51] Gollancz, *The Case of Adolf Eichmann*, p. 57.

[52] David Astor, 'The Meaning of Eichmann', *Observer*, 26 March 1961, p. 10. He reminds his readers that 'our own relatives and their wives who settled in North America and Australia found no objection to decimating the indigenous populations' (p. 10).

[53] The verdict on Eichmann was announced on 11 December 1961, and he was sentenced to death on 14 December. *Judgment at Nuremberg* was released in the UK on 19 December.

[54] Schabas, 'War Crimes, Crimes against Humanity and the Death Penalty', p. 740.

screened at the Belsen Trial and the Nuremberg IMT and which is shown being projected in the courtroom, notwithstanding that this did not happen at the actual Justices' Trial; as Ulrike Weckel notes, the material does not have a direct bearing on the offences under scrutiny in the film.[55] But *Judgment at Nuremberg* is interesting to me not only for its use of this footage as a form of evidence that acts as a stark reminder of the wider context for the trial, but because it centres on a trial that examines the conduct of earlier trials. The correctness of the Americans', and by extension, the Allies', own legal procedures, as representative of the democratic judicial process, is thus shown as directly countering the corrupt practices of the Nazi regime, such as the 'Special Courts' I discussed in Chapter 3.

As Robert Moeller suggests, part of *Judgment at Nuremberg* focuses on the Nazis laws relating to 'race defilement', and this was likely to have been selected as a narrative strand by director Stanley Kramer in order to prompt self-critique on the part of the film's audience in still-segregated America.[56] In a British context, though the film was reviewed as a serious-minded attempt to engage with the aftermath of the Nazi regime, it gained darker associations when, in the wake of the trial and sentencing of Myra Hindley and Ian Brady, it was suggested that the pair had been to see the film together.[57] This was one of a number of details about the interest that Brady in particular had in Nazism that led commentators to question the place that the crimes of the Nazis had in contemporary culture, especially

---

[55] Ulrike Weckel, 'The Power of Images: Real and Fictional Roles of Atrocity Film Footage at Nuremberg', in *Reassessing the Nuremberg Military Tribunals: Transitional Justice, Trial Narratives, and Historiography*, edited by Kim C. Priemel and Alexa Stiller (Oxford: Berghahn Books, 2012), pp. 221–48 (p. 241).

[56] Robert G. Moeller, 'How to Judge Stanley Kramer's *Judgment at Nuremberg*', *German History* 31.4 (2013): pp. 497–522 (pp. 514–15).

[57] In comments that are relevant to Hansford Johnson's discussion of Brady and Hindley, the reviewer for the *Guardian* commented positively on the absence from the film of archive footage of 'Hitler foaming and of his grey legions marching', noting that this meant the film avoided 'the specious appeal of such memories to the bored and repressed elements in our affluent society'. J O'C, 'At the Cinemas', *Guardian*, 15 January 1962, p. 15. In relation to the suggestion that Brady and Hindley saw the film together, in an article published shortly after the verdict, Elwyn Jones (not to be confused with his namesake MP and prosecutor at the trial) stated that the couple saw 'Trial at Nuremberg', presumably his misremembering of the title *Judgment at Nuremberg*, though he notes that this was not mentioned during the trial evidence and he does not provide a source for this information. 'The Truth —But Not the Whole Truth', *Sunday Telegraph*, 8 May 1966, p. 5. Pamela Hansford Johnson (who had an article about Brady and Hindley on the same page as Jones's) wrote in *On Iniquity* that Brady took Hindley to see 'a film of the Nuremberg rallies' (p. 79). The claim that they went to see *Judgment at Nuremberg* was repeated in various news items about the case in subsequent years. Whether they actually saw Kramer's film together is perhaps less significant than the construction that commentators have put on the fact that they might have.

popular culture. This was partly an issue of the types of representation that were in circulation, but even an apparently well-meaning and 'respectable' representation like *Judgment at Nuremberg* could be engaged with in an 'inappropriate' manner.

One prominent commentator who foregrounded these aspects in order to develop a wider argument about the moral and spiritual temper of early 1960s Britain and its relation to the recent past was novelist and journalist Pamela Hansford Johnson, who attended the trial of Brady and Hindley in Chester, reported on it for the *Sunday Telegraph* newspaper, and expanded these reports into her book *On Iniquity* (1967). The surfacing of the Holocaust as a point of reference in the case leads Hansford Johnson to argue that Nazism, and in particular, the Holocaust, has not been remembered in the 'correct' way. For instance, Brady's nickname for Myra Hindley was 'Hessie', arrived at by a chain of association leading from Hindley's partial namesake Dame Myra Hess, the British Jewish pianist best known for the morale-boosting concerts she gave at the National Gallery during the Second World War, to Rudolf Hess, Hitler's deputy, who was arrested after landing in Scotland in 1943 and imprisoned after the IMT. Following her arrest, Hindley was found to have a photograph of Irma Grese in her purse, and the supposed trip to see *Judgment at Nuremberg* was described in some accounts as the couple's first date (they met at work).[58] What might in other circumstances be dismissed as a joke in rather poor taste, or a disjunctive choice of viewing for an encounter that presumably was intended to have a romantic flavour, became, in the context of the couple's crimes, pathological symptoms.

Hansford Johnson herself uses Nazism as a reference point when describing the demeanour of Brady and Hindley during the trial. Brady's appearance seems to Hansford Johnson to offer support for the discredited theories of Cesare Lombroso and she describes him as looking like 'a cross between Joseph Goebbels and a bird'.[59] She admits that: 'On the whole, he looks ordinary', but if Brady presents a banal image of evil for Hansford Johnson, Hindley seems to be a figure of almost mythic proportions: 'she could have served a nineteenth-century Academy painter as a model for Clytemnestra'.[60] But,

---

[58] Later Hindley denied that it was *Judgment at Nuremberg* she and Brady saw on their first date, claiming that they had gone to *King of Kings*, a film based on the life of Jesus, which has in common with Kramer's film only its longer than average running time. See Carol Ann Lee, *One of Your Own: The Life and Death of Myra Hindley* (London: Mainstream, 2010), p. 76.

[59] Hansford Johnson, *On Iniquity*, p. 22.

[60] Hansford Johnson, *On Iniquity*, p. 22.

perhaps inevitably, Hansford Johnson reaches for another comparison, noting that with her 'Nordic blonde' hair, and her 'grey double-breasted suit', Hindley has 'the kind of authority one might expect to find in a woman guard of a concentration camp'.[61] As in the representations of the Belsen Trial defendants that I discussed earlier, appearance is here shown to encode behavioural tendencies, and what might in other contexts be seen as benign or even positive (Hindley's blondeness) is reframed to fit the sinister actions for which she is being tried.

But Hansford Johnson goes further, because for her, it is not simply a case of two individuals engaging with Nazism in what she deems a distasteful or inappropriate way. This engagement is in turn constructed as symptomatic of a wider social problem, a product, in Hansford Johnson's view, of the relaxing of moral standards in the years since the end of the war: 'We demand sex without love, violence for "kicks". We are encouraging the blunting of sensibility: and this, let us remember, is not the way to an Earthly Paradise, but the way to Auschwitz.'[62] Thus an interest in Nazism is both the cause and the product of the kind of 'blunting of sensibility' that underpinned the rise of the Nazis in the first place. Later in the book, Hansford Johnson explores the idea that this 'blunting of sensibility', and specifically its manifestation in a more liberal attitude towards the subject matter for art works, may lead to the repetition of the trajectory of recent European history:

At present, we are looking, in the arts, less like an up-and-coming society than like the last days of the Weimar Republic.
All right: what happened after that?
Hitler.
But must we take this to mean that if we raise the slightest protest against sadistic seediness and more sadistic seediness, Hitlerism will result? If so, we have abrogated moral responsibility [...] We are behaving like cowards.[63]

---

[61] Hansford Johnson, *On Iniquity*, p. 23.
[62] Hansford Johnson, *On Iniquity*, p. 18.
[63] Hansford Johnson, *On Iniquity*, pp. 42–43. Citing similar comments made in 1969 by morality campaigner Mary Whitehouse, Christopher Hilliard notes: 'Parables about Nazism were common among advocates of censorship [at this period]; opponents of censorship could counter with the spectacle of Nazi book-burning', *A Matter of Obscenity: The Politics of Censorship in Modern England* (Princeton: Princeton University Press, 2021), p. 135.

Unfettered freedom to read about Nazism has resulted in a society resembling Weimar Germany: Nazism is positioned as part of an unescapable feedback loop because it can never be culturally assimilated. Reacting against liberal attitudes might be the only choice, albeit a potentially dictatorial one, but for Hansford Johnson, taking action to break this cycle would have a protective aspect.

In this connection, she points to causes celebres that would have been familiar to her readers and that still resonate today, including the 1959 case of *Regina v Penguin Books* (the *Lady Chatterley* trial) and the Lord Chamberlain's refusal of a licence to Edward Bond's play *Saved* (1965), which was one of the precipitating factors for the ending of stage censorship in Britain in 1968. While conceding that, at the time of the *Chatterley* trial, she might have been inclined to speak up on behalf of Penguin Books, despite her doubts about the literary quality of the novel, she suggests that Brady and Hindley's trial raises the question of the 'mass availability' of certain types of material, particularly the works of de Sade, cited during the trial as having possibly provided Brady with a mean of justifying his acts to himself and Hindley. De Sade's suggestion that 'murder is a horror, but a horror often necessary, never criminal' is described by Hansford Johnson as 'the stuff of fantasy [...] but it is nevertheless dangerous fantasy, of the kind the Nazis were finally able to put into a practice on a mass scale, in the "Final Solution"'.[64] This is a reading of Nazism that depoliticizes it, and evades consideration of the particular reasons, other than the fulfilling of a fantasy of omnipotence, why the Jews specifically were marked as a target. Brady and Hindley are again positioned as both repeating the developmental trajectory of Nazism and being influenced by widely circulated representations of the failed Nazi project.

Linking Nazism and sadism in this way emphasizes the sense that, as Lisa Downing points out, Hansford Johnson 'assumes that they are causally linked and selfsame'.[65] This is emphasized when, listing some of the books Brady owned, Hansford Johnson divides them into three categories: 'Sado-masochistic', 'Titillatory', and 'Dealing with Fascism and Nazism'. In another context, the books in this final category, which include

---

[64] Hansford Johnson, *On Iniquity*, p. 59. Ruth Dudley Edwards notes that Gollancz drafted a letter to *The Times*, 'implying that contemporary literary depravity played a part in inspiring the Moors murders', but that he did not send it, and 'declared himself to be against' censorship. *Victor Gollancz*, Kindle edition.

[65] Lisa Downing, *The Subject of Murder: Gender, Exceptionality, and the Modern Killer* (Chicago: University of Chicago Press, 2013), p. 117.

G. M. Gilbert's *Nuremberg Diary* (1948), might be considered quite differently, as historical sources for instance, but here they are smirched by association with their disreputable reader and with the other books he owned. This evidences Hilliard's observation that, where censorship and the regulation of reading are concerned, 'a book's acceptability depends on who is reading it as well as the book itself'.[66] Similarly Hansford Johnson notes that Brady had 'two books on how to teach oneself German'.[67] This comment is notable not least because Hansford Johnson stresses that although Brady and Hindley both had high IQs, neither of them had extensive formal education. What might otherwise have been viewed as an attempt at self-improvement—'teaching oneself German'—is framed instead as a means of enabling access to more obscure, tabooed, and potentially dangerous knowledge.

The issue here is that for Hansford Johnson there does not seem to be any 'other' context within which Nazism might better be considered. Having offered her reader a glimpse of the perverse world of Brady and Hindley, she laments the fact that:

> It has degraded us all, it has soiled our imaginations. Yet we dare forget it no more than we dare forget Belsen or Auschwitz, unless we are trying to prove the Moors Case was an isolated incident, having no springs in our society. Nobody, I think, has cared to say the same about the Nazi murderers.[68]

These comments develop an earlier observation of Hansford Johnson's, when she admits that although the details of Brady and Hindley's crimes 'sickened' her, she nevertheless 'wanted to know *all* the details, not solely because it was my job to do so, but because there was in them an element of repulsive stimulation'.[69] She compares this to an account she quotes by a 'young Englishman' who 'happened to be in Nuremberg at the times when the Nazis were publicly degrading Jewish man and women in the streets'. This young man is sickened and shocked the first time he sees such actions, then later tells himself he has a duty to observe and report on what he has seen, before finally realizing that he 'was in serious danger of becoming acclimatized', at which point he leaves and returns to England.[70] In Hansford

---

[66] Hilliard, *A Matter of Obscenity*, p. 2.
[67] Hansford Johnson, *On Iniquity*, p. 31.
[68] Hansford Johnson, *On Iniquity*, p. 134.
[69] Hansford Johnson, *On Iniquity*, pp. 59–60.
[70] Hansford Johnson, *On Iniquity*, pp, 60–61.

Johnson's analysis, it is vital that the dangerous feelings experienced at times even by herself, even by the sensitive Englishman, remain repressed, but she can offer no way of achieving this while fulfilling a duty not to forget.

As I have noted, capital punishment was in a pre-abolition period of suspension when Brady and Hindley's trial took place and Hansford Johnson, in common with some other commentators, felt that the case brought abolition into question, or, as she more bluntly puts it, as with the 'war criminals in the Nuremberg trials' it would have been preferable if Brady and Hindley could have been 'caught red-handed [...] and simply shot down', rather than the public having to be confronted with the details of their crimes by reading about the trial.[71] Hansford Johnson's invocation of Belsen and Auschwitz in her account can be seen as an attempt to find a more appropriate focus for the memory of the Nazi period, though like some of the writers I discussed in the introduction, she relies on her reader already understanding, or rather sharing her own understanding of, what is encoded by each of the proper names she uses. Not 'daring to forget' is at a remove from the active remembering that, even as Hansford Johnson was writing, was emerging as a way of attempting both to understand the Holocaust and to memorialize its victims.

No sooner does the Holocaust come into view as an historical event than it begins to slip out of focus, or, rather, it is never, was never, a single, monumental event but always the product of intersecting narratives, inflected by the receiver's own subject position and prejudices. The glimpses of the Holocaust that were discerned in British accounts in the years following the Second World War were enough to convey the horror of what had happened, but they raised questions that commentators and readers would struggle to answer, questions that related not only to the reasons why these things had happened but also to what, if anything, might be learned from the fact that they had. Given the scope and gravity of these questions, it is perhaps unsurprising that one response, and one that can be found even among survivors, was to turn away, or to engage with them only indirectly. The work of articulating and assessing the impact of the Holocaust was one that could not be contained by judicial processes, however protracted, and it is one which continues still.

[71] Hansford Johnson, *On Iniquity*, p. 89.

Works Cited

Printed Sources

Anon, '13000 People Died in Six Weeks at Belsen', *Manchester Guardian*, 18 September 1945, p. 5.

Anon, '4 Women Whose Names Will Never Be Known', *Daily Mail*, 30 May 1946, p. 1.

Anon, 'Briton Ate Grass in Belsen Camp', *Daily Express*, 18 September 1945, p. 4.

Anon, 'Doctor Describes Routine of Gas Chambers', *Manchester Guardian*, 2 October 1945, p. 6.

Anon, 'Final Stages in Belsen Trial', 9 November 1945, p. 3.

Anon, 'Irma Put on Her Silk Stockings', *Daily Express*, 22 September 1945, p. 4.

Anon, 'Just Published', *Times Literary Supplement*, 17 November 1950, p. 731.

Anon, 'Kramer in the Box', *The Times*, 9 October 1945, p. 3.

Anon, 'Reports of Threats', *Manchester Guardian*, 27 September 1945, p. 5.

Anon, 'Two Death Sentences to Stand', *The Times*, 11 November 1948, p. 4.

Anon, 'War Criminals' Defence', *The Times*, 29 October 1945, p. 2.

Anon, 'The Women Who Died for Their Country: Courageous Secret Service Agents', *Illustrated London News*, 22 May 1948, p. 573.

Anon [Ashley Price], 'Benevolent Crochet' [rev of Christopher Lloyd, *The British Navy and the Slave Trade*], *Times Literary Supplement*, 7 October 1949, p. 650.

Adorno, Theodor, 'The Meaning of Working through the Past' (1960), in *Critical Models: Interventions and Catchwords*, translated by Henry W. Pickford (New York: Columbia University Press, 1998), pp. 89–103.

Arata, Stephen D., 'The Sedulous Ape: Atavism, Professionalism, and Stevenson's "Jekyll and Hyde,"' *Criticism* 37.2 (1995): pp. 233–59, doi: 10.1017/cbo97805 11553585.003.

Arendt, Hannah, 'Personal Responsibility under Dictatorship', in *Responsibility and Judgment*, edited by Jerome Kohn (New York: Schocken Books, 2003), pp. 17–48.

Arnold, Jane, 'Jews in the Works of Agatha Christie', *Social History* 49.3–4 (1987): pp. 275–82.

Ashbrook, Harry, 'Belsen Blonde is on Her High Horse', *Daily Mirror*, 17 September 1945, p. 8.

Ashbrook, Harry, 'Block 18—Men Died in 12 Days', *Daily Mirror*, 18 September 1945, p. 8.

Astor, David, 'The Meaning of Eichmann', *Observer*, 26 March 1961, p. 10.

Auden, W. H., 'The Guilty Vicarage' (1948), in *The Dyer's Hand and Other Essays* (London: Faber & Faber, 1962), pp. 146–58.

Baigorri-Jalon, Jesus, *From Paris to Nuremberg: The Birth of Conference Interpreting*, translated by Holly Mikkelsen and Barry Slaughter-Olsen (Amsterdam: John Benjamins, 2014).

Bailey, Victor, 'The Shadow of the Gallows: The Death Penalty and the British Labour Government, 1945–51', *Law and History Review* 18.2 (2000): pp. 305–49, doi: 10.2307/744298.

Bardgett, Suzanne, 'What Wireless Listeners Learned: Some Lesser-Known BBC Broadcasts about Belsen', in *Belsen 1945: New Historical Perspectives*, edited by Suzanne Bardgett and David Cesarani (London and Portland: Vallentine Mitchell, 2006), pp. 123–52.

Bartov, Omer, et al., 'An Open Letter to the Director of the US Holocaust Memorial Museum', *New York Review of Books*, 1 July 2019 https://www.nybooks.com/daily/2019/07/01/an-open-letter-to-the-director-of-the-holocaust-memorial-museum/?fbclid=IwAR1AoKWPKzbxZfxd8ia48BuBjDfbyerfRizy7SZziGGWqnCShfUQ8LFZjyY. Accessed 1 October 2019.

Basu, Shrabani, *Spy Princess: The Life of Noor Inayat Khan* (London: History Press, 2008).

Bauman, Zygmunt, 'Allosemitism: Premodern, Modern, Postmodern', in *Modernity, Culture and 'the Jew'*, edited by Bryan Cheyette and Laura Marcus (Cambridge: Polity Press, 1998), pp. 143–56.

Bazyler, Michael J., and Julia Y. Scheppach, 'The Strange and Curious History of the Law used to Prosecute Adolf Eichmann', *Loyola of Los Angeles International and Comparative Law Review* 34.3 (2021): pp. 417–61.

Bazyler, Michael J., and Frank M. Tuerkheimer, *Forgotten Trials of the Holocaust* (New York: NYU Press, 2014).

Beckman, Morris, *The 43 Group: Battling with Mosley's Blackshirts* (1992; London: The History Press, 2013).

Berk-Seligson, Susan, *The Bilingual Courtroom: Court Interpreters in the Judicial Process* (Chicago: University of Chicago Press, 2002).

Bleicher, Hugo, *Colonel Henri's Story: The Memoirs of Hugo Bleicher, Former German Secret Agent*, edited by Ian Colvin (London: William Kimber, 1954).

Bloxham, Donald, 'Punishing German Soldiers during the Cold War: The Case of Erich von Manstein', *Patterns of Prejudice* 33.4 (1999): pp. 25–45, doi: 10.1080/003132299128810687.

Bloxham, Donald, *Genocide on Trial: War Crimes Trials and the Formation of Holocaust History and Memory* (Oxford: Oxford University Press, 2001).

Bloxham, Donald, 'British War Crimes Trial Policy in Germany, 1945–1957: Implementation and Collapse', *Journal of British Studies* 42.1 (2003): pp. 91–118, doi: 10.30965/9783657767434_009.

Boswell, Matthew, *Holocaust Impiety in Literature, Popular Music and Film* (Basingstoke: Palgrave, 2012).

Brand, Christianna, *Heads You Lose* (Harmondsworth: Penguin, 1954 [1941]).

Brand, Christianna, *Green for Danger* (London: Pan, 1999 [1945]).

Brand, George, 'Introduction', in *The Trial of Heinrich Gericke and Others (The Velpke Baby Home Trial)*, edited by George Brand (London: William Hodge, 1950), pp. xvii–liv.

Brown-Blake, Celia, 'Fair Trial, Language and the Right to Interpretation', *International Journal on Minority and Group Rights* 13 (2006): pp. 391–412, doi: 10.1163/157181106779848368.

Bryant, Michael, 'Punishing the Excess: Sadism, Bureaucratized Atrocity, and the US Army Concentration Camp Trials, 1945–47', in *Nazi Crimes and the Law*, edited by Nathan Stoltzfus and Henry Friedlander (Cambridge: German Historical Institute and Cambridge University Press, 2008), pp. 63–85.

Bryant, Michael and Wolfgang Form, 'Victim Nationality in US and British Military Trials: Hadamar, Dachau, Belsen', in *Justice, Politics and Memory in Europe after the Second World War: Landscapes after Battle Volume 2*, edited by Suzanne Bardgett, David Cesarani, Jessica Reinisch, and Johannes-Dieter Steinert (London: Vallentine Mitchell, 2011), pp. 19–42.

Bunting, Aimee, 'Britain and the Holocaust: Then and Now', unpublished PhD thesis, University of Southampton, 2006.

Bunting, Aimee, and Tony Kushner, 'Co-Presents to the Holocaust: The British in Auschwitz and Belsen', David Cesarani Memorial Lecture 2018, 30 January 2018. Podcast, backdoorbroadcasting.net. Accessed 12 June 2018.

Burney, Christopher, *The Dungeon Democracy*, in *Solitary Confinement and The Dungeon Democracy* (London: Macmillan, 1984 [1945]), pp. 137–248.

Carroll, Tim, *The Dodger: The Extraordinary Story of Churchill's Cousin and the Great Escape* (London: Random House, 2012).

Caven, Hannah, 'Horror in Our Time: Images of the Concentration Camps in the British Media, 1945', *Historical Journal of Film, Radio and Television* 21.3 (2001): pp. 205–53, doi: 10.1080/01439680120069399.

Celinscak, Mark, *Distance from the Belsen Heap: Allied Forces and the Liberation of a Nazi Concentration Camp* (Toronto: University of Toronto Press, 2015).

Cesarani, David, 'Great Britain', in *The World Reacts to the Holocaust*, edited by David S. Wyman (Baltimore: Johns Hopkins University Press, 1996), pp. 599–641.

Cesarani, David, *Major Farran's Hat: Murder, Scandal and Britain's War Against Jewish Terrorism, 1945–1948* (London: Vintage, 2009).

Cesarani, David, 'How Post-War Britain Reflected on the Nazi Persecution and Mass Murder of Europe's Jews: A Reassessment of Early Responses', *Jewish Culture and History* 12.1–2 (2010): pp. 95–130, doi:10.1080/1462169x.2010.10512146.

Cesarani, David, 'A New Look at Some Old Memoirs', in *Justice, Politics and Memory in Europe after the Second World War: Landscapes After Battle Volume 2*, edited by Suzanne Bardgett, David Cesarani, Jessica Reinisch, and Johannes-Dieter Steinert (London: Vallentine Mitchell, 2011), pp. 121–68.

Cheyette, Bryan, *Constructions of 'the Jew' in English Literature and Society: Racial Representations, 1875–1945* (Cambridge: Cambridge University Press, 1993).

Christie, Agatha, *A Murder Is Announced* (London: HarperCollins 2005).

Christie, Agatha, *N or M?* (London: HarperCollins, 2015 [1941]).

Churchill, Peter, *The Spirit in the Cage* (London: Hodder & Stoughton, 1954).

Cohen, Elie A., *Human Behaviour in the Concentration Camp*, translated by M. H. Braaksma (London: Jonathan Cape, 1954).

Cole, G. D. H., and Margaret Cole, *Toper's End* (London: Collins, 1942).

Cooper, Katherine, 'Figures on the Threshold: Refugees and the Politics of Hospitality, 1930–51', *Literature and History* 27.2 (2018): pp. 189–204, doi: 10.1177/0306197318792374.

de Mildt, Dick, *In the Name of the People: Perpetrators of Genocide in the Reflection of Their Post-War Prosecution in West Germany* (The Hague: Martinus Nijhoff, 1996).

Diefendorf, Jeffrey M., ed., *Lessons and Legacies VI: New Currents in Holocaust Research* (Evanston: Northwestern University Press, 2004), pp. 300–21.

Douglas, Lawrence, *The Memory of Judgment: Making Law and History in the Trials of the Holocaust* (New Haven, CT: Yale University Press, 2001).

Downing, Lisa, *The Subject of Murder: Gender, Exceptionality, and the Modern Killer* (Chicago: Chicago University Press, 2013).

Drumbl, Mark A., *Atrocity, Punishment, and International Law* (New York: Cambridge University Press, 2007).

Du Bois, W. E. B., 'The Negro and the Warsaw Ghetto', *Jewish Life* (May 1952): pp. 14–15.

Dudley Edwards, Ruth, *Victor Gollancz: A Biography* (London: Victor Gollancz, 1987).

Duranti, Marco, *The Conservative Human Rights Revolution: European Identity, Transnational Politics, and the Origins of the European Convention* (Oxford: Oxford University Press, 2017).

Eaglestone, Robert, 'Avoiding Evil in Perpetrator Fiction', in *Representing Perpetrators in Holocaust Literature and Film*, edited by Jenni Adams and Sue Vice (London: Vallentine Mitchell 2013), pp. 13–24.

Eaglestone, Robert, *The Broken Voice: Reading Post-Holocaust Literature* (Oxford: Oxford University Press, 2017).

Evans, Vincent, 'The Belsen Gang Stops Smiling', *Daily Express*, 19 September 1945, p. 4.

Evans, Vincent, 'The Death Music of Auschwitz', *Daily Express*, 2 October 1945, p. 4.

Falcon, Richard, 'Images of Germany and the Germans in British Film and Television Fictions: A Brief Chronological Overview', in *Anglo-German Attitudes*, edited by Cedric Cullingford and Harald Husemann (Aldershot: Avebury, 1995), pp. 67–89.

Farrar-Hockley, Anthony, *The British Part in the Korean War: Volume II an Honourable Discharge* (London: HMSO, 1995).

Felman, Shoshana, 'Theaters of Justice: Arendt in Jerusalem, the Eichmann Trial, and the Redefinition of Legal Meaning in the Wake of the Holocaust', *Critical Inquiry* 27.2 (2001): pp. 201–38, doi: 10.1086/449006.

Flanagan, Ben, and Donald Bloxham, eds., *Remembering Belsen: Eyewitnesses Record the Liberation* (London: Vallentine Mitchell, 2005).

Foot, M. R. D., *SOE in France: An Account of the Work of the British Special Operations Executive in France 1940–1944* (London: Her Majesty's Stationery Office, 1968).

Fulbrook, Mary, *Reckonings: Legacies of Nazi Persecution and the Quest for Justice* (Oxford: Oxford University Press, 2018).

Garland, David, 'British Criminology before 1935', *The British Journal of Criminology* 28.2 (1988): pp. 1–17.

Gaskin, Hilary, *Eyewitnesses at Nuremberg* (London: Arms and Armour, 1990).

Godwin, George, 'Introduction', in *The Trial of Peter Griffiths (The Blackburn Baby Murderer)*, edited by George Godwin (London: William Hodge, 1950), pp. 13–65.

Gollancz, Victor, *Our Threatened Values* (London: Victor Gollancz, 1946).

Gollancz, Victor, *In Darkest Germany* (London: Victor Gollancz, 1947).

Gollancz, Victor, *The Case of Adolf Eichmann* (London: Victor Gollancz, 1961).

Grant, Matthew, 'The Trial of Neville Heath, the Popular Press, and the Construction of the Memory of the Second World War in Britain, 1945–1946', *English Historical Review* 133.564 (2018): pp. 1156–77, doi: 10.1093/ehr/cey209.

Greene, Graham, *The Ministry of Fear* (Harmondsworth: Penguin, 1973 [1943]).

Haag, John, 'Helene Bauer (1871–1942)', in *Women in World History: A Biographical Encyclopaedia*, http://www.encyclopaedia.com. Accessed 15 June 2018.

Hall, J. W., 'Introduction', in *Trial of William Joyce*, edited by J. W. Hall (London: William Hodge, 1946), pp. 1–36.

Hamilton, Patrick, *Hangover Square* (Harmondsworth: Penguin, 2001 [1941]).

Hansford Johnson, Pamela, *On Iniquity: Some Personal Reflections Arising Out of the Moors Murders Trial* (London: Macmillan, 1967).

Hanyok, Robert J., *Eavesdropping on Hell: Historical Guide to Western Communications Intelligence and the Holocaust* (New York: Dover, 2012 [2005]).

Hare, Cyril, *An English Murder* (London: Hogarth, 1987 [1951]).

Hayton, D. W., *Conservative Revolutionary: The Lives of Lewis Namier* (Manchester: Manchester University Press, 2019).

Helm, Sarah, *A Life in Secrets: The Story of Vera Atkins and the Lost Agents of SOE* (London: Abacus, 2006).

Helm, Sarah, *If This Is a Woman: Inside Ravensbrück, Hitler's Concentration Camp for Women* (London: Abacus, 2015).

Heschel, Susannah, 'Does Atrocity Have a Gender? Feminist Interpretations of Women in the SS', in *Lessons and Legacies VI: New Currents in Holocaust Research*, edited by Jeffry M. Diefendorf (Evanston: Northwestern University Press, 2004), pp. 300–21.

Hewitt, Kathleen, *Plenty under the Counter* (London: Imperial War Museum, 2019 [1943]).

Hilliard, Christopher, *A Matter of Obscenity: The Politics of Censorship in Modern England* (Princeton: Princeton University Press, 2021).

Hirsch, Francine, *Soviet Judgment at Nuremberg* (New York: Oxford University Press, 2020).

Hodge, James, 'Introduction', in *Notable British Trials and War Crimes Trials* (Edinburgh: William Hodge, 1949), pp. 5–7.

Holmes, Rose, 'Love, Labour, Loss: Women, Refugees and the Servant Crisis in Britain, 1933-1939', *Women's History Review* 27.2 (2018): pp. 288–309, doi: 10.1080/09612025.2017.1327096.

Hucko, Elmar H., ed., *The Democratic Tradition: Four German Constitutions* (Leamington Spa: Berg, 1987).

Humble, M. E., 'The Stylisation of History in Bertolt Brecht's *Der Aufhaltsame Austeig des Arturo Ui*', *Forum for Modern Language Studies*, 16.2 (1980): pp. 154–71, doi: 10.1093/fmls/xvi.2.154.

Humble, Nicola, *The Feminine Middlebrow Novel, 1920s to 1950s: Class, Domesticity, and Bohemianism* (Oxford: Oxford University Press, 2001).

Huxford, Grace, *The Korean War in Britain: Citizenship, Selfhood and Forgetting* (Manchester: Manchester University Press, 2018).

Immler, Nicole L., '"Too little, too late?" Compensation and Family Memory: Negotiating Austria's Holocaust Past', *Memory Studies* 5.3 (2012): pp. 270–81, doi: 10.1177/1750698012443468.

Innes, Michael, *Operation Pax* (Harmondsworth: Penguin, 1964 [1951]).

Jones, Elwyn, 'The Truth—But Not the Whole Truth', *Sunday Telegraph*, 8 May 1966, p. 5.

Judt, Tony, *Postwar: A History of Europe since 1945* (London: Vintage, 2005).

Kochavi, Ariel J., *Prelude to Nuremberg: Allied War Crimes Policy and the Question of Punishment* (Chapel Hill: University of North Carolina Press, 1998).

Koestler, Arthur, 'Scum of the Earth—1942', in *The Yogi and the Commissar* (London: Jonathan Cape, 1960 [1945]), pp. 85–93.

Kogon, Eugene, *The Theory and Practice of Hell: The German Concentration Camps and the System Behind Them*, translated by Heinz Norden (New York: Berkley, 1982 [1950]).

Kushner, Tony, 'Anti-Semitism and Austerity: The August 1947 Riots', in *Racial Violence in Britain, 1840–1950*, edited by Panikos Panayi (Leicester: University of Leicester Press, 1993), pp. 149–68.

Kushner, Tony, *The Holocaust and the Liberal Imagination: A Social and Cultural History* (Oxford: Blackwell, 1994).

Kushner, Tony, 'From "This Belsen Business" to "Shoah Business": History, Memory and Heritage, 1945–2005', in *Belsen 1945: New Historical Perspectives*, edited by Susan Bardgett and David Cesarani (London: Vallentine Mitchell 2006), pp. 189–216.

Kushner, Tony, 'The Memory of Belsen', in *Belsen in History and Memory*, edited by David Cesarani, Tony Kushner, and Jo Reilly (Florence: Routledge, 2013), pp. 181–205.

Kushner, Tony, 'The Holocaust in the British Imagination: The Official Mind and Beyond, 1945 to the Present', *Holocaust Studies* 23.3 (2017): pp. 364–84, doi: 10.1080/17504902.2017.1296084.

Lafitte, F., *The Internment of Aliens* (Harmondsworth: Penguin, 1940).

Lahiri, Shompa, 'Clandestine Mobilities and Shifting Embodiments: Noor-un-nisa Inayat Khan and the Special Operations Executive, 1940–44', *Gender & History* 19.2 (2007): pp. 305–23, doi: 10.1111/j.1468-0424.2007.00477.x.

Langhamer, Claire, '"The Live Dynamic Whole of Feeling and Behavior": Capital Punishment and the Politics of Emotion, 1945–1957', *Journal of British Studies* 51 (2012): pp. 416–44, doi: 10.1086/663841.

Lasker-Wallfisch, Anita, *Inherit the Truth 1939–1945* (London: Giles de la Mare, 1996).

Le Carré, John, *Call for the Dead* (London: Penguin, 2012 [1961]).

Lee, Carol Ann, *One of Your Own: The Life and Death of Myra Hindley* (London: Mainstream, 2010).

Levi, Primo, '*If This Is a Man*' in *If This Is a Man/The Truce*, translated by Stuart Woolf (Harmondsworth: Penguin, 1987), pp. 17–179.

Levi, Primo, 'The Grey Zone', in *The Drowned and the Saved*, translated by Raymond Rosenthal (London: Abacus, 1989), pp. 22–51.

Lewy, Guenther, *Perpetrators: The World of Holocaust Killers* (Oxford: Oxford University Press, 2017).

Lombard, Nap, *Murder's a Swine* (London: British Library, 2021 [1943]).

Lustgarten, Edgar, *The Business of Murder* (New York: Scribners, 1968).

Maier, Charles S., 'Overcoming the Past? Narrative and Negotiation, Remembering and Reparation: Issues at the Interface of History and the Law', in *Politics and the Past: On Repairing Historical Injustices*, edited by John Torpey (Langham, MD: Rowman & Littlefield, 2003), pp. 295–304.

Major, Patrick, '"Our Friend Rommel": The *Wehrmacht* as "Worthy Enemy,"' in Postwar British Popular Culture', *German History* 26.4 (2008): pp. 520–35.

Marchioness of Huntly, 'Close-up of Belsen Beasts', *Aberdeen Journal*, 15 December 1945, p. 2.

Marshall, Bruce, *The White Rabbit: A British Agent's Adventures in France* (London: Pan, 1954 [1952]).

Maxwell Fyfe, David 'Foreword', in *The Peleus Trial*, edited by John Cameron (London: William Hodge, 1948), pp. xiii–xxi.

Medhurst, Jessica, 'Representing and Repetition: Victor Gollancz's In Darkest Germany and the Metonymy of Shoes', *German Life and Letters* 69.4 (2016): pp. 468–84, doi: 10.1111/glal.12131.

Mitchell, Gladys, *Tom Brown's Body* (London: Vintage, 2009 [1949]).

Mitchison, Naomi, *Among You Taking Notes ... : The Wartime Diary of Naomi Mitchison 1939–1945*, edited by Dorothy Sheridan (Oxford: Oxford University Press, 1986).

Moeller, Robert G., 'How to Judge Stanley Kramer's *Judgment at Nuremberg*', *German History* 31.4 (2013), pp. 497–522, doi: 10.1093/gerhis/ght065.

Moorehead, Alan, 'Glimpses of Germany II—Belsen', *Horizon* 12.67 (July 1945): pp. 26–35.

Moorehead, Alan, *Eclipse* (London: Granta, 2000 [1945]).

Moran, Hugh, 'How Much of This Horror Can One Stand?', *Daily Mail*, 29 April 1961, p. 4.

Nicholas, Elizabeth, *Death Be Not Proud* (London: Cresset Press, 1958).

Nicholas, Siân, *The Echo of War: Home Front Propaganda and the Wartime BBC, 1939–45* (Manchester: Manchester University Press, 1996).

Nicolson, Harold, *Why Britain Is at War* (Harmondsworth: Penguin, 1939).

O'Hara, Glen, 'The Parliamentary Commissioner for Administration, the Foreign Office, and the Sachsenhausen Case, 1964–1968', *Historical Journal* 53.3 (2010): pp. 771–81, doi: 10.1017/s0018246x10000294.

Orwell, George, 'Raffles and Miss Blandish' (1944), in *Collected Essays, Journalism and Letters of George Orwell Volume III: As I Please 1943–45*, edited by Sonia Orwell and Ian Angus (London: Secker & Warburg, 1968), pp. 212–24.

Osborne, Deirdre, '"I Do Not Know about Politics or Governments ... I Am a Housewife": The Female Secret Agent and the Male War Machine in Occupied France (1942–5)', *Women: A Cultural Review* 17.1 (2006): pp. 42–64, doi: 10.1080/09574040600628542.

Overton Fuller, Jean, *Madeleine: The Story of Noor Inayat Khan* (London: Victor Gollancz, 1952).

Paget, R. T., *Manstein: His Campaigns and His Trial* (London: William Collins, 1951).

Pargeter, Edith, *The Terezín Requiem* (London: Heinemann 1963).

Pargeter, Edith, *Warfare Accomplished* (London: Headline 1990 [1947]).

Pendas, Devin O., *The Frankfurt Auschwitz Trial, 1963–1965: Genocide, History, and the Limits of the Law* (Cambridge: Cambridge University Press, 2006).

Pendas, Devin O., 'Retroactive Law and Proactive Justice: Debating Crimes against Humanity in Germany, 1945–1950', *Central European History* 43 (2010): pp. 428–63, doi: 10.1017/s0008938910000361.

Peters, Ellis, *Fallen into the Pit* (London: Futura 1991).

Phillips, Raymond, ed., *Trial of Josef Kramer and Forty-Four Others (The Belsen Trial)* (London: William Hodge, 1949).

Pistol, Rachel, '"I Can't Remember a More Depressing Time but I Don't Blame Anyone for That": Remembering and Commemorating the Wartime Internment of Enemy Aliens in Britain', *Patterns of Prejudice* 53.1 (2019): pp. 37–48, doi: 10.1080/0031322x.2018.1539288.

Plain, Gill, *Twentieth-Century Crime Fiction: Gender, Sexuality and the Body* (Edinburgh: Edinburgh University Press, 2001).

Playfair, Giles, and Derrick Sington, 'Clinic for Murderers', *Picture Post*, 3 December 1956, pp. 21–24.

Playfair, Giles, and Derrick Sington, *The Offenders: Society and the Atrocious Crime* (London: Secker & Warburg, 1957).

Postgate, Raymond, *Somebody at the Door* (London: British Library, 2017 [1943]).

Priemel, Kim Christian, 'Cunning Passages: Historiography's Ways in and out of the Nuremberg Courtroom', *Central European History* 53 (2020): pp. 785–810.

Prittie, Terence, 'A Victim of Nazism Still Awaits Her Compensation', *Manchester Guardian*, 2 November 1965, p. 12.

Prittie, Terence, 'Nazi Concentration Camp Victim Is Still Denied Justice', *Manchester Guardian*, 23 January 1967, p. 3.

Pronay, Nicholas, 'Introduction: To Stamp Out the Whole Tradition', in *The Political Re-Education of Germany and Her Allies after World War II*, edited by Nicholas Pronay and Keith Wilson (London: Croom Helm, 1985), pp. 1–36.

Prusin, Alexander Victor, '"Fascist Criminals to the Gallows!": The Holocaust and Soviet War Crimes Trials, December 1945–February 1946', *Holocaust and Genocide Studies* 17.1 (2003): pp. 1–30, doi: 10.1093/hgs/17.1.1.

Przyrembel, Alexandra, 'Transfixed by an Image: Ilse Koch, the "Kommandeuse of Buchenwald"', translated by Pamela Selwyn, *German History* 19.3 (2001): pp. 369–99, doi: 10.1191/026635501680193915.

Quinn, Joseph, 'The British Sailor Murdered at Bergen-Belsen' https://blog.nationalarchives.gov.uk/the-british-sailor-murdered-at-bergen-belsen-the-75th-anniversary-of-the-bergen-belsen-trials/. Accessed 9 November 2020.

Ramsey, Guy, 'Heath, man-about-town at 15, played lone wolf to the end', *Daily Mail*, 27 September 1946, p.4.

Rau, Petra, *Our Nazis: Representations of Fascism in Contemporary Literature and Film* (Edinburgh: Edinburgh University Press, 2013).

Rawlinson, Mark, 'This Other War: British Culture and the Holocaust', *Cambridge Quarterly* 25.1 (1996): pp. 1–25, doi: 10.1093/camqtly/25.1.1.

Reilly, Joanne, *Belsen: The Liberation of a Concentration Camp* (London: Routledge, 1998).

Reitlinger, Gerald, *The Final Solution: The Attempt to Exterminate the Jews of Europe, 1939-1945* (London: Vallentine Mitchell, 1953).

Richardson, Maurice, 'What Is One to Make of the Moors Murders?', *Observer*, 8 May 1966, p. 21.

Rose, Gordon, 'Crime and Society', *Manchester Guardian*, 8 November 1957, p. 6.

Rothberg, Michael, *The Implicated Subject: Beyond Victims and Perpetrators* (Stanford, CA: Stanford University Press, 2019).

Rozett, Robert, and Shmuel Spector, *Encyclopaedia of the Holocaust* (New York: Taylor & Francis, 2013).

Rutland, Harriet, *Blue Murder* (London: Dean Street Press, 2015 [1943]).

Schabas, William A., 'War Crimes, Crimes against Humanity and the Death Penalty', *Albany Law Review* 60.3 (1997): pp. 733–70.

Schleunes, Karl A., 'From Civil Rights to Civic Death: Dismantling Rights in Nazi Germany', in *Two Cultures of Rights: The Quest for Inclusion and Participation in Modern America and Germany*, edited by Manfred Berg et al (Cambridge: Cambridge University Press, 2002), pp. 77–93.

Schrafstetter, Susanna, '"Gentlemen, the Cheese Is All Gone!" British POWs, the "Great Escape" and the Anglo-German Agreement for Compensation to Victims of Nazism', *Contemporary European History*, 17.1 (2008): pp. 23–43, doi: 10.1017/s0960777307004262.

Schwelb, Egon, 'Crimes Against Humanity', *The British Yearbook of International Law* 23 (1946): pp. 177–226.

Seal, Lizzie, 'Imagined Communities and the Death Penalty in Britain, 1930–1965', *British Journal of Criminology* 54 (2014): pp. 908–27, doi: 10.1093/bjc/azu045.

Seaman, Mark, *Bravest of the Brave: The True Story of Wing Commander 'Tommy' Yeo-Thomas SOE Secret Agent Codename 'White Rabbit'* (London: Michael O'Mara, 1999).

Seaman, Mark, 'Good Thrillers, But Bad History: A Review of Published Works on the Special Operations Executive's Work in France during the Second World War', in *War, Resistance and Intelligence: Essays in Honour of M. R. D. Foot*, edited by K. G. Robertson (London: Leo Cooper, 1999), pp. 119–33.

Searle, Alaric, 'A Very Special Relationship: Basil Liddell Hart, Wehrmacht Generals and the Debate on West German Rearmament, 1945–1953', *War in History* 5.3 (1998): pp. 327–57.

Segev, Tom, *Soldiers of Evil: The Commandants of the Nazi Concentration Camps*, translated by Haim Watzman (New York: McGraw-Hill, 1987).

Sharman, Claire, 'War Crimes Trials Between Occupation and Integration: The Prosecution of Nazi War Criminals in the British Zone of Germany', unpublished PhD thesis (Southampton: University of Southampton, 2007).

Sharples, Caroline, 'Holocaust on Trial: Mass Observation and British Media Responses to the Nuremberg Tribunal', in *Britain and the Holocaust: Remembering and Representing War and Genocide*, edited by Caroline Sharples and Olaf Jensen (Basingstoke: Palgrave, 2013), pp. 31–50.

Sharples, Caroline, '"Where, Exactly, Is Auschwitz?" British Confrontation with the Holocaust through the Medium of the "Belsen" Trial', in *The Palgrave Handbook of Britain and the Holocaust*, edited by Tom Lawson and Andy Pearce (Basingstoke: Palgrave, 2021), pp. 181–200.

Shawcross, Hartley, 'Foreword', in *Trial of Wolfgang Zeuss and Others (The Natzweiler Trial)*, edited by Anthony M. Webb (London: William Hodge, 1949), pp. 13–15.

Shklar, Judith N., *Legalism: Law, Morals, and Political Trials* (Cambridge, MA: Harvard University Press, 1986 [1964]).

Sington, Derrick, *Belsen Uncovered* (London: Duckworth 1946).

Smith, Adrian, 'Berry, (James) Comer, First Viscount Kemsley (1883–1968), Newspaper Proprietor', http://www.oxforddnb.com.

Smith, Bradley F., *Reaching Judgment at Nuremberg* (London: Andre Deutsch, 1977).

Smith, Michael, 'Bletchley Park and the Holocaust', in *Understanding Intelligence in the Twenty-First Century: Journeys in Shadows*, edited by Peter Jackson and L. V. Scott (London: Routledge, 2004), pp. 111–21.

Sofsky, Wolfgang, *The Order of Terror: The Concentration Camp*, translated by William Templer (Princeton: Princeton University Press, 1997).

Sonabend, Daniel, *We Fight Fascists: The 43 Group and Their Forgotten Battle for Post-War Britain* (London: Verso, 2019).

Spender, Stephen, *European Witness* (London: Hamish Hamilton, 1946).

Stammers, Neil, *Civil Liberties in Britain during the Second World War: A Political Study* (Beckenham: Croom Helm, 1983).

Standish, Henry, 'The Living Dead of Belsen: Allied Rescue Services are Inadequate', *News Chronicle*, 21 April 1945, p. 1.

Stewart, Victoria, *The Second World War in Contemporary British Fiction: Secret Histories* (Edinburgh: Edinburgh University Press, 2011).

Stewart, Victoria, 'Representing Nazi Crimes in Post-Second World War life Writing', *Textual Practice* 29.7 (2015): pp. 1311–30, doi: 10.1080/0950236x.2015.1095453.

Stewart, Victoria, '"Commando Consciousness" and Criminality in Post-Second World War Fiction', *Journal of War and Culture Studies* 10.2 (2017): pp. 165–77, doi: 10.1080/17526272.2016.1215683.

Stewart, Victoria, *Crime Writing in Interwar Britain: Fact and Fiction in the Golden Age* (Cambridge: Cambridge University Press, 2017).

Stewart, Victoria, 'The Criminal Type in Mid-Twentieth Century Britain: Hamilton, Gorse and Heath', *Open Library of Humanities* 5.1 (2019) https://olh.openlibhums.org/articles/10.16995/olh.472/.

Stola, Dariusz, 'Early News of the Holocaust from Poland', *Holocaust and Genocide Studies* 11.1 (1997): pp. 1–27.

Stollery, Malcolm, '"The Hideous Difficulty of Recreating Nazism at War": Escaping from Europe in The Wooden Horse (1950) and the British Prisoner of War Film', *Historical Journal of Film, Radio, and Television* 37.3 (2017): pp. 539–88.

Stone, Dan, *Concentration Camps: A Short History* (Oxford: Oxford University Press, 2017).

Stonebridge, Lyndsey, *The Judicial Imagination: Writing After Nuremberg* (Edinburgh: Edinburgh University Press, 2011).

Templewood, Viscount (Samuel Hoare), *The Shadow of the Gallows* (London: Victor Gollancz, 1951).

Thomas, Jack, *No Banners: The Story of Alfred and Henry Newton* (London: W. H. Allen, 1955).

Thompson, Laura, *Agatha Christie: An English Mystery* (London: Headline, 2007).

Thurlow, Richard, *Fascism in Britain: From Oswald Mosley's Blackshirts to the National Front* (London: IB Tauris, 1998).

Tickell, Jerrard, *Odette: The Story of a British Agent (Odette Churchill G. C. M. B. E.)* (London: Pan, 1955 [1949]).

Timm, Annette F., ed., *Holocaust History and the Readings of Ka-Tzetnik* (London: Bloomsbury, 2018).

Tobia, Simona, 'Questioning the Nazis: Languages and Effectiveness in British War Crime Investigations and Trials in Germany, 1945–48', *Journal of War and Culture Studies* 3.1 (2010): pp. 123–36, doi: 10.1386/jwcs.3.1.123_1.

Tusa, Ann, and John Tusa, *The Nuremberg Trial* (London: Macmillan, 1983).

United Nations War Crimes Commission, *Law Reports of Trials of War Criminals Selected and Prepared by the United Nations War Crimes Commission Volume II: The Belsen Trial* (London: HMSO, 1947).

United States Holocaust Memorial Museum, 'Statement Regarding the Museum's Position on Holocaust Analogies', 24 June 2019. https://www.ushmm.org/information/press/press-releases/statement-regarding-the-museums-position-on-holocaust-analogies. Accessed 1 October 2019.

Walker, Patrick Gordon, *The Lid Lifts* (London: Victor Gollancz, 1945).

Walker, Patrick Gordon, 'What I Saw at Belsen', *The Listener*, 31 May 1945, p. 599.

Walker, Patrick Gordon, *Political Diaries 1932–1971*, edited by Robert Pearce (London: The Historians' Press, 1991).

Walker, Patrick Gordon, 'Belsen Facts and Thoughts', broadcast 27 May 1945. https://www.bbc.co.uk/archive/patrick-gordon-walker—belsen-facts-and-thoughts/zdsvxyc. Accessed 3 July 2019

Webb, Anthony. M., 'Introduction', in *Trial of Wolfgang Zeuss and Others (The Natzweiler Trial)*, edited by Anthony M. Webb (London: William Hodge, 1949), pp. 17–31.

Weckel, Ulrike, 'The Power of Images: Real and Fictional Roles of Atrocity Film Footage at Nuremberg', in *Reassessing the Nuremberg Military Tribunals: Transitional Justice, Trial Narratives, and Historiography*, edited by Kim C. Priemel and Alexa Stiller (Oxford: Berghahn Books, 2012), pp. 221–48.

Wentworth, Patricia, *The Key* (London: Hodder and Stoughton, 2005 [1946]).

West, Rebecca, 'The Revolutionary', in *The Meaning of Treason* (1949; rev ed London: Reprint Society, 1952), pp. 1–185.

West, Rebecca, *A Train of Powder: Six Reports on the Problem of Guilt and Punishment in Our Time* (New York: Viking Press, 1955).

White, Joseph Robert, '"Even in Auschwitz ... Humanity Could Prevail": British POWs and Jewish Concentration-Camp Inmates at IG Auschwitz, 1943–1945', *Holocaust and Genocide Studies* 15.2 (2001): pp. 266–95, doi: 10.1093/hgs/15.2.266.

Williams, A. T., *A Passing Fury: Searching for Justice at the End of World War II* (London: Jonathan Cape, 2006).

Williams, Rhys W., '"The Selections of the Committee Are Not in Accord with the Requirements of Germany": Contemporary English Literature and the Selected Book Scheme in the British Zone of Germany (1945–1950)', in *The Cultural Legacy of the British Occupation in Germany: The London Symposium*, edited by Alan Bance (Stuttgart: Verlag Heinz-Dieter Heinz, 1997), pp. 110–38.

Witter, Ben, 'Verhöre im Plauderton', *Der Zeit*, 26 March 1988, pp. 13–14.

Wittmann, Rebecca, *Beyond Justice: The Auschwitz Trial* (Cambridge, MA: Harvard University Press, 2005).

Woloch, Alex, *The One vs. The Many: Minor Characters and the Space of the Protagonist in the Novel* (Princeton: Princeton University Press, 2004).

Worpole, Ken, *Dockers and Detectives* (London: Verso, 1983).

Wylie, Neville, *Barbed Wire Diplomacy: Britain, Germany, and the Politics of Prisoners of War 1939–1945* (Oxford: Oxford University Press, 2010).

Younger, Kenneth, 'Minds Diseased', *Observer*, 3 November 1957, p. 15.

Zelizer, Barbie, *Remembering to Forget: Holocaust Memory through the Camera's Eye* (Chicago: University of Chicago Press, 1998).

Films

Carve Her Name with Pride (1958). Directed by Lewis Gilbert. Rank.
Judgment at Nuremberg (1961). Directed by Stanley Kramer. United Artists.
Odette (1950). Directed by Herbert Wilcox. British Lion.

Schindler's List (1993). Directed by Steven Spielberg. Universal Pictures.
So Little Time (1952). Directed by Compton Bennett. Associated British Picture Corporation.

Websites

BBC archive https://www.bbc.co.uk/archive/.
Belsen Trial Transcript, www.bergenbelsen.co.uk/pages/TrialTranscript/Trial_Contents.html
Encyclopaedia.com, https://www.encyclopedia.com/
Hansard, https://hansard.parliament.uk/
National Archives blog, https://blog.nationalarchives.gov.uk/
New York Review of Books, https://nyrb.com/
Oxford Dictionary of National Biography, https://www.oxforddnb.com/
Understanding Society blog, https://understandingsociety.blogspot.com
United States Holocaust Memorial Museum, https://www.ushmm.org

Archives Consulted

BBC Written Archives, Caversham.
Gerald Duckworth & Co Archives, Senate House, University of London.
Churchill Archives Centre, University of Cambridge.
Imperial War Museum, London.
National Archives, London.
Penguin Books Archive, University of Bristol.

Index